Weekends Away

New York

120 Trips to Take
Within 150 Miles of N.Y.

Edited by Mike Michaelson

E. P. Dutton   New York

Published in the United States by E. P. Dutton, a division of NAL Penguin Inc.,
2 Park Avenue, New York, N.Y. 10016.

Published simultaneously in Canada by Fitzhenry and Whiteside, Limited,
Toronto.

Library of Congress Catalog Card Number: 88-51963

ISBN: 0-525-48465-5

10 9 8 7 6 5 4 3 2 1

First Edition

 Prism Creative Group Staff

Editor and Publisher:	Mike Michaelson
Associate Publisher:	Glynis Steadman
Staff Editors:	Jean Postlewaite
	Michael Sweeney
Editorial Art:	Richard Franco
Type and Layout:	Tom Casper
	Today's Graphics

Contributing Writers:

Ken Bloom	Jean Postlewaite
Patrick Curran	Keith Ray
Jim Hargrove	Jerry Reedy
Nancy Jacobsen	Ruth Rejnis
Robert Knight	Jill Schensul
Mike Michaelson	Holly Spence
Mary O'Brien	Michael Sweeney
	Claire Walter

E. P. Dutton Staff

Editor:	Sandra W. Soule
Cover Design:	Nancy Etheredge

CONTENTS

INTRODUCTION

Escapes For All Seasons

Cities and suburbs can be great places in which to work and live. But when weekends roll around, sometimes you just have to get away. And that's what this book is all about. Escape. For a full weekend, an overnight trip, or a day's outing. Even a half-day jaunt to somewhere new and exciting may be the tonic you need to lift your spirits—spending a stimulating Saturday morning or a Sunday afternoon doing something different and entertaining.

Vacations can—and, according to recent studies, should—come in small packages. You can journey to a barrier island off the Jersey shore, unchanged in 1,000 years, where you can harvest the tart fruit of beach plums, or journey back in time and brush with living history at Old Bethpage (with political campaigning for a 19th-century election), Old Sturbridge (where you can try your hand at open-hearth cookery), and at Mystic Seaport (where you can listen to authentic sea chanteys). Or you can find adventure within the city limits of New York—a tropical rain forest or Sonoran desert in Brooklyn, a rural county fair on Staten Island. Also nearby, just beyond Manhattan's boundaries, are a bounty of world-class museums and galleries, renowned performing arts, and a mosaic of superb parks and gardens, plus vast, protected areas of forest, marshlands, and seashore. There are stately mansions to inspect, and a variety of forts, battlefields, and fighting ships to explore— the latter including a nuclear submarine, a sub from World War II, and a replica of a submarine that dates back to the Revolutionary War. As for pure natural beauty, this guide covers a region of the country that, despite its population density, is well endowed with spectacular and diverse assets ranging from talc-soft beaches, glittering bays, wild-running rivers, and rugged stretches of coast, to crystal lakes, foothills that are painted in spring with the pastel blooms of dogwoods, redbuds, and mountain laurels, and hidden valleys carpeted with wildflowers.

Recent studies show that weekend getaways are growing in popularity for a variety of reasons. These include the lack of time for long vacations and the need to relieve job stress with more frequent getaways. A report commissioned by Marriott Hotels shows that 73 percent of pleasure trips are of one-to-three-days' duration, while 28 percent of those surveyed said that they were taking more weekend pleasure trips than ever before. Most studies conclude that frequent breaks from the workday routine are important to revitalize dulled spirits and soothe frazzled nerves.

The enormous scope of diversions available over a weekend make it easy to follow this advice. A large number of them are found surprisingly close to home and are available at little or no cost. And that's what this book is all about—to help you get the most out of your weekend leisure time with suggestions for outings that will provide both a change of pace and a change of place. In these pages you'll find ideas for dozens of half-day outings perfect for a free morning or afternoon, as well as suggestions for full-day trips, overnight adventures, and weekends away.

Here is a sure antidote for the weekend blahs. If you find that your weekends are becoming a blur of dreary chores, routine shopping, and do-nothing sessions in front of the TV, it probably is time to take a fresh look at the world around you. New Yorkers are surrounded by a wealth of recreational opportunities guaranteed to stretch the mind, test the body, and soothe the soul—or simply provide pure escape and relaxation. You may be surprised at how much you can accomplish with a tank of gas (or a subway token), an open mind, and some practical suggestions that can serve as a springboard for adventure.

Head for the Bronx and the beach that is one of New York's best-kept secrets, browse a Hudson Valley antique store that specializes in Sherlock Holmes memorabilia, find out where to go on a budget-stretching shopping spree in New Jersey. See one of the earliest feature films at the studio where movies were invented, discover a "Yellowstone" at Manhattan's back door.

In these pages you'll be tempted by a Long Island restaurant that sends out its own fishing boat and another where you can choose from more than a dozen oyster dishes. You'll taste pizza from the brick oven of a pizzeria that claims to have invented the American version of Italy's famous pie and, in the same town, visit the diner that takes credit for creating the hamburger. For more innovative fare, you can test the talents of chefs-in-training at four restaurants at the Culinary Institute of America. And you'll discover the wine country of Dutchess County, of the relatively undiscovered North Fork of Long Island, and of the Hudson Valley, where you can sample award-winning vintages in a 120-year-old railroad station or take a "Lovers' picnic basket" into a vineyard. You'll explore neighborhood Italian restaurants in the Chambersburg area of Trenton—known colloquially as "the Burg"—visit a ski area that employs a German brewmaster to make its own beer, and grab a sandwich and perhaps a brew at the bar that is the Jersey City version of "Cheers."

In Brooklyn you'll visit a theater where Mark Twain spoke, a church where Charles Dickens did, and follow the footsteps of Danny Kaye, Mary Tyler Moore, and other rich and famous along the Celebrity Walk, New York's equivalent of Hollywood's Chinese Theater. You can sample the opulent lifestyle of the Great Gatsby, walk past Norman Mailer's house, and visit the homes of Eugene O'Neill and Edgar Allan Poe. You'll peek at one of Ginger Rogers' movie costumes and sleep in the bed where Meryl Streep "died" (or, at least, where one of her movie characters did). There's Woody Allen's childhood neighborhood to explore—and Bruce "The Boss" Springsteen's. And you can nibble your way through the Italian Market in the South Philly neighborhood that was Sylvester Stallone's turf in the Rocky movies.

There's adventure, too, as you are directed to gentle rivers for float trips, raging white water for rafting adventures, and languid, mule-drawn barge trips on canals. You'll fly in the open cockpit of a 1929 airplane. soar in a glider, and hike a segment of the famed 2,000-mile-long Appalachian Trail. You can watch horse racing (thoroughbreds and trotters), take in the fast-paced action of jai alai, and watch a boccie tournament. Or you can find a spot on the lawn for a symphony concert in "the Shed" at Tanglewood, or listen to jazz in the pretty Spanish courtyard at nearby Caramoor.

Ethnic adventures abound. You'll visit with the Pennsylvania Amish, steep yourself in the Queens' Greek heritage, and enjoy a Moravian-style Christmas celebration at Bethlehem, Pennsylvania. You'll discover a Polish country village, a "Little Italy" more authentic (and less expensive) than the one in Manhattan, and toss back a vodka and enjoy a bowl of borscht as you soak up Russian culture at Little Odessa-by-the-Sea. There's a real Tibetan monastery to visit and a colorful, teeming Near East bazaar where you can sample Lebanese-style "pizza."

How To Use This Guide

Arbitrarily, the trips described in this book fall within a 150-mile radius of New York City. All of these trips are outside Manhattan. After all, the object of this book is weekend getaways. Conversely, getaways don't necessarily need to encompass a great distance and we have included a good sampling of trips in and around the other boroughs. For organizational purposes, this book has been divided into nine geographic sections: Connecticut, Delaware, Massachusetts, New Jersey, New York—Boroughs, New York—Long Island, New York—Upstate, Pennsylvania, and Rhode Island. Within each area, trips are listed alphabetically by town (or borough). Where there is more than one trip in a given town, trips are subcategorized alphabetically by attraction.

Every trip has been assigned a symbol to indicate its suggested length. Although generally this takes into account traveling time from a central point in midtown Manhattan, it really is more indicative of how much there is to do at a given destination. Thus, we are suggesting trip lengths of half-day, full-day, day-and-a-half, and full weekend. To help you gain the maximum fulfillment from your weekend trips away from (and, in some cases, in and around) the city—taking a big bite out of the Big Apple, as it were—we are using symbols resembling New York's famous logo at the beginning of each trip to identify these categories:

Half-day

Day & half

Full-day

Weekend

Additionally, we are suggesting areas of specific interest. We have devised symbols to identify trips

that should be of particular interest for family outings or to couples looking for a romantic getaway. In
some cases, where a trip suited to a family outing
also may have some aspect that lends itself to a
romantic escape, both symbols are used. Of course,
the absence of one or both of these symbols does not
necessarily mean that the trip lacks suitability for
family and/or romantic outings, but simply that the
trip has broader applications. These special-interest
symbols are as follows:

family outings

romantic rendezvous

suitable for both

Help Us Help You

We thank you for purchasing this guide and trust it
will help make your leisure time more rewarding.
We believe we have devised an interesting mix of
weekend escapes. However, in future editions of this
book we will continue to add, refine, and improve
these suggestions.

We invite your assistance. As we travel, we will be
on the lookout for new attractions, restaurants, and
hotels, for exciting new things to do and places to
visit. We hope you will, too—and that you'll let us
know when you uncover some place new. If you
drop us a line at the address below, we'll consider
your suggestion for the next edition of *Weekends
Away*. If we use it, we'll send you a free copy
of the revised guidebook as a token of our apprecia-
tion.

Let us hear from you!

TO EARN A FREE BOOK, WRITE:
Prism Creative Group, Inc.
400 Federation Place
Elgin, IL 60123

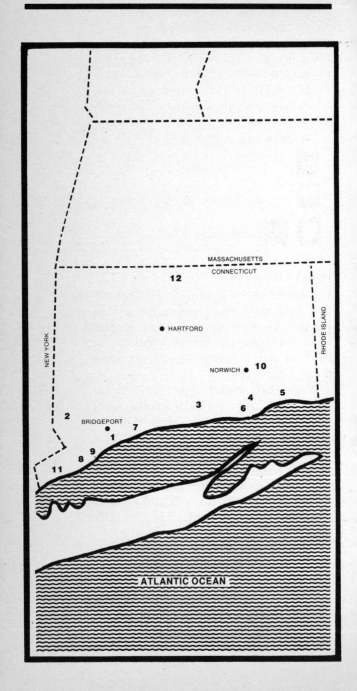

CONNECTICUT

1 Bridgeport—Various Attractions
2 Danbury—Various Attractions
3 Essex—Various Attractions
4 Groton—Various Attractions
5 Mystic—Various Attractions
6 New London—Various Attractions
7 New Haven—Various Attractions
8 Norwalk—The Maritime Center
9 Norwalk—Various Attractions
10 Norwich—Various Attractions
11 Stamford—Various Attractions
12 Windsor Locks—Various Attractions

1

Where The Circus Came To Stay

Bridgeport, Connecticut

P. T. Barnum was, and probably always will be considered the leading citizen of **Bridgeport, Connecticut.** The legendary circus entrepreneur died in 1891, but his memory lingers on. Actually, lingers is the wrong word. The memory of P. T. Barnum continues to dominate the life and times of Bridgeport as much as if he were alive today and his elephants were still plowing his yard and pulling the town's streetcars out of the mud. For Bridgeport was Barnum's hometown and the winter headquarters of his famous circus. In those days, Barnum's clowns, jugglers, aerialists, and the circus Fat Lady were a familiar sight sauntering along Cottage Street.

The major attraction in town is the **Barnum Museum,** which was recently renovated to the tune of $6 million. A building of truly Barnumesque proportions, the building includes just about everything on the man, his life and times, and his circus that anyone would want to know. It's a visual extravaganza, much as Barnum's circus was, full of all of the things that made Barnum the quintessential showman, promoter, and huckster. Here they are, ladies and gentlemen, the Siamese twins, the bearded lady, and the two-headed calf. Here's Tom Thumb—all 28 inches of him—with his little coats and carriages. And there's the "Swedish Nightingale," Jenny Lind, a virtually unknown singer from Sweden whom Barnum had made into a legend before she had even stepped off the boat or sung a note in America.

You'll also discover something else about Barnum—that he was a politician and civic booster. Barnum was elected to the Connecticut Legislature in 1865 and as mayor of Bridgeport in 1875. In between, the Republicans nominated him to run for Congress. He donated the 86 acres upon which the University of Bridgeport stands, and was an early booster of industry in Bridgeport, which now has several *Fortune* 500 corporations in residence despite its relatively small size (pop. 142,000).

But the lore, legend, and legacy of Barnum isn't all there is to Bridgeport. The city is working hard to upgrade its waterfront. **Captain's Cove Seaport,** created out of a run-down marina, now is a lovely boardwalk with shops, a 450-seat restaurant, and slips for 400 boats. It provides a showcase for an authentically-detailed replica of the HMS *Rose,* a 24-gun frigate that was launched in 1756. This reproduction of the historic *Rose* is the largest operational wooden sailing vessel in the world, and the 18th-century vessel upon which it is modeled can make an even greater claim to fame. Just before the Revolutionary War broke out the original *Rose* was assigned by the British to cut off American smuggling operations in and out of Newport, Rhode Island. The ship performed its assigned role with almost unseemly efficiency. But while it was sinking smugglers, it was also sinking the smuggling-based Newport economy. As a result, four-fifths of the citizenry soon had to leave town. These events so alarmed the Rhode Island General Assembly that they prevailed upon the Continental Congress to pass a law establishing a national navy whose ships could counteract the *Rose*. Congress obliged. So if you're glad there's a U.S. Navy, you have to thank the HMS *Rose* as its unwitting architect.

Without leaving Captain's Cove you can enjoy some splendid wharfside seafood at **The Restaurant at Captain's Cove,** which specializes in seafood, especially steamed clams and a variety of lobster entrees. The dress is casual and there are hamburgers on the menu for those who don't relish fish dishes. Also popular is **Fitzwilly's** on Main Street, offering fresh oysters, lobsters, shrimp, and other seafood, as well as satisfying sandwiches, soups, and salads.

Other interesting diversions in Bridgeport include the **Museum of Art, Science and Industry,** with its more than 50 permanent "hands-on" science exhibits, space gallery, planetarium, and Wonder Workshop Children's Programs; and **Beardsley Zoological Gardens,** the only zoo in Connecticut, with its children's zoo and Siberian tigers. You can enjoy a two and one-half mile walk along Long Island Sound at Seaside Park, and see the statue of Tom Thumb at Mountain Grove Cemetery.

Nor is there a lack of evening entertainment. Check out current schedules for the Downtown Cabaret Theatre, the Bernhard Art and Humanities Center, the Polka Dot Playhouse, and Klein Memorial Auditorium, the venue for the Greater Bridgeport Symphony, Connecticut Grand Opera, and Stamford State Opera.

To experience the fast-paced and exciting sport of jai alai, journey to nearby **Milford Jai Alai**, which offers 13 games daily and 15 on Sundays and holidays.

DESTINATIONS

Bridgeport Convention and Visitor's Commission, 303 State St, Bridgeport, CT 06604. 203/576-8494. **Barnum Museum,** 820 Main St, Bridgeport, CT 06604. 203/384-5381. **Captain's Cove Seaport,** 1 Bostwick Ave, Bridgeport, CT 06605. 203/335-1433.

RESTAURANTS

The Restaurant at Captain's Cove, 1 Bostwick Ave, Bridgeport, CT 06605. 203/335-7104. Apr-Oct daily 11 am-10 pm. **Fitzwilly's,** 2536 E Main St, Bridgeport, CT 06606. 203/334-1775. Daily 11:30 am-midnight.

2

Hats Off To Danbury

Danbury, Connecticut

The road into **Danbury, Connecticut,** is a trail of history. Motorists travel over the concrete ribbon of I-84, unaware that beneath the super-highway is a dirt road rutted by the wheels of wagons and packed by the boots of soldiers during the Revolutionary War. This was the way of the Hartford-Hudson route, ordered built by George Washington to speed movement of men and supplies between the Hudson and Connecticut rivers. Before that, it was a narrow, foot-worn trail, marked by the Pahquioque Indians who farmed in this area for centuries before the arrival of the first settlers. These Indians also named the valley that is home to Danbury and its sister towns, Ridgefield and Bethel. They called it "Housatonic," their word for "the place beyond the mountains."

Today, Danbury is a pleasant mix of the past and present. The town seems equally proud of and comfortable with both its many historic sites *and* its recent citation by Money magazine as the "most livable" place in the United States. The area is, at once, both a quintessential New England village (with its 18th-century architecture and folksy charm) and a vibrantly cosmopolitan commuter suburb (midtown Manhattan is only 90 minutes away).

Part of Danbury's heritage is preserved at the **Scott-Fanton Museum,** which consists of three 18th-century homes and a display of artifacts from the valley's history. The museum's John and Mary Rider House (1785) has been restored and furnished to its early-19th-century appearance, and includes an extensive collection of carpenters' tools from that period. The Dodd Hat Shop (1790) includes exhibits tracing Danbury's growth in the hatting industry, which led it to be called the "Hat Capital of the World" during the early 20th century. The Ives House (1780) was the birthplace of Pulitzer Prize-winning composer Charles Ives, and displays memorabilia from his outstanding career.

Another repository of valley history is the **Keeler Tavern Museum,** on Main Street in Ridgefield. Also known as the Cannonball House for the British cannonball lodged in its wall since 1777, Keeler's was variously a tavern, a stagecoach stop, and a hotel between 1772 and 1907. Currently, it has been restored and furnished to reflect its appearance during the Revolutionary War. Tours of the structure are led by authentically costumed guides.

Bethel is the locale of another important Revolutionary War site in the valley—**Putnam State Park,** which commemorates the large encampment of the troops of Continental Army Gen. Israel Putnam, which was located here in the winter of 1778-1779. Every August, life at the camp is fully recreated in a weekend of living history, featuring hundreds of troops in authentic uniforms. The rest of the year, the park offers a museum of encampment artifacts, and a number of recreated camp buildings to tour.

Even Danbury's gleaming, high-tech shopping mall can trace its lineage to an earlier era. The **Danbury Fair Mall** is located on the site of the original

Danbury Fair, a county-wide agricultural event held annually for decades. At 1.3 million square feet, the Danbury Fair Mall is the largest mall in New England.

For dining, try the **Stony Hill Inn Restaurant** in Bethel. In a fitting decor of colonial-era antiques and knickknacks, this restaurant offers fresh seafood (scrod is the house specialty), thick prime rib and steaks, and hearty homemade soups.

DESTINATIONS
Housatonic Valley Tourism Commission, Box 406, Danbury, CT 06810. 203/743-0546.

RESTAURANTS
Stony Hill Inn, Danbury-Newtown Rd, Bethel, CT 06801. 203/743-5533. Mon-Thu noon-2:30 pm, 5:30-9:30 pm; Fri & Sat noon-2:30 pm, 5:30-10 pm; Sun 1-8 pm.

3

Essex Appeal

Essex, Connecticut

Connecticut is known as the capital of U.S. submarine activities, principally because the U.S. Naval Submarine Base is located in Groton (see trip #4). But while Groton is home to the USS *Nautilus*, the world's first nuclear-powered submarine, it is **Essex, Connecticut,** where the United States' very first submarine of *any* kind was built, and is commemorated in a full-size model. The *Turtle*, a one-man sub built by a Yale student in the mid-1770s, undertook a futile attempt to blow up a British ship in New York Harbor during the Revolutionary War, marking the first time a submarine had been used as an offensive weapon in naval warfare. Today, a model of the *Turtle* is on display at the **Connecticut River Museum,** at the foot of Main Street, which consists of a dockhouse, waterfront, and park. Models, paintings, objects, and photographs relating to river history are exhibited here.

Another unique, but much more conventional mode of travel is one of the highlights of a visit to Essex. The **Valley Railroad** is a vintage steam train that carries passengers through the thickly wooded countryside to Deep River for a riverboat cruise through the verdant Connecticut River Valley. Combination train and boat trips last two hours and 10 minutes, and are a particular treat during autumn, when the valley's trees show off their vibrant colors. At Christmastime, Santa Claus rides aboard the train in its incarnation as the North Pole Express. On this seasonal journey, jolly old St. Nick leads the passengers in caroling while the train passes specially lit decorations.

The boat goes north along the Connecticut River, past meadows, woods, and marinas. The cruise takes you past **Gillette Castle,** which is part of a park overlooking the river. William Gillette was a renowned actor, most noted for his portrayal of Sherlock Holmes. His 24-room castle (complete with such built-in features as one-way mirrors and hidden passageways) and estate are open for tours.

At Chester, the turning point for the cruise, you'll see an ancient ferry, one of the oldest in the United States. You'll also see the **Goodspeed Opera House,** an intricately decorated Victorian structure. The opera house was built in 1876 and is still in use today. It is known for its musical revivals, many of which have moved on to successful Broadway runs. A recent addition to the cruise includes a southern trip—the last of the day—which takes you to the Essex Harbor of the Connecticut River, on Long Island Sound. There you'll find the town of Old Saybrook, a picturesque harbor community settled in 1636, and the site of two oft-photographed lighthouses at Saybrook Point.

Essex retains the flavor of bygone days when sea captains displayed their prosperity in fine homes built on Main Street. Worth a visit in town are **Hill's Academy Museum** and the **Pratt House.** Hill's Academy was a private boarding school, one of the earliest educational facilities in the region. Here you can browse in a country store, examine shipwright's tools, and see Pratt-Read ivory (made by a local firm into piano keys) and Civil War memorabilia. The colonial Pratt House contains an outstanding collection of American furnishings of the 17th, 18th, and 19th centuries, specializing in Connecticut-related items as well as Chinese courting mirrors.

The favored place for dining in Essex is the unique **Griswold Inn** on Main Street. This lively inn, which opened for business in 1776 in a former schoolhouse from 1738, is the social nerve-center of the area. Roaring fireplaces, 200-plus years of accumulated knickknacks, and solid fare such as prime rib, roast duckling, and fresh fish make "the Gris" (as they call it locally) a welcome stop for travelers. On Sundays, try the massive Hunt Breakfast—a mountainous buffet which usually includes any of the following and more: eggs, the inn's homemade sausage, lamb kidneys, smelts, ham, grits, bacon, fried chicken, chicken livers, creamed chipped beef, and hot corn bread.

DESTINATIONS

Connecticut River Museum, Main St, Essex, CT 06426. 203/767-8269. Adults $1.50, children 50 cents. **Valley Railroad,** Railroad Ave, Essex, CT 06426. 203/767-0103. Prices vary by trip length and season. **Gillette Castle,** c/o Park Manager, 67 River Rd, East Haddam, CT 06423. 203/526-2336. May-Oct daily 9am-5 pm. Adults $1, Children 6-11 50 cents. **Goodspeed Opera House,** East Haddam, CT 06423. 203/873-8668. Tours by appt. **Hill's Academy Museum,** 22 Prospect St, Essex, CT 06426. 203/767-0681. Wed-Fri 10 am-3 pm. Adults $1.50, senior citizens $1, children under 12 free. **Pratt House,** 19 West Ave, Essex, CT 00420, 203/767-0001. Adults $1.50, senior citizens $1, children under 12 free.

RESTAURANTS

The Griswold Inn, 48 Main St, Essex CT 06426. 203/767-1812. Mon-Thu noon-9 pm; Fri & Sat noon-10 pm; Sun 11 am-2:30 pm, 4:30-9 pm.

4

Date With The North Pole

Groton, Connecticut

On August 3, 1958, the **USS Nautilus,** the world's first nuclear-powered submarine, also became the first ship ever to pass beneath the North Pole. That's right, it went under the ice. The *Nautilus* was a remarkable vessel for its day and it accomplished a remarkable feat. And now it's berthed at the **Naval Submarine Base** in **Groton, Connecticut,** where you can see it up close and find out more about its unusual voyage beneath the polar ice. At the base, you are given a taped audio explanation and are allowed to explore the "innards" of the sub on your own.

The *Nautilus* began its epic run at the Pole on August 1, when it submerged off the north coast of Alaska near Point Barrow. It passed beneath the Pole at precisely 11:15 pm and resurfaced August 5 in the Arctic Ocean between Greenland and Spitsbergen, Norway.

During the 96 hours that the *Nautilus* was submerged it covered a distance of 1,830 nautical miles and passed beneath an ice pack that ranged in thickness from 10 to 80 feet. The sub traveled at approximately 400 feet beneath the surface. In recognition of the accomplishment, President Dwight D. Eisenhower awarded the Legion of Merit to the sub's commander, William R. Anderson, and the Presidential Unit Citation to the 115 officers and men.

Boats of one kind or another are somehow involved in nearly everything you would want to see or do in Groton. On the *Enviro-Lab*, a 50-foot oceanographic research vessel, you can take educational cruises that teach you about catching fish and lobsters, analyzing plankton, operating lighthouses, avoiding navigational hazards, and using oceanographic sampling instruments. The *Hel-Cat II* will take you on a day-long fishing trip for cod, fluke, seabass, ocean bluefish, tuna, bonita, and other varieties. The *River Queen II* offers a sightseeing cruise that takes in tall ships, the *Nautilus*, the U.S. Coast Guard Academy (across the Thames River from Groton, in New London, Connecticut—see trip #6), and the U.S. Naval Submarine Base, home of the Atlantic Submarine Fleet.

At night the *River Queen II* offers a Lobster-in-the-Rough dinner cruise and a Dixieland Jazz cruise. And if the *Nautilus* has whetted your appetite for submarines, there's another one you can go aboard. It's the USS *Croaker*, a sub that fought in World War II, berthed at 359 Thames Street.

A tour of **Fort Griswold** will take you back to the Revolutionary War era. During the war, the state of Connecticut licensed a vast armada of American pirate ships, which preyed upon British supply vessels and merchant ships. For many of these privateers, New London was home port, and the town's warehouses bulged with captured British goods, including the entire cargo of the *Hannah*. The cargo consisted largely of personal supplies destined for the British officers stationed in New York City. Fort Griswold was built to protect New London from British reprisals, but ultimately it failed in this mission. In the Battle of Groton Heights, fought in 1781, a superior force of British regulars successfully attacked the fort. They set fire to it, too, but an anonymous American patriot succeeded in extinguishing the fire after the British left.

In between boarding various ships and subs in Groton, take time out for a bite to eat at **G. Willickers.** The eclectic menu of this restaurant contains American standbys, such as ribs, steaks, and burgers, as well as many ethnic specialties, including stir fry entrees, linguine, spaghetti, and a variety of Mexican dishes. The restaurant's decor includes a collection of area antiques.

DESTINATIONS

Southeastern Connecticut Tourism District, 8 Mill St, Ye Olde Towne Mill, New London, CT 06320. 203/444-2206. **Nautilus Memorial,** Naval Submarine Base, Box 571, Groton, CT 06349. 203/449-9515.

RESTAURANTS

G. Willickers, 57 King's Highway, Groton, CT 06430. 203/445-8043. Daily 6 am-10 pm.

ACCOMMODATIONS

Thames Harbour Inn, 193 Thames St, Groton, CT 06340. 203/445-8111.

5

Play Mystic For Me

Mystic, Connecticut

This authentic replica of a 19th-century seaport celebrates the sailing ships that set out from American ports between 1814 and 1914. The town didn't have a large enough harbor to compete with New London or Boston as a major port, so **Mystic, Connecticut,** took up shipbuilding. It did the job well: Some of America's fastest clipper ships first slipped into the water here. Mystic also produced some of the country's most able sea captains.

If an 1850s whaling captain were to sail out of the past and into Mystic Seaport today, he would feel right at home, for right there before him would be the last wooden whaling ship in America, the *Charles W. Morgan;* the square-rigged iron training ship *Joseph Conrad;* and the fishing schooner *L.A. Dunton.* The *Morgan* made 37 voyages over a period of 80 years, and during that time brought back 150,000 pounds of whalebone to make canes and corsets, 50,000 barrels of whale oil to light the nation's lamps, and uncounted quantities of ambergris (a waxy intestinal by-product unique to whales) to make perfume.

Other schooners, sloops, and small boats swing gently to their moorings in the harbor; and down on Seaport Street, shipwrights and other 19th century craftsmen mend nets, furl sails, and carve scrimshaw. Even old familiar sea chanteys are drifting on the salt air.

You're permitted to board and explore many of the ships on display. On the *Morgan*, for example, you can see the captain's cabin and the crew's fo'c'sle. You can also walk the decks of the square-rigged *Conrad* and the sleek fishing schooner the *Dunton*. The museum includes a total of more than 300 watercraft—all carefully restored and maintained.

Other maritime history is housed in more than 60 buildings ashore in Mystic. On a stroll along the village streets, you can enter historic New England homes, and visit a chapel, a meeting house, a store, a bank, and a schoolhouse—all virtually untouched by time. The day-to-day life of a maritime village is also re-created in shipcarvers' shops, a chandlery, rigging loft, a clock shop, and tavern. In the museum buildings you'll discover priceless collections of ship models, figure heads, scrimshaw, and sea-scapes. Planetarium shows demonstrate the principles of celestial navigation. If you get hungry during your tour of Mystic, take time out for a meal at the **Seaman's Inne,** which specializes in fresh seafood. A winner there is the pasta with shrimp and scallops.

Special events take place all year long. Late May brings the Lobster Festival; June, the Sea Music Festival; July, Independence Day festivities and the Classic Boat Rendezvous; October, the Schooner Race and the Chowderfest; November/December, Yuletide Tours; and December, Lantern Light Tours and the Community Carol Sing.

At the **Mystic Marinelife Aquarium** you can view 6,000 marine animals in 48 exhibits, plus a 2.5-acre outdoor Seal Island and hourly demonstrations of dolphin, whale, and sea lion training in a 1,400-seat marine theater.

Also in Mystic is **Old Mistick Village,** a replica of a colonial New England village, circa 1720. It contains more than 60 shops, plus the Memory Lane Doll and Toy Museum.

In historic downtown Mystic you can stroll a compact area of mid-19th century buildings and watch the ships go by when the Bascule Bridge is raised. If you're an antique-hunter, take a walk through the Mystic River Antiques Market, an historic building overlooking the Mystic River. Thirty-five dealers sell antiques, collectibles, and artwork in this enclosed shopping center.

If the Mystic experience inspires you to set sail yourself, you can take your pick of either overnight or day trips from **Voyager Cruises.** The *Voyager*, an authentic replica of a 19th-century, gaff-rigged packet, has 10 private double cabins with mahogany berths, reading lamps, and sinks with running water. Voyager Cruises also offers sunset cruises.

DESTINATIONS

Southeastern Connecticut Tourism District, Ye Olde Towne Mill, 8 Mill St, New London, CT 06320. 203/444-2206. **Mystic Seaport Museum,** 50 Greenmanville Ave, Mystic, CT 06355. 203/572-0711. Daily 9 am-4 pm. Adults $6, children 5-18 $3. **Marinelife Aquarium,** Rte 27, Mystic, CT 06355. 203/536-3323. Adults $6.75, children $3.75. **Voyager Cruises,** Steamboat Wharf, Mystic, CT 06355. 203/536-0416.

RESTAURANTS

Seaman's Inne, Mystic Seaport Museum, Mystic, CT 06355. 203/536-9649. Sun-Fri 11:30 am-9 pm, Sat 11:30 am-10 pm.

ACCOMMODATIONS

The Inn at Mystic, Junction Rtes 1 & 17, Mystic, CT 06335. 203/536-9604.

6

Short Day's Journey

New London, Connecticut

Eugene O'Neill spent 30 summers here, but it's sometimes hard to tell whether he really liked **New London, Connecticut,** or not—or even whether New London liked him. O'Neill wrote two plays based on his experiences in New London—*Long Day's Journey Into Night* and *Ah, Wilderness.* New London comes off very badly in *Long Day's Journey*, but seems quite a delightful place in *Ah, Wilderness*. To O'Neill, no doubt, it was both. Given his mercurial personality, he would be perfectly capable of both loving and hating New London, and evidence can be cited either way. O'Neill told one friend he hated the town "like poison." To another, who had mentioned O'Neill's New London home, O'Neill said, "Every time you go past, give it my love."

As for the citizenry of that era, they were old-money Yankees who lived in New London full time and tended to look askance at outsiders. The O'Neills were, by contrast, definitely *nouveau riche*, with the emphasis on the nouveau. James O'Neill, Eugene's father, made a pretty good living as an actor, but he was by no means in the same financial class as the upper crust of New London. And it certainly didn't help matters that he was Irish and a part-time resident, nor that he and his sons, Eugene in particular, were given to roistering and drinking.

As recently as 1978, there was evidence that local animosity toward the family had not totally disappeared. When a citizen's group moved to change the name of Main Street to Eugene O'Neill Drive, there were some who were bitterly opposed to it, including a former mayor who referred to O'Neill as a "stew bum" who did nothing but "write a few plays."

Nevertheless, today O'Neill is lionized aplenty in New London. Besides the street that now bears his name, there is a bronze statue of him down at the harbor, and a museum dedicated to his life and work in the town. The museum is in the former O'Neill home, and bears the same name that O'Neill's father gave the place when he bought it in 1896: **Monte Cristo Cottage.** (James O'Neill played the count in *The Count of Monte Cristo*, his most famous role.) The collection includes letters, scrapbooks, photographs, set designs, stage models, and programs and posters valued at more than $100,000. You'll also see several items that once belonged to James O'Neill, including the sword he used in *The Count of Monte Cristo*.

Eugene O'Neill won the Nobel Prize for literature and four Pulitzers, and he is ranked with Chekhov, Ibsen, and Shaw as a playwright. But were he alive today he might be more proud of the belated recognition that he has received from the people of New London.

Monte Cristo is one among many fine old homes and other buildings you can tour in the town. The others include the Shaw Mansion, 11 Blinman Street, which served as naval headquarters during the Revolution; Joshua Hempsted House, 11 Hempstead Street, built in 1678 and the oldest house in the city; and Nathaniel Hempsted House, same address, built in 1759. **Ye Olde Town Mill** at Mill Street and State Pier Road, was built in 1650 for John Winthrop, Connecticut's sixth governor. It has an overshot waterwheel, an 1800 grist mill, and a picnic ground. **Nathan Hale Schoolhouse,** located on the Captain's Walk, was built in 1774 and has been faithfully restored. Hale taught here before enlisting in Washington's army.

While you're in the neighborhood, try some oysters, lobster, scampi, or stuffed shrimp at the **Thames Landing Oyster House.** The restaurant overlooks the river, with an especially good view from the second floor. The first floor dining room is decorated with nautical items.

The **Lyman Art Museum,** 625 Williams Street, has not only works of art, but an outstanding collection of dolls, doll houses, and toys. If you're ready for some outdoor activity, take a stroll along Long Island Sound at **Ocean Beach State Park.** The park has rides, an amusement arcade, water slide, pool, bathhouse, and concessions, all complementing a wide and popular beach, which was planned by the designer of New York's famous Jones Beach. The **Coast Guard Academy,** located on Mohegan Avenue, offers tours, and you can steep yourself in other maritime lore at the **Tale of the Whale Museum,** 3 Whale Oil Row on Huntington Street. Auto ferries leaving from New London go to Long Island, New York, and Block Island, Rhode Island.

Directly across the Thames River from New Lon-

don is Groton, Connecticut, home of the U.S. Naval
Submarine Base (see trip #4).

DESTINATIONS

Southeastern Connecticut Tourism District, 8 Mill St, Ye
Olde Towne Mill, New London, CT 06320. 203/444-2206. **Monte
Cristo Cottage,** 325 Pequot Ave, New London, CT 06320. 203/
443-0051. Mon-Fri 1-4 pm and by appointment.

RESTAURANTS

Thames Landing Oyster House, 2 Captain's Walk, New London, CT 06320. 203/442-3158.

ACCOMMODATIONS

Travelodge Connecticut Yankee, Box 479, Niantic, CT 06357.
203/739-5483.

7

Burger's King At Old Eli

New Haven, Connecticut

There must be something strange in the air in **New
Haven, Connecticut.** It's the home town of the one
of the nation's most prestigious universities, **Yale,**
yet it wants to be credited with inventing pizza pie
and hamburgers. Maybe the Yalie sense of humor
has something to do with it. After all, noted esoteric
humorist and talk show host Dick Cavett graduated
from here, as did former Chicago Bear Gary Fencik,
long considered the "thinking man's football
player" (who never let his intellect get in the way of
the stinging hits he delivered on the field).

But don't let the strange claims and the high jinks
deter you. Yale and the city of New Haven which
surrounds it, are well worth seeing. The university
even offers free guided tours. You don't have to buy
a ticket or make a reservation. If you want to go, just
show up at the Visitor Information Center, on College Street between Chapel and Elm Streets. The
tours last about an hour. If you'd rather go on your

own, pick up a copy of the Walking Tour pamphlet that includes a map, a suggested route, and a brief history of the university.

Yale University was founded by 10 Connecticut ministers and named for Elihu ("Old Eli") Yale, one of the early benefactors. At the South end of the Old Campus is Connecticut Hall, once home to such illustrious figures as Nathan Hale, William Howard Taft, and Noah Webster. The **Yale University Art Gallery** at 1111 Chapel Street is said to be the nation's oldest college art museum. Look at the varied collections—Italian Renaissance and 19th- and 20th-century American painting, African sculpture, pre-Columbian objects, art from the Near and Far East—then take a stroll in the extensive sculpture garden. The **Yale Center for British Art** contains an outstanding collection of paintings that survey the development of English art, life, and thought from the Elizabethan period onward. The collection puts major emphasis on the period between the birth of Hogarth (1697) and the death of Turner (1851), considered by many to be the "golden age" of English art. Look for outstanding examples of the work of Thomas Gainsborough, Sir Joshua Reynolds, and John Constable.

The **Sterling Memorial** and **Beinecke Rare Book and Manuscript Libraries** contain a Gutenberg Bible and several exquisite illuminated manuscripts from the medieval period. In the **Peabody Museum of Natural History** you can see the remains of great dinosaurs, as well as "The Age of Reptiles," a Pulitzer Prize-winning mural that stretches to a length of 110 feet. The Peabody is the largest natural history museum in New England.

The **Yale Collection of Musical Instruments** documents developments in the history of European and American music with 850 items. There are also concerts, lectures, and changing exhibits there.

Before you start on New Haven, head for the **Top of the Park** in the Park Plaza Hotel and enjoy a panoramic view of the city and Yale campus. The restaurant specializes in prime rib and fresh seafood. Then take a walk around New Haven's **His-**

toric Green, a National Historic Landmark and one
of the nine original squares in the city's 1683 village
plan. Its three churches represent Gothic, Federalist,
and Georgian architecture.

If you have young children with you, give them a
break from the heavy-duty culture tour by taking
them to the **Connecticut Children's Museum.** It contains a play village with shops, a hospital, and many
other buildings, all designed to challenge the imaginations of those under seven.

A couple of good places to stretch the legs and get
some fresh air are **Lighthouse Point Park** and **East
Rock Park.** The 82 acres of Lighthouse park face
Long Island Sound and offer swimming, nature
trails, and a bird sanctuary. Take a look at the
wooden carved carousel set in a turn-of-the-century
beach pavilion. At East Rock Park you can hike self-
guided nature trails, visit a rose garden, and enjoy a
splendid view of the harbor and Long Island Sound.

Before you call it day, check out those stories
about the birthplaces of the pizza and the hamburger. **Pepe's Pizzeria Napoletana** says it invented
the American version of pizza in 1925. Try their
unique clam-and-white-sauce pizza, prepared in an
authentic Italian brick oven. **Louis' Lunch** is the historic site where, according to legend, in 1900, Louis
(pronounced, like the name of his eatery, "LOO-ie")
Lassen slapped together ground-up leftovers from
the steak sandwiches he was making, and grilled it
for a customer who was in a hurry. Today, in the
same store, using the same 1896 stove as his grandfather did, Kenneth Lassen continues to serve up
hamburgers and cheeseburgers (added to the menu
in 1930). Louis' Lunch is only open during the
week, but is well worth a lunch-time visit.

DESTINATIONS

Convention and Visitors Bureau, 900 Chapel St, New Haven,
CT 06510. 203/787-8367. **Visitor Information Office,** Yale University, Box 1942 Yale Station, New Haven, CT 06520. 203/432-
2300. Campus tours: Mon-Fri 10:30 am & 2 pm, Sat & Sun 1:30
pm.

RESTAURANTS

Top of the Park, Park Plaza and Conference Center, 155 Temple St, New Haven, CT 06510. 203/772-1700. 6:30 am-10 pm. **Pepe's Pizzeria Napoletana,** 157 Wooster St, New Haven, CT 06519. 203/865-5762. Mon-Thu 4-10:30 pm, Fri & Sat 11:30 am-midnight, Sun 2:30-10 pm. **Louis' Lunch,** 261-263 Crown St, New Haven, CT 06510. 203/562-5507. Mon-Fri 9 am-4:30 pm.

ACCOMMODATIONS

The Inn at Chapel West, 1201 Chapel St, New Haven, CT. 06511.

8

Water, Water, Everywhere

The Maritime Center
Norwalk, Connecticut

For those who enjoy novel educational experiences—especially ones that are entertaining as well—**The Maritime Center** at **Norwalk, Connecticut,** is an ideal destination, great for a family outing. It presents one of the more innovative approaches to learning you'll find, principally because it's so much fun that visitors—particularly young ones—are not aware that they are "going to school" at the same time.

The center is built in and around a restored 19th-century factory on five acres of waterfront in the historic South Norwalk (or "SoNo") section of town (see trip #9). Activities and attractions are offered both inside the center and outdoors, in the immediately surrounding area. On any given day, you can see a high-tech film in the IMAX theater, explore ancient sea artifacts in the Maritime Hall, witness a historic vessel being restored in the courtyard, watch seals at play in the Great Hall, and participate in a "field trip" class held on the Long Island Sound.

Your sensory experience begins in the **Aquarium** where a lifelike mural portrays a prehistoric salt marsh. On a gradually descending walkway you'll encounter more than a dozen aquariums housing close to 175 different species of marine life in realistic environments. The habitats these tanks represent range from shallow tidal areas teeming with minuscule brine shrimp to the deep sea, where sting rays and 10-foot-long sharks menacingly swim. All of the inhabitants of the tanks are native to the Sound and/or to the ocean beyond.

A variety of interactive devices help you get the most out of the displays. At one tank, which is precisely synchronized with the ebb and flow of the tides of Long Island Sound, you can operate a video camera to zoom in on a crab and see its image magnified on the monitor. At the touch-tank, with the aid of an aquarium assistant, you can get your hands wet handling starfish and mussels. With the aid of another device you can look through a pair of lenses and experience how a fish sees. And for an insider's overview of the functioning of the aquarium, there's an exhibit that takes you behind the scenes and shows you its day-to-day workings in detail.

In the IMAX Theater you can enjoy the thrilling effects of Image Maximum cinema on an 80-foot screen that curves around you. The movies shown are loaded with special effects designed to make you feel as if you're in the middle of the action. For example, the movie *Silent Sky* presents a bird's-eye view of what it's like to soar through the heavens, while *Nomads of the Deep* creates the illusion that you're swimming along with a school of humpback whales. The special effects that makes these films seem so real are achieved by using film three times the size of standard 70-mm film and a special IMAX projector. The curved screen is six stories high and 80 feet wide, extending beyond the edges of your peripheral vision and immersing you, almost literally it seems, in the image.

In the old factory building you'll see the 30-foot steam tender *Glory Days*, poised on a boat cradle. Move on to a futuristic twin-hull racer that nicely illustrates the design approach that won back the America's Cup for the United States. To test your sailing skills, try the video display simulator; it realistically creates conditions of fog and wind for would-be skippers to handle.

In the courtyard of the Maritime Center, master shipwrights and volunteer apprentices are painstakingly restoring the 56-foot *Hope*, the last of the wooden-hulled, sail-powered oyster sloops to be built on Long Island Sound. The center's **Great Hall** is home to an indoor/outdoor tank of harbor seals, which is always a hit with visiting children.

The center also offers a gift shop, and two seafood "snack bars," **The Oyster Bar** and **The Clam House;** each specializes in its namesake shellfish. There are also a number of good seafood restaurants nearby on historic South Main Street. An example is the **Portofino Clam House,** offering fresh clam specialties as well as a variety of fish grilled over hardwood.

DESTINATIONS

The Maritime Center at Norwalk, North Water St, South Norwalk, CT 06854. 800-243-2280. Daily 11 am-6 pm. The IMAX Theater remains open until 10 pm, Thu-Sat. Admission: $5.50 for either the IMAX Theater, or the Aquarium and the Maritime Hall; $9.50 for combined admission.

RESTAURANTS

The Oyster Bar and **The Clam House** (see Destination). **Portofino Clam House,** 18 S Main St, Norwalk, CT 06854. 203/838-8605. Mon-Thu 11 am-9 pm, Fri & Sat 11 am-11 pm, Sun 2-8 pm.

9

SoNo Sojourn

Norwalk, Connecticut

Scenic and historic **Norwalk, Connecticut,** describes itself as being "where the city ends and the weekend begins"—a perfect appellation for this seaside community an hour northeast of Manhattan. Along with neighboring Wilton, Norwalk offers a combination of rich colonial charm and contemporary culture that makes it a consummate year-around getaway.

One of the newest and most exciting sights in Norwalk is **The Maritime Center,** housed in what was once a run-down 19th-century factory building. It showcases nautical artifacts, denizens of the deep in natural-setting aquariums, a six-story-tall movie that seems to surround you, and even seals at play (see trip #8).

The Maritime Center is located in **Historic South Norwalk** or "SoNo," in local argot, a beautifully restored 19th-century waterfront neighborhood that's listed in the National Register of Historic Places. Antique shops and specialty boutiques are mingled with restaurants specializing in Mexican and Italian cuisine and seafood. Also here is the **Brookfield/SoNo Craft Center,** a well-known craft education institution. The center also has a gallery shop where you can buy one-of-a-kind craft items.

The most impressive site in town—and one of the most majestic houses in New England—is the **Lockwood-Mathews Mansion,** a four-story Victorian extravaganza that contains 50 rooms arranged around a great rotunda. This sprawling, castle-like mansion was built in 1868 for financier LeGrand Lockwood, who apparently wanted a domicile that would live up to his first name. The rich interior was decorated by artisans from Europe, and everything has been restored to its original splendor. Notably beautiful are the woodwork, period furnishings, carved marble, and frescoes.

Very near the Lockwood-Mathews Mansion is **Stew Leonard's Dairy,** known as the "Disneyland of Supermarkets." Leonard's is not only a supermarket offering top-quality meat, fish, fruit, vegetables, and baked goods, but also includes a display of singing bears (a la Disney's Bear Country Jamboree), a petting zoo, and a working dairy that visitors can tour.

For another view of area history, visit **Mill Hill Historic Park,** a charming complex of 18th- and 19th-century buildings, including a one-room schoolhouse, a jail, a stable, a townhouse, and the law office of 18th-century Governor Thomas Fitch.

Spend a quiet moment or two on adjacent **Norwalk Green,** the archetypal New England village green with its ornate gazebo. Just down East Street from the green is the restored **City Hall,** which showcases 33 Works Progress Administration murals from the 1930s, depicting Connecticut life and history. This is the largest surviving collection of WPA murals in the country. City Hall is also the site of a concert hall that is home to the Norwalk Symphony.

Each September, Norwalk throws a weekend-long party to honor *Crassostrea virginica,* better known as the common East Coast oyster. The **Oyster Festival** is held in the waterfront Veteran's Memorial Park, and includes fireworks, arts and crafts, dancing, bands, and, of course, a multitude of delectable oysters.

In SoNo, a fine dining (and shopping) spot is **Pasta Nostra Trattoria.** This restaurant (recipient of a three-star review in the *New York Times*) offers Italian specialties featuring homemade pasta, and boasts a cellar of more than 80 Italian wines. The Pasta Nostra also includes a store, which sells the restaurant's pasta and sauces for home preparation. Another place for lunch or dinner in Norwalk is the **Silvermine Tavern,** a charming, early American inn with superb country dining. Specialties include a massive seafood dinner (which includes clam chowder, mussels, soft shell crab, and a two-pound lobster) and roast duckling with apple cider sauce.

DESTINATIONS

Yankee Heritage District, 297 West Ave, Norwalk, CT 06850. 203/854-7825. **Stew Leonard's Dairy,** 100 Westport Ave, Norwalk, CT 06851. 203/847-7213. Daily 7 am-11 pm.

RESTAURANTS

Pasta Nostra Trattoria, 116 Washington St, Norwalk, CT 06854. 203/854-9700. Restaurant: Tue & Wed 11:45 am-2:25 pm, Thu-Sat 6-9:30 pm. Store: Tue-Sat 10:30 am-6 pm. **Silvermine Tavern,** Perry & Silvermine Aves, Norwalk, CT 07850. 203/847-4558. Mon-Sat noon-3 pm, 6-9 pm; Sun 11 am-2:30 pm, 3-9 pm.

10 🍎 🍎

Lincoln Slept Here, Too

Norwich, Connecticut

Located midway between Boston and New York, **Norwich, Connecticut,** was founded in 1659 and became one of the busiest commercial centers in the northeast. It was also a hotbed of activity during both the American Revolution and the Civil War. Samuel Huntington, a signer of the Declaration of Independence, lived here and is buried in the Colonial Cemetery, along with both American and French soldiers. Marquette and his soldiers made camp here, and Benedict Arnold, a hero of the Revolution until he changed his mind and switched sides, was born here.

It seems that almost every city in the northeast claims that Washington slept there. Norwich is no exception, but it is one of only a few that can say, with absolute verity, that Lincoln stayed overnight, too. During the Civil War the Great Emancipator traveled to Norwich to confer at the home of Governor William Buckingham.

Today, the small city on Connecticut's southeast coast continues as a bustling commercial center, but its primary charm lies in the loving care with which its residents have preserved the reminders of their prominent place in history. Many old buildings have been preserved and restored. A stroll around town reveals Colonial saltbox houses, magnificent Greek Revival and Victorian mansions, and commercial buildings constructed by wealthy industrialists of the 19th century. The best place to see the colonial-era homes is around the lovely **Norwichtown Green.** You'll find magnificent 19th-century residences along Broadway and Chelsea Parade. Downtown, look for the Queen Anne-style City Hall built in 1892.

When Washington was here, he stayed at the **Leffingwell Inn,** built in 1675 and opened as an inn in

1701. The room he slept in now bears his name. During the American Revolution angry colonists conferred at the Leffingwell, and made impassioned speeches on the nearby village green. The Leffingwell Inn is considered to be one of the most outstanding Colonial dwellings in the state of Connecticut. The inn uniquely illustrates the development from a simple but sturdy 17th-century house to a mid-18th-century townhouse befitting its prosperous owner, Christopher Leffingwell, one of Norwich's leading citizens. By 1770 he had established the first paper mill in Connecticut, plus a stocking factory, pottery, chocolate factory, fulling mill, clothier's shop, and dye house. Many of the products Leffingwell's various enterprises turned out went to supply the Colonial Army. In 1775 he was appointed to the Committee of Correspondence, and when the citizens of Norwich heard the news about the battles of Lexington and Concord, Leffingwell was the one they heard it from.

Another worthwhile stop in Norwich is the **John Baldwin House,** which dates back to 1660. Baldwin was one of the 35 founders of Norwich, and the Baldwin name is prominent in Connecticut history. Three Baldwins occupied the state's governor's chair. Today the house functions as a demonstration center for colonial crafts, including spinning, weaving, natural dying, bread baking, soapmaking, and the drying of herbs for cookery. No advanced schedules are published. What you see is whatever the craftspeople feel like doing while you're there.

The area that is now Norwich was formerly occupied by the Mohegan Indians. The European settlers obtained the land from a Mohegan chief by the name of Uncas, who is buried in Norwich's Indian Burial Grounds. You can visit the **Tantaquidgeon Indian Museum** to see Mohegan artifacts, as well as authentic baskets, bowls, and other handmade items. The operator of the museum is Harold Tantaquidgeon, a Mohegan craftsman whose work is on display here.

One of the area's highly regarded full-service resorts is the **Norwich Inn and Spa.** Head there for a refreshment in the Prince of Wales bar, or a relaxing meal on the terrace or in **The Grill** room. A few of the restaurant's specialties are country-style pâté with Cumberland sauce, rack of lamb, tortellini, and other pasta dishes. Guests can also order from the spa menu, which includes selections for the health-conscious, with an emphasis on vegetables. If you're in the mood to experiment, try the Spa Pizza, made with a whole-wheat tortilla, topped with goat cheese, homemade tomato sauce, and shiitake mushrooms.

DESTINATIONS

Norwich Area Chamber of Commerce, 35 Main St, Norwich, CT 06360. 203/887-1647.

RESTAURANTS

The Grill, Norwich Inn and Spa (see Accommodations). 203/886-2401. Mon-Fri 7-10 am, noon-2:30 pm, 6-10 pm; Sat 7-10:30 am, noon-2:30 pm, 6-10 pm; Sun 7-10:30 am, noon-3 pm, 6-9 pm.

ACCOMMODATIONS

Norwich Inn and Spa, Rte 32, Norwich, CT 06360. 203/886-2401. 800/892-5692.

11

Housewrecker's Delight

Stamford, Connecticut

The **United Housewrecking Company** in **Stamford, Connecticut,** doesn't sound like the kind of place that would attract a lot of visitors, but it is and it does. That's because it's actually a sprawling six-and-one-half-acre indoor/outdoor collection of the weirdest, coolest, tackiest, rarest, most unexpected *stuff* that you've ever seen. What started out, as the name implies, as a liquidator of materials salvaged from condemned buildings has grown into the

Smithsonian of flea markets. There you can buy tables, chairs, bureaus, chests, shelves, barrels, bath tubs, posters, prints, paintings, and beautiful mantels in oak, pine, and marble. Or maybe you're in the market for church pews, chandeliers, traffic lights, street signs, bars, weathervanes, carved decoys, iceboxes, or ship's lanterns. You'll find all of this—and much more—at United Housewrecking. Whether you like to shop for antiques, or just plain junk, this may well be the place you've always wanted to visit.

And, even if a treasure trove of funky finds isn't your cup of tea, you'll still find plenty to interest you in Stamford. Like many other cities and towns in New England, Stamford took its name from a much older city—in this case, from a city in Lincolnshire, England. Stamford, Connecticut, was founded in 1641 by 29 secessionists from the Weathersfield Church. It became part of Connecticut by virtue of being part of the New Haven colony and later the Hartford colony. By the time of the American Revolution about 5,000 people lived in Stamford, and it has grown steadily ever since.

Despite the city's proximity to the Big Apple, it offers a respectable number of sights and attractions of its own. At the **Stamford Museum and Nature Center,** for example, you can experience a genuine New England farm, complete with livestock, tool exhibits, country store, and wildlife center. There are also a planetarium, an art gallery, and natural-science exhibits. The museum's shop carries an eclectic stock of merchandise, including yard goods, candles, tinware, pottery, wooden items, jams, syrups, relishes, stoneground flour, bird feeders, and a variety of cookbooks.

The **Hoyt-Barnum Farmhouse,** circa 1699, is Stamford's oldest house. It's decorated with period furnishings and contains exhibits of early dolls and costumes. At the **Stamford Historical Society Museum** you can bone up on local history, and admire collections of Early American furniture, farm tools, dolls, and quilts.

The **First Presbyterian Church,** although built in

recent times (1958), is worth a stop for its unusual design—curiously, it is shaped like a fish. It also boasts beautiful stained-glass windows by the Frenchman Gabriel Loire. And if you've admired New York's Whitney Museum, you can find a little bit of it here in the **Whitney Museum of American Art, Fairfield County.** This branch of the world-famous museum displays visiting exhibits (including items from the Whitney in New York) and presents lectures about art and artists. The museum is in the lobby of the Champion International Corporation headquarters building in downtown Stamford.

For seafood and a harbor view, try **The Restaurant at Stamford Landing.** This restaurant's specialties include a variety of fresh fish dishes; for a light meal, sit at the raw bar to enjoy your choice of oysters or sushi.

DESTINATIONS

City of Stamford, Stamford Government Center, 888 Washington Blvd, PO Box 10152, Stamford, CT 06904. 203/359-3220. **United Housewrecking Company,** 535 Hope St, Stamford, CT 06906. 203/348-5371. **Stamford Museum & Nature Center,** 39 Scofieldtown Rd, Stamford, CT 06903. 203/322-1646. **Stamford Historical Society Museum,** 1508 High Ridge St, Stamford, CT 06903. 203/329-1183. **First Presbyterian Church,** 1101 Bedford, Stamford, CT 06905. 203/324-9522.

RESTAURANTS

The Restaurant at Stamford Landing, 78 Southfield St, Stamford, CT 06902. 203/067 0777. Sun-Thu 11:30 am-3:30 pm, 5-10 pm; Fri & Sat 11:30 am-3:30 pm, 5-11 pm.

ACCOMMODATIONS

Stamford Marriott, 2 Stamford Forum, Stamford, CT 06901. 203/357-9555. **Inn at Mill River,** 26 Mill River St, Stamford, CT 06902. 203/325-1900.

12

Top Gun Fun

Windsor Locks, Connecticut

If you number Charles Lindbergh, "Pappy" Boyington, and Chuck Yeager among your heroes—or just want to pretend that you're Tom Cruise for an afternoon—file your flight plan and take off for the **New England Air Museum,** in **Windsor Locks, Connecticut.** There you'll find one of the most comprehensive collections of flying machines and other aeronautic miscellany in the United States, if not in the entire world. Airplane buffs, military-history fans, and future would-be "Top Guns" will find artifacts from all eras of motorized flight, including fighters, bombers, helicopters, commercial jets, and other planes.

One of the highlights of the museum is the jet-fighter cockpit simulator, which is guaranteed to make even the most jaded armchair pilot feel like a jet ace soaring into the wild blue yonder. The computer programs are extremely realistic, going from takeoff, through a flight profile, to touchdown. Although this exhibit is especially exciting for children, you may find that it's the big kids in your group who are reluctant to leave the simulator and their moments of glory in the sky.

The museum's collection includes examples of planes from both sides of both World Wars. These are accompanied by models, photographs, and text, showing and telling more about the planes. A recently restored diorama depicts an aerial dogfight over the French countryside during World War I. The diorama features models of British fighters in hot pursuit of a German Fokker Triplane. The Fokker is the most easily recognized World War I German fighter, and is symbolic of the technological achievements of aviation in World War I, which boosted the development of the airplane from the crude box-kite apparatus in which man first learned to fly to a highly accurate and deadly instrument of war. The Fokker Triplane on display at the museum conjures up visions of Manfred von Richthofen, the German ace who was the famous "Red Baron," maneuvering his deadly Fokker behind a British Sopwith Camel, firing the machine guns mounted on the upper fuselage in front of the cockpit, and slipping back into the clouds. Contrasting with this 1917 scene, directly behind the Fokker is a modern F-100 Super Sabre jet, looking all the more space-age when viewed next to the World War I relic. Another modern marvel of military aviation at the museum is an F-4 Phantom II, which flew in battle in Vietnam and scored one "victory," as shown by a red star prominently displayed on each side, under the cockpit area.

The museum houses approximately 40 planes, while another 100 or so are stored outdoors or in other buildings, and are rotated to the main display periodically. Exhibits of numerous small artifacts, such as tools, models, and rare photographs, are shown in the lobby. Authentically costumed mannequins are displayed near some of the aircraft in the main exhibition building.

As you stroll about you'll see aircraft in various stages of restoration, photographic exhibits on the history of manned flight, and a vintage balloon basket. A 1938 Packard Brewster touring car is on display next to the Stinson Detroiter airplane, powered with a Packard diesel engine. The glider exhibit is complemented by a Monnett Monderai sailplane suspended from the ceiling of the main exhibition building. Throughout the year a number of non-aviation oriented exhibits—car shows, for example— are held at the museum. If you visit around Christmastime, you might even see Santa Claus, seated in the festively-decorated Sud Caravelle jet transport.

This area of north-central Connecticut is home to a number of other sites of interest. Also in Windsor Locks is the **Noden-Reed Farm Museum,** consisting of an 1840 house and 1825 brick barn containing historic farm-oriented tools and other artifacts from the early part of the state's history. This was also the site of the first Christmas tree exhibited in Connecticut. In East Windsor is the **Trolley Museum,** which displays steam and electric streetcars, trolleys, and other light railroad cars and equipment dating from the late 1800s. Daily during summer or on weekends the rest of the year, you can hop aboard a restored trolley for a ride through the countryside surrounding the museum. Also on the grounds is the **Connecticut Fire Museum,** a collection of historic fire-fighting equipment ranging from horse-drawn, hand-pumped wagons of the mid-1800s to shiny chrome-and-metal pumping trucks of the 1950s.

For dining in the area, try **Dunfey's Tavern,** at the **Tobacco Valley Inn** in neighboring Windsor. Hearty steaks, swiss- or cheddar-burgers, seafood combination platters, and homemade soups are the specialties there.

DESTINATIONS

New England Air Museum, Bradley International Airport, Windsor Locks, CT 06096. 203/623-3305. Daily 10 am-5 pm. Adults $5, seniors $4, children $2. **Noden-Reed Farm Museum,** 58 West St, Windsor Locks, CT 06096. 203/627-9212. **Trolley Museum** and **Connecticut Fire Museum,** CT 140, East Windsor, CT 06088. Daily 10 am-4 pm.

RESTAURANTS

Dunfey's Tavern (see Accommodations—Tobacco Valley Inn). 203/688-5221. Daily 7 am-10 pm.

ACCOMMODATIONS

Tobacco Valley Inn, 450 Bloomfield Ave, Windsor, CT 06095. 203/688-5221. **Koala Inn,** 185 Ella T. Grasso Turnpike, Windsor Locks, CT 06096. 203/623-9417.

DELAWARE

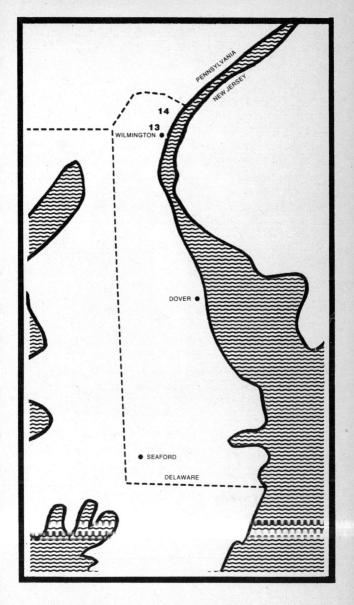

13 New Castle—Various Attractions
14 Winterthur—Winterthur Museum
And Gardens

13 🍎 🍎

Old Charms In New Castle

New Castle,
Delaware

As you stroll past Federal mansions and manor houses on the original cobblestone streets of **New Castle, Delaware,** you can almost hear the carriages bringing the wealthy to market at the village green. New Castle's houses convey the history of Dutch, Swedish, and British colonial settlement, as well as the promise of the new republic. These five square blocks along the west bank of the Delaware River, just 20 miles from the Brandywine Valley's attractions, have been a well-kept secret. Less visited than the Brandywine's better known attractions, historic New Castle boasts many 17th- and 18th-century buildings clustered around a town square paced out by Peter Stuyvesant in 1651. A visit here conveys the magic of the first settlers' visions of the new land along the mighty river.

The strategic location on the west bank of the Delaware River made New Castle a prominent 17th century burg with gracious brick homes surrounded by tidy gardens. After Stuyvesant bought a parcel of land from the Indians in 1651, he established Fort Casimir. But the valued location created turf wars. In the first 30 years of settlement, the town changed hands from Dutch to Swedish to English, becoming part of William Penn's New World land grant in 1682.

But while the town prospered as a colony and leading new republic center, mid-19th century malaise—the diversion of the railroad to Wilmington—curtailed growth, and left intact the plainly elegant 18th- and early-19th-century buildings. From the Strand, a wide expanse of park that stretches toward the shimmering Delaware, walk along 2nd, 3rd, and 4th streets and down Delaware and Market streets. This is where you'll find cobblestones, manor houses, and mansions. And you can walk through the brick arch cut wide enough for the wagon trains.

In May many of these gracious private homes open to the public, but you can tour three homes anytime. The **Old Dutch House Museum,** the only 1600s house to survive in its original form, features a collection of Dutch shoes, along with 17th-century furniture. The **Amstel House,** built by a Dutch settler in 1680, and enlarged in 1738, hosted George Washington, who grabbed kisses from the local belles at the wedding of Ann Van Dyke and Kensey Johns.

George Read II House, built between 1797 and 1801, is the grandest. This prominent attorney, and son of a signer of the Declaration of Independence, wanted his home to proclaim his stature. From the gilded fanlights, to the interior arches, carved woodwork, and formal gardens, the Georgian-style house flows with a fine Federal flair.

Approximately 15 miles west of New Castle is **Newark,** another Delaware town that offers a mix of the historic and the contemporary. This thriving small town (pronounced "New-ARK") got its start as a tavern at a crossroads of two heavily used Indian trails. Although the original tavern is long since gone, Newark does have its share of historical sites. Nearby Cooch's Bridge is known as the site of the only Revolutionary War battle fought in Delaware. According to legend, it was in this battle, on September 3, 1777, that Betsy Ross' new Stars and Stripes flag was flown for the first time. A 90-foot tall observation tower affords scenic views of the battlefield. The surrounding Iron Hill Park has hiking, nature, and bicycling trails, as well as picnic facilities.

Other historic structures in the area include the Hale-Byrnes House, where General George Washington and his staff met during the Revolutionary War's Brandywine Campaign (visits by reservation); and the Old Welsh Tract Baptist Church, dating from 1703, which is the oldest primitive Baptist church in the U.S.

Newark is also home to the **University of Delaware,** the campus of which is known for its scenic beauty. Georgian-style brick structures surrounded by broad grassy areas sprawl across the campus. A natural spot for strolling and taking in the sites is the stately, elm-lined Mall, which extends from the venerable Old College building to Laurel Hall. Formal tours of the campus are available.

Just north of town is the **Walter S. Carpenter, Jr. State Park.** Its 551 acres include forest, streams, and farmland. It's a perfect spot for fishing, hiking, or horseback riding. Special fitness, nature, and equestrian trails are laid out for visitors to follow.

For dinner in New Castle, try the **David Finney Inn,** a three-story restaurant with lodging, part of which dates to 1685. Amid a colonial decor mixing country pieces and antiques, enjoy such house specialties as sole papillote, rack of lamb, and filet mignon, as well as black forest cake and chocolate mousse. For comfortable family dining in Newark, the **T'Adelphia Restaurant** is a good choice. T'Adelphia means "the brothers" in Greek, and the restaurant's Pappanicholas brothers serve up lamb, poultry, fish, and Greek-American specialties. Also notable is the large salad bar and Sunday breakfast buffet.

DESTINATIONS

Old Dutch House Museum, 32 E Third St, New Castle, DE 19720. 302/322-9168. Apr-Nov Tue-Sat 11 am-4 pm, Sun 1-4 pm. Adults $1, children 50 cents. **Amstel House,** 4th and Delaware Sts, New Castle, DE 19720. 302/322-8411. Apr-Nov Tue-Sat 11 am-4 pm, Sun 1-4 pm. Adults $1, children 50 cents. **George Read II House,** 42 The Strand, New Castle, DE 19720. 302/322-8411. Mar-Dec Tue-Sat 10 am-4 pm, Sun noon-4 pm. Adults $3, children $1.50. **New Castle County Chamber of Commerce,** 250 Main St, Newark, DE 19711. 302/737-4343. **University of Delaware,** Hullihen Hall, Rm 116, Newark, DE 19716. 302/451-8123. **Walter S. Carpenter, Jr. State Park,** DE 896, Newark, DE 19711. 302/731-1310.

RESTAURANTS

The David Finney Inn (see Accommodations). 302/322-6367. Daily 7-10:30 am, 11:00 am-2 pm, 5:30-9:00 pm. **T'Adelphia Restaurant,** Newark Shopping Center, Newark, DE 19711. 302/368-9114. Mon-Sat 11 am-10 pm; Sun 9 am-1:30 pm, 4-10 pm.

ACCOMMODATIONS

The David Finney Inn, 216 Delaware St, New Castle, DE 19720. 302/322-6367.

14 🍎 🍎

A Winterthur Wonderland

Winterthur Museum and Gardens
Winterthur, Delaware

At the **Winterthur Museum and Gardens** you will find not only the lifestyle of the very rich and famous—the home of Henry Francis du Pont—but also one of the most formidable collections of furniture, textiles, and other objects made or used in America between 1650 and 1850. The 196 rooms of this magnificent country estate nestled in the rolling Delaware hills near the Brandywine River offer American history with a high-style flair.

At Winterthur the early American lifestyle comes alive. You can imagine political dinners at tables set with silver, and elaborate punchbowls; games of whist; glasses of port in drawing rooms graced with elegant card tables; and cold nights when the intricate tapestries were drawn close about the canopied beds. Room settings display more than 71,000 antiques, including William and Mary carved wardrobes, 18th-century Pennsylvania blanket chests, silver tankards by Paul Revere, and fine examples of Chippendale styling.

While you can't see all of Winterthur in one trip, highlights include the elegant Port Royal parlor, with its balance of matched Chippendale highboys, and lavender and yellow color scheme—du Pont's favorite; the Chinese parlor, noted for its vivid green Oriental wallpaper, with scenes of Chinese village life flowing panoramically across four walls; and the gracefully curved Montmorenci stairway, which was rescued from an 1822 home in North Carolina.

Try the Two Centuries Tour for a 1640-1840 overview, or the spring-time Port Royal tour for a peek at 16 elegant rooms. For a dashing display of Christmases past, reserve tickets for Yuletide at Winter-

thur, a 1½-hour guided tour of 21 specially decorated rooms recreating holiday traditions of early
America. Other special gifts for the eye are the collections of silver, textiles, ceramics, and paintings.

Fine furniture merits an equally fine setting—
Winterthur, named after the Swiss town of du
Pont's ancestors, sits on 963 elaborately maintained
acres full of roses, tall oaks, and towering beeches.
Don't miss the gardens. Walk or take a tram ride
(April-October) through the elaborately manicured
grounds that are vibrant with color spring and fall.

To see more of how du Pont money makes a garden grow, tour **Longwood Gardens,** the 350-acre
former summer estate of Pierre du Pont, the one-
time chairman of General Motors. The dazzling display includes fields of roses, 13 pools of waterlilies,
and three acres of conservatories housing bonsai,
cacti, and rare orchids. The cascading fountains, a
du Pont fancy, include a summertime show of colored lights and shooting sprays.

At the **Hagley Museum and Library** nearby, see
where the du Pont fortune began. Tour the gunpow-
der mills along the Brandywine River that Eleuthere
I. du Pont built in 1802 to supply black powder to
the United States Army. This 225-acre park depicts
19th-century industrial life. There is a restored
workers' community, and on weekends baking demonstrations are given. Also at the site of the museum
is Eleutherian Mills, the first du Pont estate in the
area. Built by E. I. du Pont in 1803, this Georgian-
style mansion is furnished with antiques and other
authentic family pieces. Another du Pont family attraction in the area is the Nemours Mansion and
Gardens, a 103-room art- and antique-filled French-
style chateau that was once the home of Alfred I. du
Pont.

Buckley's Tavern, housed in a 160-year-old building in the historic town of Centerville, near Winterthur and Longwood, is a fitting stop for lunch or
dinner. The continental specialties with a French
flair include onion soup, chicken salad with grapes
and walnuts, seafood pastas, and trout in champagne.

The nearby city of **Wilmington** is also home to historic sites and interesting attractions. These include the Delaware Art Museum, which features an extensive collection of English pre-Raphaelite paintings; the Delaware Museum of Natural History, which displays such natural oddities as a 400-pound clam shell and the world's largest known bird egg; and Holy Trinity Church, which dates from 1698, and is believed to be the oldest active Protestant church in North America.

To dine in the grand style of the du Ponts, try **Bellevue in the Park,** located in the antique-filled 1855 Greek Revival mansion of William du Pont, Sr. Fresh seafood specialties are highlighted among the restaurant's French and American cuisine. Luxurious accommodations can be found at the **Hotel du Pont,** a venerable hotel of 290 lavishly decorated rooms. Among the hotel's points of interest are its intricately carved ceilings, its antique furnishings, and its million dollar collection of Wyeth-family paintings. The renowned and impeccable service of the hotel's friendly staff will make you feel like one of the du Ponts.

DESTINATIONS

Winterthur Museum and Gardens, Winterthur, DE 19735. 800/448-3883, 302/654-1548 Tue-Sat 9 am-5 pm, Sun 12-5 pm. Adults $8, seniors and students under 17 $6.50; under 12 free. Reservations suggested. **Longwood Gardens,** Rte 1, Kennett Square, PA 19348. 215/388-6741. Hours vary by season and special events.

RESTAURANTS

Buckley's Tavern, 5812 Kennett Pike, Centreville, DE 19807. 302/656-9776. Mon-Sat 11:30 am-1 am, Sun 11:30 am-11 pm. **Bellevue in the Park,** 911 Philadelphia Pike, Wilmington, DE 19809. 302/798-7666. Daily 11 am-2:30 pm, 5-9:30 pm.

ACCOMMODATIONS

Hotel du Pont, Rodney Sq, Box 991, Wilmington, DE 19899. 302/594-3100 or 800/441-9019.

MASSACHUSETTS

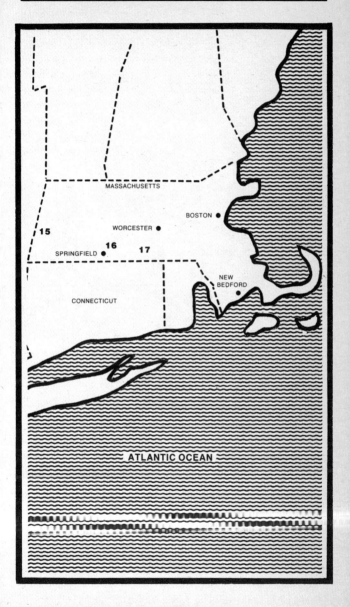

15 Lenox—Tanglewood Music Festival
16 Springfield—Various Attractions
17 Sturbridge—Old Sturbridge Village

15

Symphony Under The Stars

Tanglewood Music Festival
Lenox, Massachusetts

The Berkshire hills communities, especially around
Lenox, Massachusetts, have beguiled generations of
visitors, attracted not only by the scenic beauty of
this area of western Massachusetts but also its glittering musical and literary heritage, a tradition that

continues unabated. During the 1988 summer season, the Boston Symphony Orchestra celebrated its 50th anniversary of summer concerts in the Tanglewood Music Shed. Tanglewood is also the campus for an illustrious school of music at which, at one time or another, about a fifth of all members of America's leading symphony orchestra have studied. In Lenox and neighboring Stockbridge, writers and artists as diverse as Norman Rockwell, Nathaniel Hawthorne, Edith Wharton, and Norman Mailer have lived and worked. The rustic ambiance of the Berkshires and the energetic quest for perfection by world renowned artists working there makes this an unusual and memorable place to visit.

For lovers of classical and modern orchestral music, the annual July and August **Tanglewood Music Festival** is a total delight. The sonorities are mostly in the classical vein, with occasional performances of popular and rock music. On most Friday, Saturday, and Sunday evenings during the two-month festival, the Boston Symphony Orchestra, led by its permanent music director or by a guest conductor, is the main attraction. The orchestra is often supplemented by well-known instrumental and vocal soloists and, at times, by the Tanglewood Festival Chorus.

All of the full orchestra concerts take place in a large open-air, 6,000-seat building that is modestly called the Music Shed. (When an eminent architect designed a structure in the late 1930s, his plans had to be simplified to fit within the $100,000 construction budget. He peevishly remarked that for that amount of money the orchestra would have "just a shed [which] any builder could accomplish without the aid of an architect." The current building was designed by an engineer from neighboring Stockton). The main shed is also used for annual concerts by the Boston Pops, the Tanglewood Music Center Orchestra, guest orchestras, and occasional recitals. Well-attended open rehearsals of the BSO are held some Saturday mornings.

Concert-going purists usually opt for the more expensive seats inside the shed. There, the musicians on the stage can be seen and the music heard in the natural acoustic setting of the hall. But thousands of festival-goers choose to bring blankets, folding chairs, picnic meals, and potables to spend a relaxing evening or afternoon on the huge lawn that spreads out in front of the shed. At best they get only glimpses of the stage, but the atmosphere is festive and informal. The Tanglewood Music Center includes a number of other buildings and performance centers. Most important for visitors is the Theatre-Concert Hall, where recital and chamber music events are scheduled on selected days during the festival season.

The little town of Lenox, just a mile or two northeast of the music center, has a number of fine, if somewhat pricey, inns and restaurants. One of the best values, featuring French and American cuisine served in a romantic atmosphere, is **Lenox House,** located just north of the village on Pittsfield-Lenox Road. The restaurant's specialties include a variety of duck dishes, bouillabaisse, and veal piccata. A number of other excellent restaurants are in the fine inns of Lenox. Also in town is **Eastover Resort,** offering luxury accommodations and pools, tennis courts, a riding stable, and skiing facilities in winter.

When in Lenox, be sure to stop by **The Mount,** which from 1902 to 1911 was the summer estate of Pulitzer Prize-winning novelist Edith Wharton. Tours of the restored house and gardens are conducted from June through October. During most of July, The Mount serves as home for the Shakespeare & Company repertory theater group. Performances of the Bard's plays, as well as works by Edith Wharton, are conducted on both indoor and outdoor stages.

There are a number of bed-and-breakfast inns in and around Lenox. For a brochure listing accommodations in the area, contact the Berkshire Visitors Bureau.

DESTINATIONS

Tanglewood Music Center Lenox, MA 01240. Recorded information (in season): 413/637-1666. Additional information (in season): 413/637-1940. For out-of-season info call Boston Symphony

Hall: 617/266-1492, ext. 281. Tickets through various Ticketmaster locations; by mail after Jun 7 (Tanglewood Ticket Office, Tanglewood, Lenox, MA 01240) or in person at the Tanglewood Box Office. Late Jun-late Aug. Major symphony orchestra concerts in the shed Jul & Aug Fri 9 pm (often preceeded by smaller "Prelude" concert at 7 pm), Sat 8:30 pm (open rehearsals, if scheduled, at 10:30 am), Sun 2:30 pm. Shed seating ticket prices $10.50-$44, sometimes higher for special events. Lawn admission $8 ($9 for special events.) **The Mount,** Plunkett St & Rte 7, Lenox, MA 01240. 413/637-1899. Jun-Oct, Tue-Sat, 10 am-5 pm, Sun 9:30-5 pm. Fees vary by activities.

RESTAURANTS

Lenox House, Rte 7 & 20 Pittsfield-Lenox Road, Lenox, MA 01240. 413/637-1341. Daily 11:30 am-10 pm (Sat to midnight).

ACCOMMODATIONS

Eastover Resort, 430 East St, Lenox, MA 01240. 413/637-0625. **Berkshire Visitors Bureau,** Berkshire Common, Pittsfield, MA 01201. 413/443-9186.

16
Born In The USA

Springfield, Massachusetts

The fourth largest city in New England is the site of a surprising number of American firsts: The earliest American automobile, Thomas Blanchard's steam carriage, and the world's first gasoline powered motorcycle, George Hendee's "Indian Motorcycle," were both made here. Not surprisingly, the first working gasoline pump was developed in the same city, which also gave its name to the famous Springfield rifle. As if all this were not enough, the game of basketball was played for the first time in this Massachusetts city, and volleyball was developed in the nearby town of Holyoke, a few miles up the Connecticut River.

Springfield, Massachusetts is at the southern end of the Pioneer Valley, a wide area straddling the Connecticut River and extending northward to the Vermont border. The Valley was first settled in the 1600s and is now a variegated vacation land. Consider using Springfield as a jumping off place to explore the early industrial centers, modern hamlets, and lovely rural lands of the northern valley, a microcosm of New England. But save a couple days to discover the historical charms of Springfield.

The sport of basketball was invented in December, 1891, when Dr. James Naismith, an instructor at the Springfield Y.M.C.A. Training School (now Springfield College), sought to develop an indoor activity to keep his students physically fit during the cold New England winters. He attached an empty peach basket to the wall, organized several nine-man teams, tossed in a volleyball, and *voila!* The **Naismith Memorial Basketball Hall of Fame**, along the Connecticut River just south of downtown Springfield, is housed in a beautiful building decorated with huge outdoor murals of players in action, and is a familiar sight to travelers on I-91.

The Basketball Hall of Fame features a number of ingenious displays honoring people who have contributed to the game that now is played competively in close to 150 countries. Visitors can try their hands at shooting baskets from a moving walkway, watch a movie that puts them smack in the middle of a rousing game, and even walk through a locker room filled with personal memorabilia from some of the game's legendary players. Among the outsized equipment on display are the size 20 sneakers that belonged to Bob Lanier of the Detroit Pistons.

North and east of the downtown area, off Page Boulevard, is the **Indian Motorcycle Museum and Hall of Fame,** which commemorates the development of the world's first motorcycle. Historians say that the Springfield area was a mecca for bicycling enthusiasts in the late 19th century. In 1901, George Hendee and Oscar Hedstrom managed to attach a gasoline engine to a modified bicycle and gave birth to the Indian Motorcycle. Until its demise in the 1950s the company they founded went on to produce airplane and boat motors, lawnmowers, street cleaners, and snowmobiles. Most of these products can be viewed in the museum.

For nearly two centuries, the historic Springfield Armory east of downtown was both the city's largest employer and the area's major claim to fame. From its inception in 1794 by President George Washington, until its closing in 1968, the facility manufactured small arms and automatic weapons for the US Army. Today, the **Springfield Armory National Historic Site** has on display examples of every weapon ever produced there, including the famous Springfield Rifle used in World War I and the World War II-vintage Garand M-1. Also shown are some of the tools of Thomas Blanchard, developer of the first American steam carriage.

Four museums and the municipal library surround the tree-shaded **Quadrangle,** a few blocks east of I-91 and the Connecticut River. Period and modern arts and crafts, and entire rooms moved from historic neighborhood homes, grace the **Connecticut Valley Historical Museum.** Oriental armor, jade, and rugs from the 19th century, as well as American art from the same era, are the prime attractions at the **George Walter Vincent Smith Art Museum.** Eclecticism is the spirit at the **Museum of Fine Arts,** housing works by European masters including Picasso, Monet, Chardin, and Pissaro, as well as American artists such as Winslow Homer and Chester Harding. The **Science Museum** doubles as the home of the Seymour Planetarium, boasting the first American-built sky projector, completed in 1937.

As you'd expect from any sizable city, Springfield has a wide assortment of restaurants and accommodations. For an unusual experience in international fast-food cuisine, try the **Picnic in the Shops** in the downtown area, a collection of 10 different establishments with a full bar. For a variety of continental dishes, ranging from beef Marsala to homemade linguine in a delicate white sauce, try **Monte Carlo,** a Springfield-area favorite since the 1930s. Accommodations in the heart of downtown Springfield include hotels run by the Holiday Inn, Marriott, and Sheraton chains.

For a look back at a typical Massachusetts village of the 18th and 19th centuries, visit **Storrowtown Village,** in West Springfield. This restored village includes a schoolhouse, a meeting hall, a blacksmith's shop, homes and gardens, and a gift shop. Guided tours of the structures include crafts demonstrations. For a meal fit for an old-time Yankee, try the colonial-style beef, veal, poultry, and seafood dishes at the **Old Storrowtown Tavern.** Both the village and the tavern are located on the fairgrounds of the **Eastern States Exposition Park,** home to a two-week exposition each September, which includes a horse show, agricultural and historical exhibits, games, and big-name entertainment.

DESTINATIONS

Basketball Hall of Fame, E Columbus Ave at Union St, Springfield, MA 01101. 413/781-6500. $3. **Indian Motorcycle Museum,** 33 Hendee St, Springfield, MA 01103. 413/737-2624. Open Dec-Feb 1-5 pm, Mar-Nov 10 am-5 pm. Adults $4, children $2. **Springfield Armory National Historic Site,** Armory Square Green, Springfield, MA 01105. 413/734-8551. Daily 8 am-4:30 pm. **Springfield Library & Museums Association at the Quadrangle,** 220 State St, Springfield, MA 01103. 413/739-3871. Hours for all museums and library, Tue-Sun noon-5 pm. **Storrowtown Village,** Eastern States Exposition Park, West Springfield, MA 01089. 413/787-0136.

RESTAURANTS

Picnic in the Shops, 1500 Main St, Springfield, MA 01103. 413/733-2171. Mon-Wed, Fri 9:30 am-6 pm; Thu 9:30 am-9 pm; Sat 9:30 am-5:30 pm. **Monte Carlo,** 1020 Memorial Ave, West Springfiled, MA 01089. 413/734-6431. Mon-Fri 11:30 am-10 pm, Sat & Sun 4-10 pm. **Old Storrowtown Tavern,** Eastern States Exposition Park, West Springfield, MA 01089. 413/732-4188. Mon-Sat 11:30 am-9 pm.

ACCOMMODATIONS

Springfield Marriott, Vernon & Columbus Sts, Springfield, MA 01115. 413/781-7111. **Sheraton Tara,** Monarch Pl, Springfield, MA 01103. 413/781-1010.

17
A Living History—Yankee Style

Old Sturbridge Village
Sturbridge, Massachusetts

The seasonal rhythms of early 19th-century rural

living abound in this authentically recreated New England village circa 1830. The nearly 40 homes, shops, and public buildings in **Old Sturbridge Village,** a number of them surrounding an historic green, literally bustle with life throughout the year. In the winter, firewood is delivered on ox-drawn sleighs to cozy hearths, where Yankee-style dishes are prepared over open fires. Workers head for the woods in early spring to tap maple trees and prepare for sugaring, following Mother Nature's calendar just as their forebears did. The **Freeman Farm,** complete with period implements, is busiest at spring planting and fall harvest times. Throughout the year, artisans trained in the skills of yesteryear demonstrate the crafts of early Americana. Visitors are always welcome to watch, and sometimes help out, in the day-to-day and season-to-season workings of this popular living museum.

The historic town is about 35 miles west of Boston and just south of the busy intersection of the Massachusetts Turnpike and I-84. But the closeness of the superhighways only emphasizes the dramatic time change visitors feel as they enter the town. Time is certainly the hallmark of the J. Cheney Wells Clock Gallery in the Visitor Center, where more than 100 early timepieces sound, more or less on the hour, year-around.

Automobiles are prohibited inside the reconstructed village, and so many first-time guests begin their visits by taking in the sights from a horse-drawn wagon. But the buildings are close enough on the 200-acre site to make strolling an easy alternative. To see the interiors of the buildings in the central village, it is necessary to join one of the group tours, which are organized at the Visitor Center.

The working businesses present a microcosm of 19th century Yankee self-reliance. In the **Mill Neighborhood,** a pond and several flumes created by water diverted from the Quinebaug River provide the power to turn the waterwheels of three separate mills, a gristmill, a saw mill, and a carding mill which prepares wool and cotton for spinning. A blacksmith shop has frequent demonstrations, as does a newspaper office with an old flatbed press that is several centuries old. There are other shops, offices, and cottage industries, a general store, a lovingly restored meetinghouse, a schoolhouse, an historic tavern, and, of course, a number of authentic homes.

Depending on the time you visit, you may be fortunate enough to see a Justice of the Peace hearing conducted in the general store or, perhaps, in the tavern. From time to time, you may see village construction workers raise a barn or repair clapboard siding much as it was done a century and a half ago. In the summer, concerts are performed on the village commons. Demonstrations of nearly forgotten crafts, such as candle dipping, tinsmithing, sausage making, spinning, weaving, and pottery-making are supplemented by classes and seminars on the same types of early American craftsmanship, often divided into beginning and more advanced groups. Numerous classes are offered on collecting and care of antiques.

Special seasonal programs are scattered throughout the year. Around Washington's birthday and the Fourth of July, for example, celebrations are historically accurate. Often, ladies preparing to socialize with their neighbors can be seen arranging the very latest hairstyles—of 1830. Preparations for Thanksgiving take a full week and include turkey hunts, old-fashioned religious services at the Center Meetinghouse, and open-hearth cooking. Opportunities in the area for seasonal sports abound, including swimming, hiking, cross-country skiing, and more.

History and food combine for a tasty treat that, if not quite haute cuisine, can still charm and satisfy most visitors. In the Great Room of Bullard Tavern, guests can often help to cook their own meals in the fireplace following historic recipes. Reservations usually are required to enjoy the oyster bisque, roast beef and turkey, cornbread, puddings, and pies featured there. Hot mulled cider is a favorite on cold winter afternoons in the taproom. Also during winter, up to 14 people can sign up for a program to prepare and enjoy a 19th century family meal at the Parsonage, using a brick oven, open fireplace, and reflecting oven to prepare onion soup, roast beef, curried chicken, and pie.

Old Sturbridge Village is located in the modern, but still historically quaint, village of Sturbridge. The town has a number of inns, taverns, and restaurants that carry on the flavorful tradition of the museum. Crabapples and Publick House, two eateries at the **Publick House Inn,** are noted for their seafood, duckling, and home-baked goodies. People who have had their fill of Americana and traditional dishes often flock to **Rom's,** featuring Italian cooking, Wednesday evening smorgasbords, and moderate prices. For a change of pace in accommodations, you might want to try one of the numerous bed and breakfast-style establishments in Sturbridge and nearby towns. The **Berkshire Bed and Breakfast Connection** can help with reservations, particularly at unusual inns and on farms..

An unusual attraction is **Bethlehem in Sturbridge,** an automated, laser-lit diorama depicting the birth of Jesus. The real highlight of the area, however, is old Sturbridge Village, one of the finest and best run living-history museums in America.

DESTINATIONS

Old Sturbridge Village, 1 Old Sturbridge Village Rd, Sturbridge, MA 01566. 508/347-3362. (Winter activities info: Tri-Community Chamber of Commerce, Southridge, MA 01550. 508/764-3283.) Daily 10 am-4 pm. Closed Christmas, New Year's, and Mondays Dec-Mar. Adults $12, ages 6-15 $5. **Bethlehem in Sturbridge,** Station Hill Rd, Sturbridge, MA 01566. Daily 2 & 7 pm Thanksgiving-Jan 8; 2 pm Palm Sun-Easter Sun; 2 pm Jul 4-Lab Day. Donation of $3 requested. 508/347-3013.

RESTAURANTS

Publick House Inn, Rte 101, Sturbridge, MA 01566. 508/347-3313. (Crabapples: Daily 11:30 am-11 pm; Publick House: Daily 7:30 am-11 pm) **Rom's,** Rte 131, Sturbridge, MA 01566. 508/347-3349. Daily 11 am-9 pm (Sat to 10 pm).

ACCOMMODATIONS

Sheraton Sturbridge Center, Rte 20, Sturbridge, MA 01566. 508/347-7393. **Colonial Quality Inn,** Rte 20, Sturbridge, MA 01566. 508/347-3306. **Berkshire Bed and Breakfast Connection,** 413/268-7244.

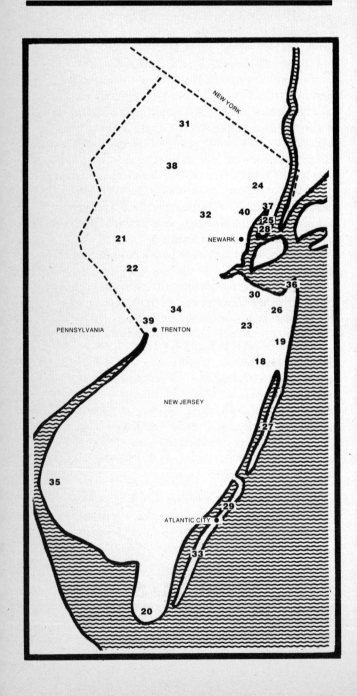

NEW JERSEY

18 🍎

Forging Ahead

Allaire State Park, New Jersey

More than 160 years ago, the area occupied by pristine **Allaire State Park,** on New Jersey's Coastal Plain, was a burgeoning industrial region that blackened air and lungs with the smoke of its furnaces and decimated the land. Trees were cut down for wood and charcoal, swamps were dredged for iron ore, and villages sprung up to provide homes for the influx of workers. Today, the area has been wonderfully reclaimed by nature. Stands of hardwoods surround the Manasquan and Mingemanhone rivers, trails for hikers and horseback riders wind through fields of wildflowers and over grassy hills, and migrating birds feed and rest in the trees there during their annual treks north and south.

At the heart of this transformation is **Allaire Village,** once a bustling "company town" where iron and brass objects were created from bog iron and where the iron workers lived in sturdy brick rowhouses; now it's a ghost town of preserved buildings. From the late 1700s until the mid-1800s, the village's blast furnace turned out iron that was used to make pots, stoves, pipes, screws, and other objects. Up to 400 workers and their families lived and worked in the village, which had grown to more than 60 buildings and structures. In the 1800s, as higher grades of iron ore became more accessible, the forge became uneconomical, and was eventually shuttered around 1853. The sturdy brick structures of the village have survived the years and now serve as a museum, allowing visitors to get an idea of what a busy industrial town of the 18th and 19th centuries was like. You can tour the furnace, blacksmith's shop, bakery, general store, post office, community church, and some of the workers' homes, all restored to their approximate 1853 condition.

Other park activities include fishing for trout in the Manasquan River (and, for kids *only,* fishing in the stocked Lower Mill Pond in the village), golf at the 18-hole Spring Meadow Golf Course, and canoeing on the Manasquan (rentals available). Campsites are available in a heavily wooded and particularly scenic section of the park.

The state park is also the site of the **Pine Creek Railroad,** which offers narrow-gauge steam train rides through the park; each circuit lasts approximately 20 minutes. The only railroad of its kind in New Jersey, the Pine Creek runs during summer and also offers a special "Christmas Express" run—

hosted by jolly ol' St. Nick, of course—on selected dates in December.

South of the park is the town of Lakewood and **Winkelmann's,** a Bavarian-style restaurant offering specialties such as weiner schnitzel, knockwurst, and rich tortes for dessert. The towns of Asbury Park (see trip #19) and Freehold (see trip #23) are also nearby.

DESTINATIONS

Allaire State Park, PO Box 220, Allaire, NJ 07727. 201/938-2371. Daily dawn-dusk; Allaire Village buildings daily May-Sep; Pine Creek Railroad wknds Apr-Jun & Sep-Oct, daily Jun-Sep.

RESTAURANTS

Winkelmann's, 945 River Ave, Lakewood, NJ 08701. 201/363-6294. Mon-Sat 11:30 am-9:30 pm, Sun noon-9 pm.

19

Greetings From Asbury Park

Asbury Park, New Jersey

When local rock-and-roller Bruce Springsteen titled his first album "Greetings From Asbury Park, NJ" (and adorned it with a colorful postcard-like cover), he seemed to be summing up the implied philosophy of this long-time seaside resort town: Having a wonderful time—wish you were here.

Asbury Park has been attracting vacation visitors since its founding in 1871. The general Asbury area includes several small shore communities adjacent to it with marvelous beaches stretching for miles in both directions along the coast. And although tens of thousands of city-dwellers make a mass exodus there every weekend from Memorial Day through Labor Day to enjoy the attractions of the beach, Asbury Park has more to offer than merely seaside amusements.

The famous mile-long boardwalk has been undergoing a big change as part of a multi-million-dollar renovation project. The town's Waterfront Redevelopment Plan, which involves 48 acres and 2,700 units of residential housing and related business—such as boutiques and restaurants along the ocean and Wesley Lake—also includes renovation of two landmarks: the **Convention Hall** and **the Paramount Theater.** The Paramount Theater has long been the site of concerts, operas, and ballets, and was personally selected by actor (and former Asburian) Danny DeVito to hold the world premiere of the film that marked his directorial debut, *Throw Momma From the Train.* The Convention Center, site of major musicals since the 1930s, hosts such events as a national boccie tournament and two big boat shows. The center is also historically significant in that a fire-damaged ship, the *Morro Castle,* ran aground near here in 1934, killing 122 persons.

The one-time "Queen of the Jersey Shore," the **Berkeley-Carteret Hotel,** has been restored to its former elegance. Built in 1925 and opened in the height of an opulent era, the once-glamorous hotel was closed in 1976. Its rebirth as a fully modern resort hotel offering such amenities as a heated pool, concierge services, golf and tennis privileges, and a health club was part of the $550-million Waterfront Redevelopment Plan.

Asbury Park plays host to a number ethnic festivals, including the Festival of Clowns and the Columbus Day Landing Ceremony, which commemorates the Italian seafarer's discovery of the New World. Just to the south of Asbury Park is **Ocean Grove,** noted as a National Historic site. Many of the old hotels there are being converted into condominiums. Ocean Grove is home to the Methodist-sponsored Camp Meeting Association and the 7,000-seat Great Auditorium, which features a musical potpourri of pop and symphony concerts, as well as cultural and religious programs. The state's largest auditorium, it was built in 1893 at a cost of $69,000; recent repair work to the roof alone is valued at almost $1 million. If you're keen on organ music, you won't want to miss the auditorium's 1908 Hope-Jones pipe organ, which is featured in several concerts a week.

For dinner or lunch, try **Christie's,** an Italian restaurant known for its special veal dishes and its own fresh-baked bread, pastries, and desserts.

DESTINATIONS

Greater Asbury Park Chamber of Commerce, Lake & Ocean Aves, PO Box 649, Asbury Park, NJ 07712. 201/775-7676. **Berkeley-Carteret Hotel,** Ocean Avenue, Asbury Park, NJ 07712. 201/776-6700.

RESTAURANTS

Christie's, 1 English Ln, Wanamassa, NJ 07712. 201/776-8558. Tue-Fri 11:30 am-2 am, Sat 5 pm-2 am, Sun 1 pm-2 am.

20

Victoriana By The Sea

Cape May, New Jersey

This is the place to rent a bicycle or take a long walk and enjoy cool sea breezes and soak in the sights of rolling dunes, marshlands, and the towers, turrets, and cupolas of pastel gingerbread houses with rockers and swing seats on their wraparound verandas. **Cape May, New Jersey,** takes you back to the Victorian era when architects let their imaginations be their guide. To walk along the Washington Street Mall and Ocean Avenue is like reliving the horse-and-buggy days when the elite of New York, Philadelphia, and Washington spent their summers where Delaware Bay flows into the Atlantic. Cape May was the summer place of the rich and famous of a bygone era and hosted such luminaries as Abraham Lincoln, Henry Clay, John Philip Sousa, and Lilly Langtry, as the spa became the summer White House for five presidents. Since 1816 Cape May has hosted visitors who are drawn there for the fishing, swimming, clambakes, birding, boating, and bandstand concerts.

With more than 600 homes predating 1900, the entire city is a registered National Historic Landmark. Most of the older homes were built after fire levelled 30 acres of the town in 1878. Today, many of these mansions and villas have been renovated, as picturesque bed-and-breakfast inns. One, an 1881 villa, unabashedly claims the name Queen Victoria. A good way to see these homes is to take a walking tour or trolley tour—stop at the Welcome Center for details. Of special interest is the **Emlen Physick Estate,** erected in 1879 at 1048 Washington Street. This 16-room Victorian mansion was designed by Frank Furness, who turned away from the gingerbread style. The house-museum exhibits Victorian toys, costumes, and artifacts. The adjoining carriage house, which predates the main building, serves as the headquarters of the Mid-Atlantic Center for the Arts (MAC), the nonprofit group that offers the trolley and walking tours of the historic district. If you visit in early October, you can join in the activities of Victorian Week, a 10-day affair which includes home tours, period fashion shows and antique shows, entertainment, and more.

Actually, Cape May has a heritage that extends to the 1630s when Dutch migrants from Nieuw Amsterdam and Pilgrims from England settled the area. One of the Dutch settlers, Captain Cornelius Mey, gave the town its name, which was later anglicized to May.

Be sure to explore Cape May Point to see the lighthouse or watch the sunset, and if you happen to spot something glistening in the sand, you have probably have found a Cape May "diamond," a piece of wave-smoothed quartz, which can be very pretty when polished up. Cape May Point displays one of the East Coast's most unusual shipwrecks, that of the concrete vessel *Atlantus*. It was one of three experimental ships built in World War I in an attempt to overcome a wartime steel shortage. *Atlantus* remained afloat until 1926 when it was blown aground here and has since settled into the sand. The nearby Cape May lighthouse was built in 1859. Its predecessors warned ships of hazardous shoals as early as 1774.

Birdwatchers are attracted to the **Cape May Bird Observatory** on East Lake Drive at Cape May Point.

This is the heart of coastal birdwatching in spring and fall, with upward of 400 species having been documented in this area. As many as 85,000 hawks have been spotted in one of the annual hawk watches that are in effect from mid-August until November.

Washington Inn, originally a plantation house of 1848, is among the well-regarded restaurants in Cape May. The continental menu features veal and seafood specialties, including the popular lobster Washington (several types of shellfish in sherry cream sauce piled into the cavity of lobster) accompanied by a variety of home-baked breads and pastries. Dining alfresco, overlooking a colorful garden, is especially delightful on a cool summer's evening. Another historic restaurant, Watson's Merion Inn is housed in an 1885 mansion that retains its Victorian decor. Specialties include stuffed lobster and fresh broiled fish. The flounder is especially tasty.

Fisherman's Wharf at Shellenger's Landing is something of a local landmark. It is the center of fishing in the area, with dozens of boats coming and going daily. It's great fun to buy a box lunch at the seafood market, consisting of fresh fish sandwiches, cole slaw, and fries to munch away on at one of the nearby docks. Also popular is the **Two Mile Landing** area north of Cape May at the drawbridge on Ocean Highway, where you can take a cruise aboard the cruise boat *Big Flamingo.*

Many visitors arrive in Cape May from Delaware via the **Cape May-Lewes Ferry,** but if you drive in on the Garden State Parkway or the slower but more scenic Ocean Highway, you may want to take a round-trip ride on the ferry (2-1/2 hours) just for the fun of it. There are frequent crossings, from 7 am to 10:20 pm in summer, but the best time is late afternoon when you capture unexcelled views of the sunset beyond Delaware Bay.

Cape May is at the tip of the peninsula that makes up Cape May County, with a number of other oceanfront communities serving the sea-loving public from early in May until late October. If you're more inclined for family amusements or a lively nightlife, plan to visit Wildwood, the principal beach town north of Cape May. Here the 2.5-mile boardwalk and downtown area bustle with an array of shops, arcades, amusement parks, restaurants, and night clubs. (The three boardwalk amusement parks claim to have more rides than Walt Disney World.)

North Wildwood was among the largest settlements north of Cape May in the 1890s when it was known as Anglesea. Scandinavians who settled there developed a major commercial fishing center comparable to the one in Gloucester, Massachusetts. Even today, an ocean expanse eight miles offshore remains a prime fishing area. Fishing for blue fish, sea trout, and striped bass is popular from bulkheads on the ocean side in North Wildwood. You can also rent a boat for fishing in the Intracoastal Waterway that extends from Ocean City through the Wildwoods to Cape May. Historic **Hereford Lighthouse** (1874) now serves as the North Wildwood Information Center and Museum.

This area is not without its own Victoriana. The four-story Queen Anne style **Candlelight Inn** is now a bed-and-breakfast inn. And the popular **Ed Zaberer's** restaurant features prime rib and seafood in a Victorian setting said to contain the "world's largest" collection of Tiffany lamps.

Stone Harbor, north of North Wildwood, has a year-around population of 1,200. At the **Wetlands Institute** off Stone Harbor Boulevard you can tour an environmental museum, climb an observation tower, hike a trail through the marshlands, and learn more about the area's ecological concerns. The **Cape May County Historical Museum** is north of Cape May in the **John Homes House** on Shore Road in the town of Cape May Court House. The museum contains Indian artifacts, ship models, whaling equipment, and antique furniture in an early-19th-century dining room and an 18th-century kitchen, doctor's room, and military room.

Families with children enjoy the free zoo at the **Cape May County Park** on US 9 at Crest Haven Road. Sunday band concerts are performed in the park from June through September.

Another natural site worth seeing is **Bennett Bog,** a wildlife sanctuary northwest of Cape May on Shunpike south of Tabernacle Road in Erma. The bog harbors numerous rare and unusual plants, as does nearby **Yearrick Hedge Gardens** off Tabernacle Road in Fishing Creek.

DESTINATIONS

Cape May County Chamber of Commerce, PO Box 74, Cape May Court House, NJ 08210. 609/465-7181. **Cape May Welcome Center,** 405 Lafayette St, Cape May, NJ 08204. 609/884-3323. **Cape May-Lewes Ferry,** PO Box 827, N Cape May, NJ 02204. 609/886-2718. **Wildwoods Department of Tourism,** PO Box 609, Wildwood, NJ 08260, or **Wildwood Tourism Commission,** PO Box 499, Wildwood, NJ 08260. 800/WW-BY-SEA. **Cape May County Historical Museum,** Shore Rd, Cape May Court House, NJ 08210. 609/465-3535, Mid-Jun-mid-Sep Mon-Sat 10am-4pm. Closed Jan-Mar. Hours vary other months.

RESTAURANTS

Washington Inn (see Accommodations). 609/884-5697. Apr-Dec 5-10pm. **Watson's Merion Inn,** 106 Decatur St, Cape May NJ 08204. 609/884-8363. Apr-Oct 4:30-10pm. **Ed Zaberer's,** 400 Spruce Ave, N Wildwood, NJ 08260. 609/522-1423. Mid-May-mid-Sep daily 4-10pm.

Washington Inn, 801 Washington St, Cape May, NJ 08204. 609/884-5697. **Candlelight Inn,** 2310 Central Ave, N Wildwood, NJ 08260. 609/522-6200.

21

Hot Air And History

Clinton, New Jersey

Even unabashed boosters of **Clinton, New Jersey,** will tell you that one of the things the town is most well-known for is its profusion of hot air. Notwithstanding the verbosity of local politicos, the hot air referred to here is the kind used to power balloons, and it's found in Clinton in abundance each August when the town plays host to the **Northeast Regional Balloon Championships.** One weekend each year, the skies above this sleepy, historic town are filled with colorful hot-air balloons from throughout the East Coast and other parts of the country. Games, entertainment, and balloon rides make this celebration a complete summertime happening.

Long before balloons soared over Clinton, milling was the town's claim to fame. Remnants of that activity, usually dating from the mid-1800s, are plentiful in and around the town. One mill, built in 1837 on the site of an even earlier mill, is now the home of the **Hunterdon Art Center.** The transformation of the mill has resulted in an appealing structure that retains much of its rustic charm. The stone exterior of the mill has been revealed for the first time in nearly a century. Formerly encased in a layer of oatmeal-colored stucco, the rugged beauty and impressive character of the building's striking gray fieldstone exterior can now be fully appreciated.

Hunterdon features galleries where nationally known artists display and sell their works. Functional ceramics, jewelry, glassware, hand-woven items, and prints are just a few of the craft objects on display. Prominent artists also conduct workshops from time to time.

In 1957, printmaker Anne Steel Marsh, also a Center trustee, curated the first National Print Exhibition at the Center. It now averages more than 600 entries, of which about 150 are juried for the exhibit; they then tour both in and out of state.

More area history—again, connected to the era of the mills—can be found at the **Clinton Historical Museum Village,** which includes the four-story 1763 Old Red Mill. The mill was once the center of the town's industry, and its water-power was used to grind various grains, limestone, graphite, and talc, as well as to produce the town's first electricity. Today, the mill provides display space for artifacts and memorabilia of more than 200 years of rural life in New Jersey's Delaware Valley.

The museum village offers a panorama of life in the 18th, 19th, and early 20th centuries, focusing on day-to-day family and work activities. The village includes a one-room schoolhouse, log cabin, lime kiln, blacksmith shop, and other historic buildings, each displaying typical artifacts of particular eras. Period furniture and appropriately dressed mannequins complement the historic buildings.

The limestone cliffs near the mill make a natural outdoor amphitheater, which is utilized for weekly concerts during summer. The type of music varies from folk and jazz to blues and country. For area dining, head for the **Clinton House,** a restaurant housed in a 1743 structure that was once a stagecoach stop. House specialties include steak, prime rib, stuffed game hens with wild rice, lobster, and an ocean-fresh catch-of-the-day.

DESTINATIONS

Hunterdon Art Center, 7 Center St, Clinton, NJ 08809. 201/735-8415. Daily 9 am-5 pm. **Clinton Historical Museum Village,** 56 Main St, Clinton, NJ 08809. 201/735-4101. Apr-Oct Mon-Fri 1-5 pm, Sat & Sun noon-6 pm. Adults $5, children 6-12 $2.

RESTAURANTS

The Clinton House, 2 W Main St, Clinton, NJ 08809. 201/735-5312. Mon-Sat 11:30 am-2:30 pm, 5-10 pm; Sun 11:30 am-2:30 pm, 5-9 pm.

22 🍎

Sale Of The 18th Century

Flemington, New Jersey

Whether you prefer historic registers or cash registers, there's something for everyone in **Flemington, New Jersey.** At this early farming community (the site in late August of the annual New Jersey State Agricultural Fair), dedicated history buffs can immerse themselves in the town's 18th-century atmosphere, and do a little shopping on the side. Conversely, steadfast outlet shoppers can add a little diversion to their bargain hunting by enjoying some of the historic sights that made Flemington famous.

Flemington was established in 1756 when Samuel Fleming built his home on 105 acres in the heart of New Jersey's Skylands, the mountainous northwest region, 55 miles from New York City. His home, **Fleming Castle,** still stands on Bonnell Street. It serves as the headquarters of the Daughters of the American Revolution, and can be seen by appointment.

The seat of Hunterdon County since 1785, Flemington displays its history through an impressive array of preserved Colonial, Greek Revival, and Victorian buildings. Visit the Civil War Monument on Main Street and stop at the County Court House, site of the famous Lindbergh baby kidnapping trial. This Greek Revival building is the center of the town's Main Street area.

The **Black River & Western Railroad** operates one-hour, round-trip steam train excursions through the historical district and into rural farm country, to Ringoes, New Jersey, with connecting trains on Sundays to Lambertville on the Delaware River. The station is easy to find—it's in the heart of **Liberty Village and Turntable Junction,** the city's main shopping areas.

Liberty Village is no ordinary shopping center. More than 80 manufacturers operate factory outlets here, but what makes these stores special are the very buildings that house them. In a unique combination of restoration and re-creation, the outlet center consists of a mixture of 1800s buildings (on the site of an old foundry) and contemporary structures designed to look like 18th- and 19th-century shops and homes. Strolling through Liberty Village, one can appreciate the effort to preserve an 18th-century atmosphere, and that can make a long day's shopping all the more pleasant.

Of course, the shopping itself is a major attraction. Unlike many outlet centers which specialize in clothes, Flemington shops sell a much wider range of merchandise. The city became famous in the early 1900s for Flemington Cut Glass and it is now also known for its selection of china, housewares, gifts, jewelry, and, yes, clothes—particularly coats and furs. (And, as you're shopping, remember that New Jersey levies no sales tax on clothing, unlike New York City's hefty 8-1/4 percent.)

Liberty Village has stores representing Corning, Calvin Klein, Waterford Crystal, and Harve Bernard, plus at least 50 more stores selling a variety of merchandise, from shoes to chocolates. In adjoining Turntable Junction, visitors can shop for old-fashioned sweets, Oriental gifts, and country lace.

You can easily spend an entire day here, going from shop to shop, without seeing the same goods over again. To help you get the most out of your shopping time, the Flemington Trolley runs every half-hour to carry your tired body to the next street filled with stores. Timetables and maps are available at most shops; a $1 ticket is good all day.

And when the day is done, have dinner at **The Union Hotel,** a 214-year-old landmark in Flemington's historic district. This is a casual, family restaurant with a lively pub and a varied menu, highlighting meats, pasta, and seafood. The Tuesday night special is a particular hit—a 20-ounce T-bone steak for $7.95.

DESTINATIONS

Fleming Castle, 5 Bonnell St, Flemington, NJ 08822. 201/782-6472. By appointment. **Black River & Western Railroad,** Mine St, Flemington, NJ 08822. Mid-Apr-early Dec. Adults $5, ages 5-12 $2.50, ages 3-4 $1. **Liberty Village and Turntable Junction,** 1 Church St, Box 161, Flemington, NJ 08822. 201/782-8550. Mon-Sun 10 am-5:30 pm.

RESTAURANTS

The Union Hotel, 76 Main St, Flemington, NJ 08822. 201/788-7474. Mon-Sat 11 am-4 pm, 5 pm-midnight; Sun 12-8 pm.

23

Cowboys, Molly, And The Boss

Freehold, New Jersey

It's pretty obvious, really. If you're in the vicinity of New York City and you want to see cowboys, you should head west. Well, at least as far west as **Freehold, New Jersey,** where, it is estimated, there are more working cowboys than in any state east of Texas. This is horse country, and raising horses is one of Monmouth County's principal industries. Horse farms are common here, and mares with young colts can often be seen frolicking in fields from area roads.

Horses from the area—as well as from the rest of the East Coast racing circuit—compete at two racetracks in Monmouth County. **Freehold Raceway** is one of the oldest harness racing tracks in the nation. Races are run there every day of the year beginning at 1 pm (except Sundays and from June until August). Thoroughbreds race at **Monmouth Park,** in Oceanport. Monmouth offers racing from late May to early September; daily post time is 1:30 pm.

To see horses and their owners compete for ribbons instead of purses, check out **East Freehold Park Showgrounds,** an 81-acre park for equestrian events and animal shows. It provides comfortable viewing for the casual observer. Inquire ahead for details on upcoming shows and competitions.

Freehold also has some interesting historical sites. The town was the location of the Battle of Monmouth on June 28, 1770, which is today remembered not for acts of war, but for an act of brave compassion. Molly Hays emerged a heroine from the battle, and was memorialized as "Molly Pitcher," for carrying water to artillerymen in a pitcher on that hot June day. Molly also helped keep an artillery gun in action after her husband was wounded and another member of his gun crew was killed. For these actions, Molly was thanked on behalf of the army by Gen. Nathanael Greene, and was later presented to George Washington himself for commendation. Today, the **Monmouth Battlefield State Park** marks the site of the engagement and commemorates Molly and the battle with exhibits at its visitor center and tours of the battlefield.

More area history is preserved at the **Monmouth County Historical Museum and Library,** which displays Revolutionary and Civil War weapons, as well as collections of ceramics, silver, and paintings. Early 17th-, 18th-, and 19th-century furniture is featured in the galleries. The attic museum stuffed with historic toys, dolls, and doll houses is a special treat for youngsters. Near Freehold Raceway is **Covenhoven House,** an 18th century home with period furniture used as headquarters by British Gen. Henry Clinton prior to the Battle of Monmouth. For the art connoisseur, there's a notable collection of Currier and Ives prints at the **American Hotel,** one of the oldest in this area and a stagecoach stop during the 19th century.

Many rock and roll fans may not be familiar with Freehold, but they certainly know her most famous son. Singer Bruce "The Boss" Springsteen grew up here, making the town's grammar school and high school, as well as the star's boyhood home, points of curious interest to his devoted fans.

Not far from here, a mile south on NJ 79, is **Van's Freehold Inn,** offering a menu of solid favorites, such as lobster, shrimp, prime rib, and thick steaks. The restaurant's homemade cakes, pies, and other desserts make it a local mecca for anyone with a sweet tooth.

DESTINATIONS

Western Monmouth Chamber of Commerce, 49 E Main St, Freehold, NJ 07728. 201/462-3030. **Freehold Raceway,** Park Ave at US 9 and NJ 33. Freehold, NJ 07728. 201/462-3800. **Monmouth Park,** Oceanport Ave, Oceanport, NJ 07757. 201/222-5100. **East Freehold Park Showgrounds,** Kozloski Rd, Freehold, NJ 07728. 201/842-4000. **Monmouth Battlefield State Park,** NJ 33, Freehold NJ 07728. 201/462-9616. **Monmouth County Historical Museum and Library,** 70 Court St,

Monmouth, NJ 07728. 201/462-1466. Tue-Sun 9 am-5 pm. **Covenhoven House,** 150 W Main St, Freehold, NJ 07728. 201/462-1455. Jun-Oct Tue, Thu, Sat, & Sun 9 am-5 pm.

RESTAURANTS

Van's Freehold Inn, South St, Freehold, NJ 07728. 201/431-1500. Mon-Thu 11:30 am-10 pm, Fri & Sat noon-10:30 pm, Sun noon-9 pm.

ACCOMMODATIONS

American Hotel, PO Box 350, 18 E Main St, Freehold, NJ 07728. 201/462-0819.

24 🦅

The Bridge That Saved A Nation

Hackensack, New Jersey

Tucked into a dead-end street, just a few steps from the shopping malls and frenetic parkways for which New Jersey is infamous, is a gentle reminder of what New Jersey once was. The **New Bridge Landing Historic Park** in River Edge, a small town north of Hackensack, is home to the **Steuben House,** which sits at the edge of the Hackensack River. The Jersey Dutch sandstone building is one of the rarest types of Colonial architecture, and is found nowhere else in the world. The oldest part of the house dates to about 1710, when Johannes Ackerman, a shoe-maker, acquired the land. The Ackermans later sold the land to Jan Zabriskie; the estate was eventually confiscated from Zabriskie's son, who was accused of being a British informant. The government gave it to Maj. Gen. Baron von Steuben, a Prussian officer, for his efforts on behalf of the American troops during the American Revolution.

Today, four rooms are open to the public, exhibiting items from the collections of the Bergen County Historical Society. Most of the items on display were made and used in the area. There is an outstanding collection of local pottery, including a large display of pie dishes made in the town. Children enjoy the collection of dolls and toys; a wax doll from about 1700, named Betsy Cox, is thought to be the oldest surviving doll in America. The attic is filled with maps, toys, and antique signs. There's even a wooden dugout canoe.

Also on the property is the two-century-old **Campbell-Christie House,** a 19th-century barn, and the **Demarest House,** thought to be more than 300 years old. These buildings are open only during special events at the park. Civil War re-enactments, concerts, and festivals are held throughout the year.

Also of interest in the park is the **New Bridge.** Although its current reduced state makes it hard to imagine now, the Hackensack River played a significant role in commerce and combat in the 18th century. In 1744, the New Bridge, a wooden drawbridge, was built across the Hackensack, the first river crossing above Newark Bay. Commercial traffic followed as soon as the bridge was built. On November 20, 1776, 6,000 British and Hessian troops crossed the Hudson at the Lower Closter Landing to attack Fort Lee. Gen. George Washington rode out from his headquarters in Hackensack and led the fleeing men from the fort over the New Bridge. For its role in saving the American troops, the wooden bridge was later called "The Bridge That Saved a Nation." In 1888, it was replaced with an iron truss swing-bridge which was mounted on a turntable to open to river traffic. In 1956, it was closed to vehicle traffic, but visitors are welcome to investigate.

Another link with the Dutch past is found by driving about five minutes from New Bridge Landing to Hackensack. The **First Reformed Protestant Dutch Church,** known as the Church on the Green, celebrated its 300th birthday in 1986. The congregation is the oldest in Bergen County. The big stone church currently on the site was built in 1791, and incorporates stones from the original building.

For history of a different era, navigate a little farther downriver from the Steuben House to the **USS Ling,** a World War II submarine. The *Ling* was commissioned just a little too late to see combat: on its way from the Panama Canal to the Pacific, the war ended. Visitors can tour the submarine, which is as cramped as you might imagine. The adjoining museum houses photos of venerable subs, memorabilia, and a periscope to peer in for views outside. On the lawn are torpedoes and other submarine-related items.

For a meal from the depths of the sea, try lunch or dinner at the nearby **Sea Shack.** The Shack is a casual establishment whose specialty is blackened swordfish. Another choice is **Pizza-Town USA.** This faded little red, white, and blue restaurant serves some of the best pizza in town.

DESTINATIONS

New Bridge Landing Historic Park, 1209 Main St, River Edge, NJ 07661. 201/487-1739. Wed-Sat 10 am-noon, 1-5 pm; Sun 2-5 pm. **First Reformed Protestant Dutch Church,** 42 Court St, Hackensack, NJ 07601. 201/342-7050. **USS Ling,** Court & River Sts, Hackensack, NJ 07601. 201/342-3268. Daily 10 am-5 pm, last tour at 4 pm. Dec-Jan closed Mon & Tue. Adults $2.50, children under 12 $1.50.

RESTAURANTS

Sea Shack, 293 Polifly Rd, Hackensack, NJ 07601. 201/489-7232. Tue-Fri 11:30 am-10:30 pm, Sat 4:30-11 pm, Sun & Mon 11:30 am-10 pm. **Pizza-Town USA,** 492 Hackensack Ave, River Edge, NJ 07661. 201/342-1030. Daily 10 am-10 pm.

25

A Square Mile Of Fascination

Hoboken, New Jersey

Marlon Brando battled on the docks and back alleys of **Hoboken, New Jersey,** in *On the Waterfront,* and Woodrow Wilson sailed to France for the Versailles Peace Conference from the city's piers. Stephen Foster wrote *I Dream of Jeannie with the Light Brown Hair* in a rented room at Sixth and Bloomfield (a plaque marks the building), and G. Gordon Liddy of Watergate fame grew up in a Hudson Street brownstone (no plaque). In the 1830s, fur baron John Jacob Astor built a summer place at Second and Washington, and Hetty Green, the "Witch of Wall Street," who was nearly as rich as Astor but far more eccentric, later lived in a cold-water flat nine blocks uptown.

That's Hoboken, a vibrant town with a rich history. Hemmed in by the Holland and Lincoln Tunnels, the Palisades and the river, it retains a streetscape from bygone days and a small-town flavor that is unique in the New York area. You'll find that its accessibility by excellent public transportation makes it ideal for a spur-of-the-moment excursion.

Nicknamed the "Mile Square City" and once known as a rough port town, rapidly gentrifying Hoboken today invites ambling and exploring. Washington Street, the main drag which locals call "the avenue," has enticing restaurants, antique shops, and boutiques. Between Newark and First streets is City Hall, a hulking yellow brick building where the **Hoboken Historical Museum** maintains changing displays. There still are mansions on Castle Point Terrace, rows of brownstones along Hudson and Bloomfield streets, and elsewhere five-story tenements, either in their original state or remodeled into efficient condos for the yuppies who have all but turned Hoboken into New York's sixth borough.

Castle Point, a dramatic promontory high above the river, is the only outcropping of green serpentine rock along the Hudson. It is now the campus of **Stevens Institute of Technology.** From the lookout beside Stevens Center, you will marvel at the eye-popping panorama of Manhattan. On a clear day, this million-dollar view stretches from the George Washington Bridge on the north to the Verazanno Bridge on the south.

Fine art is flourishing in Hoboken. Small galleries showing local artists' work come and go in storefronts all over town, while Stevens houses a notable collection. At the **Samuel C. Williams Library** is a brass stabile by alumnus Alexander Calder, plus changing exhibitions and a permanent collection of memorabilia of the Stevens family on whose estate the engineering college is located. Nearby is Elysian Park, a remnant of the historic greenspace called Elysian Fields, where America's first organized baseball game was played in 1846.

Several Hoboken firehouses are listed on the National Register of Historic Places, as is the **Holy Innocents Church,** a Gothic jewel built by Martha Bayard Stevens in memory of a son who died, decorated with a theme of children and angels. Also listed is the Erie-Lackawanna Terminal, with its leaded-glass ceiling and unusual European-style train sheds.

Some people come to Hoboken just to eat, and once you have sampled its terrific restaurants, you will, too. The **Clam Broth House,** arguably Hoboken's best-known eatery, serves bargain seafood. **Gerrino's Ristorante** and **Da Vinci** both specialize in northern Italian cuisine. **Talbot's** and **On the Waterfront** are refined and elegant culinary oases, while **Maxwell's** is a noisy pub where many New Wave bands have made their debut.

Hoboken has no visitors' bureau or chamber of commerce. From New York, it can be reached by bus every 15-20 minutes from the Port Authority bus terminal via New Jersey Transit or the Red Apple bus or by PATH from Herald Square, Chelsea, Greenwich Village, and the World Trade Center.

DESTINATIONS

Hoboken Historical Museum, City Hall, 94 Washington St, Hoboken, NJ 07030. Weekdays (except gov't holidays), 9 am-5 pm. **Samuel C. Williams Library, Stevens Institute of Technology,** Castle Point, Hoboken NJ 07030. 201/792-5239. Mon-Thu 8-1 am, Fri 8 am-9 pm; Sat 10 am-5 pm, Sun noon-1 am. **Holy Innocents Church,** Willow Ave & Sixth St. Inquire at All Saints Rectory, Washington and 7th Sts. 201/792-3563.

RESTAURANTS

Clam Broth House, 38 Newark St, Hoboken NJ 07030. 201/

659-2448. Sun-Thu 11:30 am-11:30 pm; Fri, Sat 11:30-12:30 am.
Gerrino's Ristorante, 96 River St, Hoboken NJ 07030. 201/
656-7731. Mon-Thu noon-3 pm, 5-10 pm; Fri noon-3 pm, 5-11 pm,
Sat 5-11 pm. **Da Vinci,** 411 Washington St, Hoboken, NJ 07030.
201/659-2141. Mon-Thu 11:45 am-2:45 pm, 5-10 pm; Fri 11:45 am-
2:45 pm, 5-11 pm. Sat 5-11 pm. **Talbot's,** 61 Sixth St, Hoboken NJ
07030. 201/795-4515. Tue-Fri, 5-9:30 pm; Sat 5-10 pm, Sun 3-8
pm. Reservations suggested. **On the Waterfront,** 163 14th St,
Hoboken NJ 07030. 201/420-7711. Mon-Fri noon-4 pm, 5-11 pm;
Sat 5-11 pm; Sun noon-3:30 pm. **Maxwell's,** 1039 Washington St,
Hoboken, NJ 07030. 201/798-4046. Tue-Sat 11 am-12 am, Sun 12
pm-12 am.

26

Life On The Farm

Longstreet Farm
Holmdel, New Jersey

It's a normal day out on the farm: the bright sun
shines from an azure sky, the sweet smell of freshly
cut hay fills the clean air, and green hills roll gently
to the horizon. Cows stand solidly out in the pasture, chewing their cud and lazily swishing their
tails; geese and chickens flap around the barnyard,
chattering noisily; high-spirited lambs gambol like
children in a playground.

To get away from the city and experience life as it
was lived on an East Coast farm in the 1890s, journey to **Longstreet Farm,** in **Holmdel, New Jersey,**
once among the largest and most prosperous farms
in Monmouth County. Now confined to just nine
acres, the original farm covered 495 acres, assem-
bled in 1806 by Hedrick Longstreet from several existing farms.

Even in the 1890s, when steam and gas power
were replacing horse power, Longstreet Farm was
considered old fashioned. At that time, farm practices in Monmouth County were changing in re-
sponse to competition from midwestern farmers and
to mechanization sparked by the Industrial Revolution, but Longstreet continued with its time-tested

methods, raising cereal grains and livestock, with potatoes as a cash crop.

The farm remained in the family until it was purchased by Monmouth County in 1967. It has since been preserved as a slice of the county's rural past, and was opened to the public in 1972.

While the farming methods were leisurely in style, there was—and remains—a lot to do. Visitors can watch costumed interpreters perform seasonal chores at the farm, opting to try their hand at a bit of work if they so desire. In the spring, sheep are shorn of their winter coats; barnyard manure, spread during the winter, is turned under by the plow; disk and harrow rake the fields before crops are planted. Public programs include demonstrations of plowing, milking, spring cleaning, pumpkin planting, blacksmithing, cooking, and needlework.

The long, hot days of summer slow the pace. Winter wheat and rye are harvested, hay is cut and stored, and crops are cultivated. There are ice cream socials and county fairs, and large straw hats to help beat the heat.

The pace quickens in the fall. Home-grown garden vegetables are canned for the winter. Extra workers are employed to help with harvesting and threshing. You see potatoes being dug and stored in the cellar of the potato house. Farmers pick corn in late fall and store it for use later as feed.

When cold weather comes, wood is gathered and cut and split for firewood. Repairs are made on the various buildings, fences, and equipment, and holiday activities include ice cutting and sleigh rides.

Numerous buildings dot the nine-acre farm. The best place to begin exploring is at the carriage house, which serves double duty as the orientation center and meeting place for programs. Exhibits familiarize you with the farm, and there is additional literature available in the gift shop. Guided or self-guiding tours are available.

The farmhouse, built in the late 1700s and expanded and redesigned several times since, has been restored and furnished to resemble its appearance in the 1890s. Most of the other buildings have retained their practical uses. There is a stable for horses and mules, a pump house for farm water and a well house for drinking water, an ice house, and an "out kitchen" where cooking and other kitchen demonstrations are given. On weekends, you can watch apples being pressed into cider and then sample the tasty results.

For country dining with a touch of history, head east about five miles to the **Lincroft Inn.** The restaurant is housed in a building that was an old stagecoach stop, part of which dates to 1697. Try the medallions of veal or the fresh ocean seafood; steaks and prime rib are also popular there.

DESTINATIONS

Longstreet Farm, Holmdel Park, Holmdel, NJ 07738. 201/946-3758. Mem Day-Lab Day daily 9 am-5 pm, Lab Day-Mem Day daily 10 am-4 pm.

RESTAURANTS

Lincroft Inn, 700 Newman Springs Rd, Lincroft, NJ 07738. 201/741-8170. Tue-Sat 11:30 am-10 pm, Sun noon-9 pm.

27

Serene Seaside

Island Beach State Park
Seaside Park, New Jersey

It's early morning in spring and you share the 10-mile sliver of sand at **Island Beach State Park** with few others. A lone fisherman in hip waders casts into the Atlantic surf. In a beach buggy nearby, awaiting the skillet, is a freshly caught striped bass, weighing close to 10 pounds. Two teenagers comb the white sand for the driftwood that the powerful tides pile on the shore. A retired couple pore over a field guide, examining a pile of shells they have collected—blue mussels, soft-shelled clams, whelks, periwinkles, and long, narrow razor clams. About

40 species of shells are common to these shores, with as many more rare varieties, mostly storm-washed from deeper water. There is a solitary bird watcher, although it is a little early for the spring arrival of thousands of migratory birds and the federally-licensed banders who set up nets to temporarily capture birds for banding.

It is not always this deserted at the 2,694-acre park. On some hot summer weekends, visitors flock in and the gates are closed by 10 am. But if the magnificent bathing beaches are not an important attraction, spring and fall are a nice time to visit. In spring a profusion of beach plum bushes bloom with white flowers; in August and September locals harvest the tart fruit to make jelly and delicious pancake syrup. Fall is the time, too, for admiring the holly, when the berries have turned a deep red, the leaves dark green.

Despite its popularity and proximity to major population centers (located about midpoint between New York City and Atlantic City), the park is one of the last relatively undisturbed barrier islands in North America. It is an ocean lover's version of Walden Pond, with varied flora and fauna and the foamy surf of the blue sea fingering into the white sands. Eagle-like osprey wheel overhead, herring gulls stand to attention on weather-worn fences, and sandpipers unfailingly outrace the incoming swell.

From pirates to bootleggers, the island has had a checkered history. The object of a land grant by England's Charles I, it became the property of Lord Stirling, a Brigadier General of the Continental Army who distinguished himself in the Revolutionary War. During the 1780s, it provided cover for the New Jersey Privateers, the state's own band of pirates who were sanctioned by the government to raid British ships. Later, the island became a haven for rum-runners and then the object of grandiose plans for a magnificent seaside resort, until the stock-market crash of 1929 ended that dream. It was acquired by the State of New Jersey in 1953 and opened as a public park in 1959.

To protect the island's fragile dune ecosystem,

with vegetation that exists today as it did thousands of years ago, the island is divided into three sections. The northern and southern zones are nature preserves; the central section is a recreation area. Public use of the northern section is limited to the ocean beach, which may be used for fishing and beach-walking; use of the southern area also is limited to the beach, for picnicking, sunbathing, fishing, and nature study. Throughout the island are specified locations for diving, surfing, fishing, and swimming (in the mild waters of the bay or in the ocean surf). One mile of ocean shore in the central portion is a bathing beach staffed by lifeguards from mid-June through Labor Day.

Trees carved by wind and spray are set against a backdrop of beach plum, holly, catbrier, and beach heather, the last with a complex root system that helps to conserve the dunes. Protection of the dunes is a prime concern and tours by interpreters help visitors appreciate the delicate balance. Guides explain how beach grass thrives in shifting sand, holding the dunes together, and how a secondary grass, Japanese sedge, is believed to have sprouted from packing materials washed overboard in rough seas. They'll also tell you about the dark, matted clumps of eel grass, a flowering plant that grows in the bay. In the 1930s, a cottage industry harvested eel grass and dried it for use as house insulation, furniture stuffing, and packing material.

Although overnight camping is not permitted in the park, lodging is available within minutes' drive in the communities of Seaside Park and Seaside Heights. A popular choice is the **Aztec Motel,** where you can step out of your room onto the beach and take advantage of a heated pool.

You'll also find a varied selection of restaurants here, with emphasis on steaks, Italian fare, and seafood. Locals insist that **Bum Rogers Tavern,** one block from the ocean, has the best garlic crabs on the east coast (they're cleaned and then sautéed in wine, garlic, and butter). The large restaurant, with seating for 110 in two dining rooms, uses blue-claw crabs from nearby Barnegat Bay during the nine-month season. Other offerings include buckets of steamers, clams on the half shell, and Italian-style seafood. Popular with beef eaters is Steak Murphy, prepared with a peppery onion sauce.

The stylish **Top O' The Mast** has big picture windows that look out onto the beach (lighted at night) and the pounding Atlantic Ocean. The specialty is tableside cookery including chateaubriand, and flambéed duck and fish such as pompano and red snapper. Caesar salad is a specialty. There is live entertainment every night (weekends off-season) with the emphasis on nostalgia and oldies. It was voted the top night spot in New Jersey in a poll conducted by the *Bergen Record*.

Another popular spot (open only in season) is the **Berkeley Fish Market,** overlooking Island Beach State Park. This is both a restaurant and a fish market that also has a take-out counter for fried fish and chips. The upstairs restaurant offers a bayside view, and specializes in live lobster, scallops, stuffed flounder, and a variety of broiled and fried fish.

DESTINATIONS

Island Beach State Park, Seaside Park, NJ 08752. 201/793-0506.

RESTAURANTS

Bum Rogers Tavern, 2207 Central Ave, S Seaside Park, NJ 08752. 201/830-2770. Daily 9 am-2 am. **Top O' The Mast,** 23 Ave & Ocean, S Seaside Park, NJ 08752. 201/793-2444. Daily 11 am-midnight. **Berkeley Fish Market,** 24 & Central Ave, S Seaside Park, NJ 08752. 201/255-6333. Mid-May-mid-Sep daily 8 am-10 pm.

ACCOMMODATIONS

Aztec Motel, 901 Boardwalk, Seaside Park, NJ 08752. 201/793-3000. **Windjammer Motor Inn,** 1st Ave & Central Ave, Seaside Park, NJ 08752. 201/830-2555.

28

Behind Lady Liberty's Back

Jersey City, New Jersey

According to lore, a New Yorker and a New Jerseyan long ago had a boat race. At stake were the harbor islands. The New Yorker won, and such islands as Staten, Liberty, and Ellis now belong to the Empire and not the Garden State, although they are just a few hundred yards off the Jersey City shore. Yet only in the last decade has **Jersey City** staked a bit of a claim to the Lady of the Harbor, and given her an appropriate backdrop. Where once there were expanses of abandoned railroad yards, there now is **Liberty State Park.**

Take an afternoon or summer evening to explore this 800-acre oasis of open space in the middle of the densely built up New York-New Jersey area. Even on the steamiest days, you will catch a refreshing sea breeze on the park's walkways and meadows—and the view of the lower Manhattan skyline just across the Hudson is breathtaking.

The Jersey Central Railroad terminal, the historic conduit between Ellis Island and life in America for thousands of immigrants, hosts antique shows and other exhibits. You may remember it from the closing scene of *Funny Girl.* In the warm months, the park really shines. There are open-air concerts and **Circle Line's Liberty Island Ferry** makes frequent runs to the statue. The man-made estuary at the north end of the park, once part of a barge canal leading across the state to the Delaware, is the ferry departure point—faster, less expensive, and less crowded than its Manhattan-based counterpart. When Ellis Island, now under restoration by the National Park Service, reopens, it, too, will be accessible from Liberty State Park.

Elsewhere, Jersey City is mainly a city of neighborhoods, including three that are downtown and close to the river, with exquisite brownstone rowhouses. Paulus Hook, site of one of the more than 100 Revolutionary War skirmishes fought in New Jersey, is the oldest. The Colgate plant is now under reconstruction from industrial into commercial use, and the developers promise to keep its great clock, said to be the world's largest, a Hudson River landmark.

Van Vorst Park to the northwest has the largest brownstone concentration. On Montgomery Street, be sure to look at City Hall, an elaborate monument to the power and spoils of old-line ward politics, and the old Majestic Theater, being restored for use as a cultural center. The top floor of the nearby library serves as the **Jersey City Museum,** with changing exhibits of local art and history. Stop at **Winston's,** a lively neighborhood hangout known for reasonably priced food and good companionship. It's the "Cheers" of Jersey City.

Hamilton Park, the smallest of the brownstone areas, is within walking distance of Jersey's newest neighborhood. Newport, a massive high-rise development atop and around the Holland Tunnel, is virtually a city within a city. **Newport Centre,** a suburban-style indoor mall, boasts excellent shops (including the first Macy's Euro-trendy Aeropostale clothing specialty stores), six movie theaters, and a food court. You can hop the PATH for a quick ride to Newport. New Jersey levies no sales tax on clothing—a welcome relief from New York's 8-1/4 percent.

Uptown Jersey City is on the hill formed by the southern taper of the Palisades, which only here are inland from the Hudson. Detached houses and apartment buildings replace the downtown rowhouses. Journal Square is the uptown (though hardly upscale) shopping district and transportation hub. The Square has three grand movie palaces (one restored by the Jehovah's Witnesses, one under threat of demolition, and one in use). Nearby, the grand old County Courthouse, a Beaux Arts treasure, almost succumbed to the wrecking ball but instead has been restored and is used for court sessions again.

DESTINATIONS

Jersey City Chamber of Commerce, 574 Summit Ave, Jersey City, NJ 07302. 201/653-7400. **Liberty State Park,** Wolf Dr, Jersey City, NJ 07305. 201/915-3400. **Circle Line Statue of Liberty Ferry,** 201/435-9499 for schedules and rates. Newport Centre, **PATH** train to Pavonia Station from Herald Square, Chelsea, Greenwich Village, or World Trade Center, $1. **Jersey City Museum,** 471 Jersey Ave, Jersey City, NJ 07302. 201/547-4514. Tue, Wed, Fri, Sat 11:30 am-4:30 pm, Wed 11:30 am-8 pm.

RESTAURANTS

Winston's, 292 Barrow St, Jersey City, NJ 07302. 201/434-8694. Daily 11-2 am.

29

A Wind In Your Sails

Long Beach Island, New Jersey

When you suddenly feel the need to see rolling surf and feel fresh ocean breezes; when you get the urge to dig for clams in the wake of the receding tide, wet a line, or just wriggle your toes through warm sand, then **Long Beach Island** is the place to be. This 18-mile-long thread of land, stretching alongside the New Jersey mainland, offers every water sport you could hope for, as well as non-nautical attractions such as antique stores, historical sites, and even a unique artists' colony.

This barrier island was first inhabited by whalers in the 18th century, later supplanted by commercial fisherman. Now sportfishing probably tops the list of most popular activities; there's deep-sea fishing, surf or pier fishing, and angling in the bay.

White sandy beaches line the entire length of the eastern side of the island where the Atlantic surf rolls in. On the west are protected bays, where you'll find boat berths and bathing beaches. Boats of all types sail or motor down the calm waters of the Intracoastal Waterway, including excursion boats, some destined for mainland hotels and casinos in Atlantic City.

NJ 72 spans the bay, connecting the mainland town of Manahawkin with **Ship Bottom** at approximately the mid-point of Long Beach Island. After you cross the Manahawkin Bay Bridge you'll immediately run into Long Beach Boulevard, the only main thoroughfare, extending the length of the island.

You'll find several motels at Ship Bottom, most open year-around. **The Sandpiper,** near the beach, is moderately priced. And a pleasant restaurant is the colonial-style **Bayberry Inn,** which specializes in fresh seafood, as do many restaurants on the island. The inn's seafood specialties change seasonally, and can include grilled swordfish, clam and crab dishes, and thick chowders.

Driving north on the boulevard you'll reach **Surf City,** one of the island's original whaling towns. This is a family-oriented resort community with shops, restaurants, and a guarded bathing beach at 16th Street.

Just beyond North Beach is **Harvey Cedars,** which was the country's largest whaling settlement in the 18th century, known then as Harvey's Whaling Station. This is the spot to "hang 10" if you're a surfer, or cast a line if you prefer fishing. Restaurants line the boulevard in this tiny but charming town.

Still heading north, you'll reach **Loveladies,** a popular art colony. The area around the harbor might remind you of Cape Cod. In summer you'll find art exhibits and musical performances ranging from folk to jazz.

Finally, at the northernmost tip of the island, standing like a sentinel, is "Old Barney," the 167-foot **Barnegat Lighthouse** in the town of **Barnegat Light,** a quiet community with little traffic and a lot of character. The docks are bustling, though, for this is the center of the island's fishing industry, and boats are ready to take you to whatever is biting.

Many a ship was spared disaster on the shoals of Barnegat Inlet, thanks to Old Barney's beam of light. For a spectacular view, climb the spiral staircase. Surrounding the lighthouse are 31 acres of primitive beach in the state park, where you can fish or swim.

The **Barnegat Light Museum,** built in the early 1900s, served as a one-room schoolhouse, and now displays items from the island's past. For a meal, try **Kubel's,** just a couple of blocks from the lighthouse. It features daily "blackboard specials" and has docking facilities for patrons who wish to arrive by boat. The restaurant's menu highlights fresh seafood dishes, such as grilled tuna steaks, scallops, and homemade seafood soups.

If you decide to drive to the southern half of the island, starting again from Ship Bottom at the island's mid point, you'll first reach **Brant Beach,** where scuba equipment can be rented.

Continuing on, you begin to see the string of **Beach Haven** communities, the island's most popular resort destinations. This is an area of Victorian summer cottages, beaches, parks, and bike paths. It's the place to try windsurfing, jet skiing, or waterskiing, available at several marinas.

As a break from beaches and boating, youngsters enjoy **Fantasy Island Amusement Park,** with rides, miniature golf, and even a "kid casino." Within walking distance is **Schooner's Wharf,** a shopping complex fashioned after a New England fishing village. In summer, catch a show at **Surflight Theatre,** which features hit Broadway musicals. It also has a children's theater.

Motels and restaurants are plentiful, as well as quaint Victorian B&Bs, such as the **Bayberry Inn.** There's the full-service **Engleside Inn,** or the smaller **Sea Spray Motel,** both right on the beach. For dining try these two popular spots which overlook the bay: **Morrison's Seafood Restaurant & Marina** and **Gourmet's Mooring.** And don't forget **The Show Place,** where singing waiters deliver eye-popping (and belt-busting) ice cream concoctions.

By all means visit the island after peak season, when most of the tourists have gone home. Most restaurants and motels are open through September, and many year-around.

One of the biggest events of the year takes place in September—the Long Beach Island Fishing Tournament, which attracts thousands of fishermen, all anxious to land a prize-winning catch. Remember, for fishing or clam digging you'll need a license, obtainable at any bait and tackle shop.

DESTINATIONS

Chambers of Commerce: **Ship Bottom,** 17th St & Long Beach Blvd, NJ 08008. 609/494-2171. **Surf City,** 9th St & Long Beach Blvd, NJ 08008. 609/494-2843. **Harvey Cedars,** 76th St & Long Beach Blvd, NJ 609/494-2843. **Barnegat Light,** 10 W 10th St, NJ 08006. 609/494-9196. **Beach Haven,** 300 Engleside Ave, Beach Haven, NJ 08008. 609/492-0111. **Barnegat Lighthouse State Park,** Barnegat Light, NJ 08006. 609/494-9196. Jun-Lab Day daily 8 am-dusk. May-Oct: Sat & Sun. Adults 50 cents; under 12 and over 62 free. **Fantasy Island Amusement Park,** 320 W 7th, Beach Haven, NJ 08009. 609/492-4000. **Surflight Theatre,** Beach & Engleside Aves, Beach Haven, NJ 08006. 609/492-9477. Mid Jun-mid-Sep: 8 pm.

RESTAURANTS

Bayberry Inn, 13th St & Long Beach Blvd, Ship Bottom, NJ 08008. 609/494-8848. Daily 11:30 am-3 pm, 4-10 pm. **Kubel's,** 7th St & Bayview Ave, Barnegat Light, NJ 08006. 609/494-8592. Daily 11 am-10 pm. **Morrison's,** 2nd St, Beach Haven, NJ 08009. 609/492-5111. Feb-May & Oct Sat, Sun 11 am-9 pm. Jun-Sep daily 8 am- 9 pm. **Gourmet's Mooring,** 9th & Bay Ave, Beach Haven, NJ 08008. 609/492-2828. Mid-Mar-Dec daily noon-1 am. **The Show Place,** Centre St & Beach Ave, Beach Haven, NJ 08008. 609/492-0018.

ACCOMMODATIONS

Sandpiper, 1001 Long Beach Blvd, Ship Bottom, NJ 08008. 609/494-6909. Closed Dec-Mar. **Engleside,** 30 Engleside Ave, Beach Haven, NJ 08008. 609/492-1251. **Sea Spray Motel,** 200 S Bay Ave, Beach Haven, NJ 08008. 609/492-4944.

30

The Great Escape

Cheesequake State Park
Matawan, New Jersey

When the work week is through, and the body and

spirit ache for the outdoors, exercise, and entertainment, escape to **Cheesequake State Park.** Here you can become re-acquainted with nature, as well as enjoy an outdoor musical performance.

The name "Cheesequake" is taken from the Leni Lenape Indians, who frequented the area to hunt and fish. Evidence of their occupation dates back 6,000 years and the park office has a small display of Indian artifacts that were found in the area.

Cheesequake's vegetation is unique in the state. Marshes, a white cedar swamp, open fields, and northeastern hardwood forest make up the park's 990 acres. Visitors looking for a day of recreation and relaxation can enjoy swimming in Hooks Creek Lake, hiking, picnicking (grills and stone fireplaces are provided), camping, and fishing. There are basketball courts, a softball field, a playground for children, and a snack bar.

The park has also been designated a wildlife sanctuary, and is home to a variety of birds, as well as raccoons, foxes, and deer. Hikers are afforded the best look at the park's flora and fauna on one of three marked trails: the longest (3.5 miles) takes visitors through a pine forest, then down to a freshwater swamp and through a hardwood forest. Trail maps are available.

In winter, the hiking trails are transformed into cross-country ski trails, the swimming lake becomes a skating pond, and a hill serves as a sledding area. In the fall, the woodlands and marshes are brilliant with color.

Summer is by far the most popular time to visit Cheesequake, especially with New Yorkers, who often travel the 30 miles to the park to "get away from it all." Frequently, however, they find that many of their neighbors have had the same idea. The park fills up early on weekends, usually by 11 am, and officials will stop letting cars in. So it's best to come early.

To watch the "stars" come out at night, visit the nearby **Garden State Arts Center.** This outdoor entertainment complex schedules concerts from mid-June through September. Top musical acts, ranging from the Beach Boys to Frank Sinatra, have performed here. The complex, which opened in 1968, has 5,302 pavilion seats with lawn seating for another 5,000. Show time is 8:30 pm, but visitors who arrive early will find plenty to do. Telegraph Hill Park here has picnic tables and is a pleasant dinner spot before shows. Many also enjoy tailgate parties in the parking lot.

Come even earlier and spend the afternoon at the "Gamefield," a fitness course designed by the Raritan Bay Medical Center. Athletes of all ages and abilities can choose their activity (total conditioning, cardiovascular fitness, weight loss, body building, or sports enhancement), then follow a marked course, complete with fitness tips.

After a day in the "country," enjoy an old-fashioned American meal at **The Farm House** in Little Silver (20 minutes away, but worth the trip). Specialties are stuffed pork chops and prime rib, as well as home-baked breads and pastries, and portions are hearty. The atmosphere is "dressy casual," so you might want to bring a change of clothes if you have spent a day in the park.

DESTINATIONS

Cheesequake State Park, Matawan, NJ 07747. 201/566-2161. Open year-round, dawn to dusk. **Garden State Arts Center,** PO Box 116, Holmdel, NJ 07733. 201/442-9200. Mid-Jun-Sep. Office hours 9 am-4:30 pm. Curtain time 8:30 pm.

RESTAURANTS

The Farm House, 438 Branch Ave, Little Silver, NJ 07739. 201/842-5017. Wed-Sat 4:30-9 pm. Sun 4-9 pm.

31

Great George, Great Skiing

Vernon Valley/Great Gorge
McAfee, New Jersey

By rights, there shouldn't be skiing in northern New

Jersey, at least, not the kind of big-league skiing that exists at **Vernon Valley/Great Gorge**. After all, this ski resort perches on the outer fringes of creeping suburbia, just 47 miles and a bit more than an hour's non-peak drive from the George Washington Bridge. You can sneak off for a day or night of skiing, or better yet make a whole weekend of it, playing at a comfortable slope-side condominium and enjoying some really fine off-slope facilities.

The growing development makes the place a full resort, but what drives the behemoth is the skiing. On the hill are 52 runs, totally covered with snow-making from one of the world's highest-capacity systems, 14 chairlifts, and three beginner tows, all with an uphill capability of 17,500 an hour. The only number that reads modestly is the vertical drop—just 1,050 feet, but still greater than almost any other ski area between West Virginia and the northern Catskills.

You're right if you infer that such hefty mountain statistics also indicate a hefty population of skiers. Vernon Valley/Great Gorge is the product of the merger of two commendable ski areas. Everyone calls the duo Great Gorge, even though Vernon Valley took over its neighbor. It is the East's biggest urban ski area, where the distinctive speech and no-nonsense manners of New Yorkers dominate. The region has 14 million residents, and on weekends, school vacations, and nights, you'll feel as if you're sharing the slopes with most of them. Thousands of people stand in lift lines, crowd into one of the 10 food-service facilities, or slalom around one another—prone, supine, standing, or skiing. But most of all, they're having fun—and you will, too.

Great Gorge is a gratifyingly egalitarian place in a sport often accused of elitism. It is a ski area where blue-collar Long Islanders share the slopes with socialites, where accents from Puerto Rican to Polish to preppy are heard, where high-school ski clubbers neck on the lifts, and three-generation families find an activity to enjoy together.

Although it is easy to ski *between* the Great Gorge and Vernon Valley sectors, which are on opposite ends of a long ridge, people tend to prefer one or the other. Preferences seem to be on the basis of skill and experience. The old-line, advanced practitioners who have been coming here for years ski Great Gorge, and the newer, less skilled skiers tackle the slopes of Vernon Valley. There is still the flavor of two distinct ski areas (three, if you count the much smaller Great Gorge North, set in the middle like the point of a "W," consisting of two lifts and a handful of trails).

If you ski the Great Gorge side, you'll find yourself in the haven of hardcore skiers and long-time regulars. The lifts and trails were laid out in an instinctive, shoot-from-the-hip fashion. Trails merge, weave, and intersect, creating odd angles, funny little jughandles, and quirky intersections. The lifts have a similar scattershot layout, set at odd angles to one another. The best skiers tend to make laps on the Racing Chair plus Racing Trail or Kamikaze, the two steepest of the western pitches and the toughest duo of all the resort's terrain.

By contrast, Vernon Valley's lifts and trails are as neatly arranged as strands of spaghetti emerging from a pasta maker. Yet the trails ski with more variety than their uniform appearance on the trail map would indicate. Some fall-line trails perform with the consistency of an upended ironing board, while others resemble a tilted washboard, alternating flats with little pitches. Moonspin, Straightaway, and Zero G are the valley's steepest runs, but they don't approach the challenge of the Gorge.

At the bottom of the Vernon Valley side, you will find the broad, tame slopes accessed by slow-moving tows where new skiers are introduced to the sport by a cadre of instructors. Thousands of newcomers have been launched into the skiing life on this gentle turf.

Most people come to Great Gorge to get in the most skiing with the least driving. Some come to get in a moderate amount of skiing combined with a lot of partying—with the least driving. When the arc lights come on, they bathe the trails in the curiously shadowed bluish glow that characterizes night skiing, and the serious partying begins. The huge bars in the base lodges rock with conviviality. Vernon Valley's own beer, made on-site by a German brewmaster, is a choice beverage, on tap or bottled.

While varied terrain and terrific apres-ski combine to create a good-size ski area, it's **Great Gorge Village** that boosts it into resort status. Located at the base of Great Gorge North, the village is a complex of ski-in/ski-out or walk-to-the-slopes condos—more than 250 at last count. It's also the site of the posh **Spa at Great Gorge,** a $12 million luxury facility. The spa—all 100,000 square feet of it—is a lushly landscaped, elaborately outfitted health club and social center. It boasts seven indoor and outdoor heated pools (most open year-around); indoor tennis, squash, and racquetball courts; indoor running track; Nautilus and free-weight health club; saunas, steamrooms, whirlpools; and an exercise studio. The spa is open only to condo owners and overnight renters, and it makes a weekend at Great Gorge all the more worthwhile.

There's a great sense of luxury in driving a very short distance to arrive at a full-service ski resort in the early evening, checking in, and having the choice of swimming, playing tennis, working out, skiing, or enjoying a civilized dinner. You won't have to go far to find any one of the above. **Kites,** the graceful restaurant atop the spa, serves new American cuisine with a special flare.

In summer, the ski area and the base facilities operate as **Action Park,** the world's largest water theme park. There are also such non-wet amusements as Go-Karts, miniature golf, an Alpine Slide, shopping in Cobblestone Village, and a full calendar of ethnic festivals.

In 1988 Great Gorge Resort acquired the former Playboy Club/Hotel, built in the far reaches of Sussex County when it appeared as if all of New Jersey, and not just Atlantic City, would legalize gambling. An extensive refurbishment of the 600-room hotel has transformed it into the Mountain View Resort at Great Gorge, conveniently linked to the ski area.

DESTINATIONS

Great Gorge Resort, Rte 94, PO Box 848, McAfee, NJ 07428. 201/827-2000; 201/827-3900 snow reports; 201/287-8202 **Great Gorge Village** reservations. Mon-Thu 9 am-10 pm, Fri 9 am-11 pm, Sat 8:30 am-11 pm, Sun 8:30 am-10 pm. Lift tickets: adult, weekends and holidays, full-day $30, half-day $22, night $21; weekdays, full-day $26, half-day $19, night $21. Junior, weekends and holidays, full-day $25, half-day $19, night $18; weekdays, full-day $22, half-day $16, night $18. Limited-terrain tickets (for beginner lifts), adult $17, junior $15, at all times.

RESTAURANTS

Kites, Spa at Great Gorge. (see Destination). 201/827-6111. Tue-Thu 5-9 pm, Fri, Sat 5-11 pm, Sun 11 am-3 pm, 5-9 pm. Reservations suggested.

ACCOMMODATIONS

Great George Resort. (see Destinations).

32

Survival Of The Fittest

Morristown, New Jersey

Before George Washington and his brave troops faced the British during the Revolutionary War, they had to defeat a series of equally tough and unrelenting enemies—disease, inclement weather, and mutiny. Like Pennsylvania's Valley Forge (see trip #118), New Jersey's **Morristown** was a place where Washington and his men confronted those enemies, and emerged victorious, all the more determined to defeat the hated Redcoats.

In the late 1770s, Morristown was the site of Jacob Ford's powder mill, an important military asset. In addition, the village processed a good portion of the iron needed by the troops, at its furnaces and forges. Much of this is preserved in the **Morristown National Historical Park,** which is comprised of three units: Washington's Headquarters and the Historical Museum and Library, Fort Nonsense, and Jockey

Hollow. Two of these divisions are in Morristown; the other is about six miles south.

Fort Nonsense, near the Morristown Green, is located on the highest peak in the area. It is most likely that the fort was built to store supplies, but it got its name because no one could remember what exactly the fort was built for.

The **Historical Museum and Library** houses items relating to the 1779-1780 encampment of Washington's troops, including military weapons of the era. Literature stored here includes some 40,000 manuscripts and about 20,000 printed pieces on both the colonial and Revolutionary periods.

Approximately six miles down the road, you can get an idea of the privations endured by the troops during the hard times at Jockey Hollow. Huts, similar to those occupied both by officers and men, have been reconstructed. Staffers, costumed in period clothing, give daily presentations during the summer, and on weekends the balance of the year. Washington's Headquarters, a colonial house built by Col. Jacob Ford and furnished with several original pieces, also is located here.

Although the whims of nature were harsh on American soldiers during the Revolution, today this site can be restful and enjoyable for the casual visitor. The area is a wildlife sanctuary, and hiking trails meander through woodland hills, brooks, and flowers.

On the opposite end of the scale from the soldiers' lot was the life lived by affluent farmers of the era, revealed by the **Wick House** property, a restored farmhouse that Maj. Gen. Arthur St. Clair occupied in 1779-80.

Morristown also is home to **Historic Speedwell,** the **Frelinghuysen Arboretum,** and the **Morris Museum of Arts and Sciences.** Historic Speedwell is the home and iron works built by Stephen Vail, who manufactured the engine for the *Savannah,* the first steamship to cross the Atlantic. Stephen's son, Alfred, also made history as co-developer—with Samuel F. B. Morse—of the telegraph; they gave the first successful demonstration of the new communications device at Speedwell in 1837. Attractions there include Vail's mansion (resplendent with rooms of period furnishings), artifacts and equipment from the heyday of the iron works, and an exhibit on the development and history of the telegraph.

Pleasing to the eye is the Frelinghuysen Arboretum, a 127-acre preserve featuring peonies, roses, lilacs, trees, shrubs, and a self-guiding nature trail. Lawn concerts are given throughout the summer. At the Morris Museum of Arts and Science are exhibits of minerals, fossils, mounted and live small animals, and displays featuring Indian artifacts, computers, and fine arts.

There are several fine restaurants in the area, including the **Black Orchid** (offering veal and duck specialties) and **Rod's 1890s Ranch House** (serving steak and seafood, and famous for their homemade pastries).

DESTINATIONS

Morristown National Historical Park, Public Information, Morristown, NJ 07960. 201/539-2016, -2085. Open daily 9 am-5 pm. $2. **Historic Speedwell,** 333 Speedwell Ave, Morristown, NJ 07960. 201/540-0211. May-Oct Thu-Fri noon-4 pm, Sat-Sun 1-5 pm. Adults $2, seniors $1, children 6-16 50 cents. **Frelinghuysen Arboretum** 53 E Hanover Ave, Morristown, NJ 07960. 201/829-0474. Mid-Mar-Nov daily 9 am-dusk, Dec-mid-Mar Mon-Fri 9 am-4:30 pm. **Morris Museum of Arts and Sciences,** Normandy Heights & Columbia Rds, Morristown, NJ 07960. 201/538-0454. Tue-Sat 10 am-5 pm, Sun 1-5 pm. Adults $1.50, students and seniors, 50 cents.

RESTAURANTS

Rod's 1890s Ranch House, 1 Convent Rd, Morristown, NJ 07960. 201/539-6666. Mon-Sat 11:30 am-11 pm; Sun 11 am-3 pm, 4-11 pm. **Black Orchid,** 3 Headquarters Plaza, Morristown, NJ 07960. 201/898-9100. Mon-Fri 11:3- am-2:30 pm, 6-10:30 pm; Sun 6-10:30 pm.

33

Oceans Of Fun

Ocean City, New Jersey

These seven square miles of island city are ribboned by eight miles of sparkling water and glistening beaches—lure enough for most city dwellers. Mere geography makes **Ocean City, New Jersey,** an idyllic getaway—a breezy island resort that lies between the Atlantic Ocean and Great Egg Harbor. In addition to the draw of sun, sand, and surf, Ocean City offers free band concerts, amusement parks, shopping, and good dining, all geared toward family fun. The north end of the island offers easy access to the ocean and inland waterways, making it a favorite port with the yachting crowd.

Located on the northeastern extremity of the Cape May County coast, Ocean City is tucked among the Jersey shore resorts which run from Atlantic City in the north to Cape May in the south. Ocean City is reached easily by major highways and the Garden State Parkway.

Unlike most of its nearby neighbors, Ocean City is dry. Remaining in force is a ban on the sale and consumption of liquor in public places—in keeping with the founders' restrictions of 1879 when the island became the site of a Christian resort. However, those in search of bright lights and libation need travel only a few miles to adjacent islands or to the mainland to find nightclubs and lounges.

Although it has been a popular family resort for more than a century, Ocean City has always had to work a little harder to attract beachgoers—perhaps because of the liquor ban. But for the past couple of decades, the city has added verve with a series of whimsical events such as the Miscellaneous Tanning Contest (the best tanned bald spot and left arm, the palest ring finger, the least tanned person), an Artistic Pie Eating Contest, and, its latest competitive milepost, a French-fry Sculpting Contest.

Check out a series of annual and unusual beauty contests such as the Little Miss Splinter Boardwalk for seven-year-olds and the unforgettable Miss Crustacean Contest, a beauty pageant where comely crab contestants waddle down the runway with the winner receiving the coveted Cucumber Rind Cup. Visitors also crack up at the flurry of activity that surrounds each year's staging of the Hermit Crab Race of Martin Z. Mollusk Day, an event that attracts upwards of 200 hurrying hermits.

Since 1954, one of Ocean City's more spectacular and colorful summer events has been the annual Night in Venice Boat Parade, probably the largest and most high-spirited boat parade in the country. It takes place on Great Egg Harbor Bay in late July, when waterfront homes blaze festively with hundreds of colorful lights to welcome a procession of more than 100 boats, also elaborately decorated.

Ocean City offers traditional entertainment as well as whimsy, including concerts by well-known big bands at its landmark Music Pier. Since 1928, much of the city's activity has revolved around the pier, situated on the boardwalk at Moorlyn Terrace. It is the site of a flower show in June and an arts-and-crafts exhibit in mid-September. It also is a favorite place for friends to meet, and the Pavilion, with its arches and walkway, overlooking the beach and ocean, provides a perfect place to relax and enjoy sea breezes. Many a courting couple warmly remembers starlit evenings by the sea set to romantic tunes. Although spring and summer are the Music Pier's busiest times, activities continue into the cooler months.

An information center at the front of the Pavilion provides details about concerts, accommodations, special events, and high and low tides. The center is open on weekends during spring and fall and daily from 10 a.m. to 10 p.m. during summer.

Although Ocean City's prime beach locale connotes fun-in-the-sun, the cooler months offer frequent special activities. Christmas in Wonderland is centered around Wonderland Pier, at 6th and Boardwalk, an amusement park which opens for the holiday and Santa's arrival. While enjoying this winter rite, you may see some wet-suited surfers who are undaunted by the numbing temperature of the ocean.

Although there are ample hotels, motels, and camp sites, those seeking overnight accommodations in Ocean City might want to consider the array of classic guest houses—many charmingly restored—which dot the boardwalk and the ocean-front.

Even if you're not registered as a guest, a visit to the **Flanders Hotel,** 11th and Boardwalk, is a must. This exquisitely restored hotel is filled with antiques, and has a seaside solarium. It is one of Ocean City's oldest accommodations and two dining rooms on the boardwalk provide a luxurious days-gone-by atmosphere. A fixed-price menu (about $20) includes a multi-course meal with such entrees as boiled sea scallops with bacon, veal picante (wine sauce and mushrooms), and filet mignon. Following dessert, a fruit and cheese plate is served.

Also recommended is the **Top of the Waves** on the ocean on Central Avenue, a bed-and-breakfast establishment that serves a rather unique breakfast in the Three Stooges Room. Another charming bed-and-breakfast inn is **Laurel Hall** at 48 Wesley Road, restored to its Victorian splendor.

Seafood dishes are the specialties in many of Ocean City's restaurants, with the cuisine ranging from exquisite to down-home. For a taste of family-style cooking head for **Scotch Hall,** located in a restored house. Try the scallops parmesan or flounder stuffed with crabmeat. If seafood pasta dishes are your thing—along with an array of hard-to-resist desserts—the **Culinary Garden and Inn,** on Central Avenue, is an ideal choice.

Ocean City's full and varied calendar of events draw its share of visitors—as do the resort's natural attributes. Eight miles of beaches are perfect for swimming, sunbathing, beach games, hunting seashells, or simply lounging with a good book. There's 2-1/2 miles of boardwalk to explore and excellent boating, fishing, tennis, shuffleboard, and golf facilities.

Shoppers will get their fill of quaint shops on and off the boardwalk, open year-around. The downtown shopping area, situated on Asbury Avenue between 6th and 11th streets, is chock-full with art galleries, candy shops, bakeries, clothing, gifts and antique shops, and restaurants. Getting from place to place is relatively easy by foot, but a jitney service runs and is available for less than one dollar.

The Ocean City Historical Museum on Wesley Avenue is filled with 19th-century furnishings and costumes depicting life in Ocean City in its early years, including a notable display of rooms decorated in authentic Victorian style. It also contains marine and wildlife exhibits and whaling and Indian artifacts. An entire room is devoted to the wreck of the four-masted barque, *Sindia*, which ran aground in a gale in 1901.

The island's early history abounds with tales of shipwrecks and whaling vessels and every once in a while someone unearths a relic from the beaches. It is said that whalers used the island to launch their vessels and boil down the valuable oil. In fact, it was from one of these whalers, John Peck, that Ocean City received its first name—Peck's Beach.

In the 17th and 18th centuries, the site became known as Party Island as young people crossed the bay for celebrations, swimming, and courting. Because of its pristine beauty, four Methodist ministers chose Peck's Beach as the site of their proposed Christian resort and camp meeting ground in 1879. The clerics christened the new community Ocean City and incorporated the Ocean City Association. By a process of cross-deeding, the association secured control of every inch of the island. Today, any transfer of title in Ocean City maintains the original restrictions that keep the island a "Christian seaside resort."

DESTINATIONS

Public Relations Department, 9th & Asbury, Ocean City, NJ 08226. 800/225-0252 or 800/624-3746 (in NJ). **Music Pier**, Moorlyn Terrace at the Boardwalk, Ocean City, NJ 08226. **Historical Museum**, 409 Wesley Ave, Ocean City, NJ 08226. 609/399-1801. Open Apr-Dec.

RESTAURANTS

Scotch Hall, 435 Wesley, Ocean City, NJ 08226. 609/399-0947.
Jun-late Sep Mon-Sat 4:30-8 pm, Sun noon-8 pm; rest of year
Tue-Sat 4:30-8 pm, Sun noon-7 pm. **Culinary Garden & Inn,** 841
Central Ave, Ocean City, NJ 08226. 609/399-3713. Closed Dec-
Feb. Hours vary. **Flanders Hotel Dining Rooms,** 11th &
Boardwalk, Ocean City, NJ 08226. 609/399-1000. Daily 8:30-10
am, noon-1:30 pm, 6-7:30 pm.

ACCOMMODATIONS

Flanders Hotel, (see Restaurants). **Top of the Waves B&B,**
5447 Central Ave, Ocean City, NJ 08226. 800/322-0477. **Laurel
Hall,** 48 Wesley Rd, Ocean City, NJ 08226. 609/399-0800. B&B
Information: 609/399-8844.

34

Hallowed Halls

Princeton, New Jersey

Visit **Princeton** to see the campus of one of the
nation's finest and most attractive universities? Of
course. But this small community has many
additional lures.

The school dominates the town. **Princeton
University,** chartered in 1746 as the College of
New Jersey, was officially renamed in 1896.
Although virtually every one of its buildings is
architecturally significant and worth a studied look,
some merit particularly close attention.

You can stroll around on your own, of course, or
you can sign up for the Orange Key guided tours,
which are free. These tours provide entrance to
some areas that are off-limits to other sightseers.
One is Nassau Hall, which fronts on Nassau Street,
the town's main thoroughfare. When it was
completed in 1756, this was the largest academic
structure in the 13 colonies. Now it serves as the
university's administration building.

There are other sites worthy of note on campus,

such as the Art Museum, in McCormack Hall, with a permanent collection that includes Oriental, African, pre-Columbian, Greek, and Roman art and artifacts. The Chapel, which is located behind the imposing Firestone Library (closed to outsiders), is the third largest university chapel in the world, and contains a renowned collection of stained glass crafted by American artists. The Museum of Natural History, in Guyot Hall, is home to prehistoric animals, minerals, and fossils, as well as changing exhibits. The three-story University Bookstore, on University Place, can set you rummaging for hours in its book stacks and perusing other items for sale. Many of the stately old homes you see on Prospect Street are the school's famed private eating clubs.

The Woodrow Wilson School of Public and International Affairs—named after the former U.S. President who was also president of Princeton University—was founded in 1930. It is now housed in a sleek contemporary building, dedicated in 1966, on the corner of Prospect Street and Washington Road.

Just a short distance from the university is **Bainbridge House.** This 1766 Georgian townhouse contains period rooms, special exhibits, a gift shop, and library, and is home of the Historical Society of Princeton.

If you're into gravestone rubbings, stop by **Princeton Cemetery,** where legible tombstones date to 1760. They include those of Aaron Burr, Grover Cleveland, John Witherspoon, a signer of the Declaration of Independence, and Paul Tulane, founder of Tulane University. Every president of Princeton University from the 1700s through the early 20th century is buried there, too.

Shop until you drop types may need extra staying power to do justice to Nassau Street, the commercial section of Princeton which is about a mile long. You'll find Laura Ashley and Benetton, and many other stores and boutiques, less well known but with intriguing merchandise. (Yes, the orange and black you see all around town are the university colors.)

The Nassau Street area also abounds with more than a dozen restaurants. For a casual meal, perhaps elbow-to-elbow with students and professors, you might want to try **P.J.'s Pancake House.** The Nassau Inn, a hostelry on Palmer Square, practically smack-dab in the center of town, offers several pleasant restaurants. The glass-enclosed **Greenhouse** allows you to watch the passing parade as you munch your salad or burger. If you want to *dine*, not merely eat, there's **Lahiere's.** The country French decor is cozy and the food tantalizing, particularly the seafood specials which vary from salmon to New Zealand mussels. The chef experiments with different ways of making brioche—so far the black pepper and the parmesan and herb have been winners. Also hits are the chocolate soufflé and flourless chocolate ganache cake. You may find it difficult to select a wine; the cellar is jammed with thousands of bottles priced from $10 to more than $4,000.

Feel like taking a turn on the ice while you're in town? Princeton's three-and-a-half mile man-made **Carnegie Lake** is open to the public for ice-skating in season. Sailing is preferred in warmer weather.

For evening entertainment, try for tickets to the latest **McCarter Theatre** production. Built in 1929, the theater presents professional drama, dance, music, and special events regularly. The New Jersey State Council on the Arts has designated the theater "a regional center of artistic excellence."

DESTINATIONS

Chamber of Commerce of the Princeton Area, PO Box 431, Princeton, NY 08542. 609/520-1776. **Princeton University,** Dept. of Communications & Publications, Stanhope Hall, Princeton Univ, Princeton, NJ 08544. 609/452-3000. Orange Key Guides, Rear of MacLean House, Princeton Univ, Princeton, NJ 08544. 609/452-3603. Tours: Mon-Sat 10 & 11 am, 1:30 & 3:30 pm, Sun 1:30 & 3:30 pm. **Bainbridge House,** 158 Nassau St, Princeton, NJ 08542. 609/921-6748. Tue-Sun 12-4pm. **Princeton Cemetery,** Witherspoon and Wiggins Sts, Princeton, NJ 08542. 609/924-1369. Gates are always open. **Carnegie Lake,** entrance between Washington Rd & Harrison St bridges. 609/921-9480. Call first for skating conditions. **McCarter Theatre,** 91 University Pl, Princeton, NJ 08540. 609/683-8000.

RESTAURANTS

P.J.'s Pancake House, 154 Nassau St, Princeton, NJ 08542. 609/924-1353. Weekdays 7:30 am-10 pm, Fri to midnight; Sat 8 am-midnight, Sun 8 am-10pm. **Greenhouse,** Nassau Inn, Palmer Square, Princeton, NJ 08542. 609/921-7500. Daily 7 am-2:30 pm, 5-10 pm. **Lahiere's,** 5 Witherspoon St, Princeton NJ 08542. 609/921-2798. Mon-Thu 12-2:30 pm, 5-9:30 pm; Fri 12-2:30 pm, 5-10 pm; Sat 12-2pm, 5-10pm.

35

The Big Tomato

Salem, New Jersey

It was a hot July day in **Salem, New Jersey,** in 1820, when Col. Robert Gibbon Johnson, a respected figure in Salem county, prepared to prove conventional wisdom wrong. The town was thronging with market-day crowds, and when word got around about what Colonel Johnson was going to do, a crowd began to gather in front of the courthouse. Johnson stood on the courthouse steps with a basket of plump tomatoes at his feet. Now, everybody knew that tomatoes were poisonous, and best used only for seasonal decorations, but Johnson told the crowd that was hokum as far as he—and other men of science and agriculture—were concerned, and he was going to prove it. The Colonel picked up a tomato, and, as the crowd watched anxiously, took a bite of the juicy fruit. There were doctors in attendance in case he collapsed in pain, and some locals were making surreptitious bets as to the Colonel's survival, but the anticipated illness never struck. Johnson finished eating, calmly wiped his face and hands, and invited the gathered crowd to try his tasty red tomatoes.

Thus was born not only the use of tomatoes as food (in North America; they had been eaten for years in parts of South America), but also the birth of Salem as the state's biggest grower of tomatoes. Today, the city celebrates Colonel Johnson's "discovery'' with an annual Robert Gibbon Johnson Day, held each July. There are games (including tomato tossing and catching), judging of tomatoes for size and appearance, and a re-enactment of the Colonel's historic snack. But Salem's historic contributions and attractions are far from limited to tomatoes— the town dates from 1675, and is believed to be the oldest English settlement on the Delaware River.

One of the town's most historic sites is the Salem Oak, which dates to the 15th century. In 1675, under the tree's shady branches, John Fenwick, the town's founder, signed a peace treaty (without any blood having been shed) with the Lenni-Lenape Indians, which made the settlement and development of the area possible. Today, the mighty oak stands over the entrance to the Friends Burial Ground, where many of the early Quaker settlers and their descendants were laid to rest.

Salem has a number of other historic sites. The 1721 Alexander Grant House is the headquarters of the Salem County Historical Society. It is furnished with local antiques and includes collections of Indian relics, Wistarburg glass, and period dolls. On the grounds are the John Jones Law Office (opened in 1736, and believed to be the oldest remaining law office in the U.S.) and a formal garden.

A sad chapter in the area's history is commemorated at the Hancock House, just south of town. Built in 1734 by Judge William Hancock, the house was used as a barracks for approximately 30 local Quakers who stood watch over the nearby bridge during the Revolutionary War. Although fighting in the war was against their religion, these men acted as unarmed sentinels and contributed cattle and other food supplies to Washington's men at Valley Forge. In reprisal for this peaceful cooperation, a British force of 300 men stormed the house and massacred the Quakers on March 21, 1778. The house stands as a memorial to those men, and is furnished with period pieces.

To enjoy a trip back to a more recent bit of history, try lunch or dinner at the **Oak Diner,** across the street from the stately Salem Oak. This stainless-steel-and-formica relic of the 1950s offers basic diner fare and friendly service. Order a salad with tomatoes, or perhaps a BLT, in honor of the brave and foresightful Colonel Johnson.

DESTINATIONS

Greater Salem Chamber of Commerce, 104 Market St, Salem, NJ 08079. 609/935-1415.

RESTAURANTS

Oak Diner, W Broadway & Oak St, Salem, NJ 08079. 609/935-1305. Daily 5:30 am-9 pm.

36

Sand, Seafarers, and Spies

Sandy Hook
Gateway National Recreation Area, New Jersey

Conspiracy, war, guiding lights, and a sun so bright. Intrigued? Then head for the New Jersey shore for a day at **Sandy Hook** and the **Spy House.**

In the **Gateway National Recreation Area,** the 18th and 19th centuries come alive when you visit one of the nation's oldest lighthouses, a maritime museum, and a deserted fort. But this trio of historic sights, interesting though they are, are not even the main attraction. What lures most visitors to Sandy Hook, particularly on beautiful summer weekends, is the beach—all six, sandy miles of it—where the swimming is good and the surfing is great.

Sandy Hook is actually a sandspit peninsula with some unusual ecology. On this small, breezy peninsula are found sand dunes, holly trees (with their dark green leaves and deep crimson berries making them a visual embodiment of Christmas), mudflats, and a salt marsh, as well as the seashore. Birdwatchers find this spot just as scintillating as do bikini watchers; hundreds of species are found there. The visitor center has nature exhibits as well as free maps and brochures.

The area's historical sites are worth a tour. Fort Hancock was built in 1895 as a coastal defense post during the Spanish-American War. Walk the Old Dune Trail or tour the old coastal defense gun emplacements. Take a look at one of the oldest lighthouses in America (built in 1764), then visit the Sandy Hook Museum, where the ecology of this peninsula is interpreted through models and photographs. The museum's creaky floors add atmosphere.

Back at the beach, you can swim, hunt for sea shells, or just lie back and relax. On the bay side, the steady winds and shallow water create conditions ideal for windsurfers. Fishermen have special areas designated for them on the ocean side; surf fishing there often yields catches of bluefish and striped bass.

Because Sandy Hook is so popular in summer, the crowds can become overwhelming. By 11 am on weekends, the peninsula is usually filled and visitors may be turned away, so it's best to get an early start.

Just before you reach Sandy Hook, at the base of the peninsula, is another historical spot, the **Twin Lights of Navesink,** built in 1862. There, you can tour a maritime museum featuring exhibits on the history of the lights and that of the U.S. Lifesaving Service. Visitors can climb one of two lighthouse towers for great views of the Atlantic coast and the distant New York City skyline.

A few miles west of Sandy Hook in Port Monmouth is the Spy House, on the shore of Raritan Bay. Once called The Homestead, it was renamed the Spy House by British forces sailing into New York Harbor during the Revolutionary War because Americans used it for surveillance. The original structure, built in 1663, was the first house along the Jersey shore. Set amidst 39 acres of sand dunes, the Spy House contains the Shoal Harbor Marine Museum, which traces 300 years of local fishing and shipping history through exhibits of photographs and artifacts. Because the Spy House is in an isolated area, it can be difficult to find. Look for signs on Route 36 near Belford.

After spending time in and around the water, set sail for **Bahrs,** in the Highlands near the Twin Lights, overlooking the Shrewsbury River and Gateway National Park. Bahrs is known for its whole lobsters (one- or two-pound sizes), as well for thick chowders and dishes featuring clams and oysters; the steaks are delicious, too. This restaurant, established in 1917, nearly qualifies as an historic landmark itself; dress is casual.

DESTINATIONS

Gateway National Recreation Area—Sandy Hook, Highlands, NJ 07732. 201/872-0115. Open dawn to dusk. **Twin Lights Historic Site,** same address. 201/872-1814. 9 am-5 pm daily. **Spy House,** 119 Port Monmouth Rd, Port Monmouth, NJ 07732. 201/787-1807. Mon-Fri 9:30 am-3:30 pm, Sat 1-3:30 pm, Sun 2:30-5 pm.

RESTAURANTS

Bahrs, 2 Bay Ave, Highlands, NJ 07732. 201/872-1245. Mon-Fri 11:30 am-10 pm, Sat 11 am-10:30 pm, Sun 11 am-9:30 pm.

37

Designer Delights

Secaucus Outlet Center
Secaucus, New Jersey

Ready, Set, Charge! That's just about the ideal way to prepare for an assault on the **Secaucus Outlet Center.** You'll need to limber up those charge cards, because the bargains to be found there are unbeatable, if you know where to look and happen to be in the right place at the right time.

More than 50 designers and stores have factory outlets in Secaucus, including such famous names as Harve Bernard, Argenti, Liz Claiborne, and Bally. Some outlets feature only their own lines—others, such as Fashion Mate and United States Apparel, carry a variety of labels in a wide range of prices—a very wide range of prices.

That's really a key phrase to keep in mind if you plan to do some serious shopping. You'll need to keep a proper perspective on what constitutes a bargain. Certainly, the term "outlet center" doesn't mean you'll come away with six designer suits and a year's supply of footwear for $100. It's true that in some stores items are marked down to incredible prices, such as wool sweaters for $10 or leather shoes for $15. But don't expect to buy a designer dress that costs $400 in department stores for $25 in Secaucus. You may, however, find that same dress discounted 50 to 75 percent, which is quite a significant savings. Add to that the fact that New Jersey doesn't charge sales tax on clothing purchases (as opposed to New York City's 8-1/4 percent), and you'll realize that while there aren't any rock-bottom steals among the prices at the outlet center, you *can* save a considerable amount of money by shopping there.

If you're realistic about what you want and understand that designer clothes are expensive to begin with, you should be very pleased with the discounts here. You also have to understand that, on any given day, the suit of your dreams may or may not be available. It's all in the timing.

The Secaucus Outlet Center is situated on Meadowlands Parkway, four miles west of Lincoln Tunnel and minutes from Giants Stadium and the Harbor Cove real estate development on what used to be a pig farm and swampland. Approximate driving time from midtown Manhattan is 30 minutes. Once you arrive, you can expect to spend another hour in your car, driving from store to store. The center is spread out over at least two miles of intertwining roads, and few stores are connected. That means constantly getting in and out of the car, rechecking the map (available at any store) and, especially on weekends, searching for parking spaces. This is a crowded spot come Saturdays and Sundays. Wear good walking shoes. (While the center is accessible via PATH, the only shuttle between stores is solely for use of guests of the Hilton Meadowlands; a car is a virtual necessity for an effective and organized shopping trip there.)

One welcome sight to the weary shopper is the Castle Road section of the center. Here, most of the shops are laid out consecutively, along both sides of one street, and parking is available in the back. Once parked, you can conveniently visit about 20 stores. Some of the more interesting shops on Castle Road include Passport Foods Outlet, which carries a wide variety of international foods and gives out samples; Preganetti's Maternity Outlet, which claims to have "the largest selection of maternity wear anywhere;" and Toy Liquidators, for the child in all of us.

If you find that you've worn yourself out hunting down and bagging bargains (not to mention the wear and tear you may have put on your faithful charge card), it may be time to rest at **Junior's Restaurant.** This bright, cheery establishment serves inexpensive meals—including satisfying daily specials, such as spaghetti and meatballs, spicy Italian sausage, and thick goulash—in a comfortable ("comfortable" being the key word here) setting.

DESTINATIONS

Secaucus Outlet Center, PO Box 2187, Dept W, Secaucus, NJ 07096-2187. 201/348-1625. Mon-Wed, Fri & Sat 9:30 am-6 pm (varies by store), Thu 9:30 am-9 pm, Sun 12-6 pm.

RESTAURANTS

Junior's Restaurant, 1000 Castle Rd, Secaucus, NJ 07094. 201/864-6484. Mon-Wed 7:30 am-6 pm, Thu 7:30 am-9 pm, Fri-Sun 7:30 am-7 pm.

38

Time-Warp Town

Waterloo Village
Stanhope, New Jersey

Although the explosive growth of railroads played a major role in opening up America during the 19th century, they also nudged some historic communities into obscurity. Engineers laid track along the path of least resistance, spawning boomtowns and skipping by some communities, dooming them to become ghost towns or sleepy backwaters. One such community that was a busy hub of commerce during the mid-19th century, only to slip into decline when the railroad passed it by, now lives on as **Waterloo Village Restoration.**

The area was once rich in iron ore and supported an ironworks that supplied arms to Gen. George Washington's Continental Army. Founded in 1760 as Andover Forge, the village changed its name to commemorate Wellington's defeat of Napoleon at Waterloo. It flourished again when the Morris Canal was opened in 1831 to connect Phillipsburg on the Delaware River and Newark. Then the railroad came along, supplanting the canal and the once-busy canal town had met *its* Waterloo.

Today, the village is flourishing again as an historic restoration. Guides and artisans in period costumes add to its charm as they portray everyday life in early America—grinding grain at the water-powered grist mill, cutting wood at the sawmill, and forging tools at the blacksmith shop. You'll also see a potter at his wheel, a merchant tending the general store, and the chemist drying herbs at the apothecary.

You can stroll along the winding and scenic towpaths of the Morris Canal and visit 23 authentically restored and furnished buildings. These include a stagecoach inn, a church, various homes and tradesmen's shops, and a carriage house. At crafts barns you can see such artisans at work as candlemakers and weavers. On summer weekends, there are concerts that range from classical to popular, including symphony, jazz, and chamber music, and a celebrated bluegrass festival (usually late August).

For an extended outing that will please youngsters, travel west to **Hope, New Jersey,** and the **Land of Make Believe,** a children's theme park. Chock full of rides, shows, and attractions, this kid-size park lets children fly the Red Baron airplane, tour Santa's Enchanted Christmas Village with a stop at the Magic Fireplace to the North Pole, and enter a conversation with Colonel Corn, a talking scarecrow. At

Old McDonald's Farm there are animals to pet. A replica of a Civil War era steam train, the *C.P. Huntington*, seen in the movie *Iron Horse*, chugs through the foothills of historic Jenny Jump mountain. According to legend, the mountain, along with a state park, are named after a nine-year-old girl named Jenny who jumped off the mountain to escape Indians. The park has a half dozen eateries with fast-food fare ranging from pizza and chicken to hot dogs and hamburgers, plus homemade fudge. At the nearby village of **Hope,** take a self-guided tour of the historic stone buildings built by Moravians who came from Bethlehem, Pennsylvania (see trip #109), and founded the community in 1774.

Despite its teutonic name and classic German decor, the **Black Forest Inn** at Stanhope, housed in a turn-of-the-century stone building, isn't big on German dishes. It serves about 95 percent continental dishes, including rack, saddle, and loin of lamb, duck breast in cassis, beef Wellington, and a variety of fish, poultry, beef, veal, and seasonal game dishes. If you crave German food, you'll find a small selection of traditional dishes such as sauerbraten.

DESTINATIONS

Waterloo Village Restoration, Waterloo Rd, Stanhope, NJ 07874. 201/347-0900. Tue-Sun Apr 15-Sep 30 10 am-6 pm, Oct 1-Dec 31 10 am-5 pm. Adults $7.50, seniors $5, children $3. **Land of Make Believe,** Rte 80 (exit 12), Hope, NJ 07844. 201/459-5100. Mem Day-mid-June Sat & Sun 10 am-5 pm; mid-Jun-Lab Day daily 10 am-5 pm. Adults $7, children $8.

RESTAURANTS

Black Forest Inn, 249 US 206, Stanhope, NJ 07874. 201/347-3344. Mon, Wed-Fri 11:30 am-2 pm, 5-10 pm; Sat 5-10 pm; Sun 1-9 pm

39

Trenton Makes, The World Takes

Trenton, New Jersey

What's a poor capital to do? New York City to the

north and Philadelphia to the south get all the attention—and a sizable chunk of the traffic whizzing along the nearby New Jersey Turnpike. But **Trenton,** situated on the Delaware River about halfway between the two, truly merits a visit.

History was made here during the Revolutionary War, and events occurred that undoubtedly influence the way Americans live today. In December 1776, Gen. George Washington, with 2,400 cold and weary troops, surprised and routed a garrison of well-equipped—but totally unprepared—Hessian mercenaries in Trenton. The Continental Army's surprising victories here and in Princeton during the subsequent 10 days are recognized as being a major turning point of the Revolutionary War.

Today, on the western edge of the downtown area, you can visit the **William Trent House,** a splendid example of Georgian/Queen Anne Colonial architecture dating to 1719. At the time of the Battle of Trenton, the house was occupied by a physician, a Loyalist who nevertheless gave medical assistance to both American and British Hessian troops. William Trent, for whom the city was named, was one of the area's outstanding citizens. Today, the house has been restored and is accurately furnished to the period according to a 1726 inventory settling Trent's estate. The gardens are restored, too, with reference to colonial plantings.

Just a few blocks away is the **Old Barracks,** where you can see how the other side lived during those Revolutionary War battles. Built in 1758 to house British soldiers during the French and Indian War, this now-restored fieldstone building also served as a barracks for the unlucky Hessians who were there to meet Washington. Inside is a restored squad room, consisting essentially of wooden bunks and tables. other rooms are furnished as they might have appeared in private homes of the time. Some of the staff dress in period clothing.

The State House area is just around the corner, offering a mix of old buildings and gleaming new government complexes. The State Capitol, built in French Academic Classicism style, is, of course, open during weekday working hours. Practically next door is the very contemporary **State Museum,** which features a planetarium, rotating exhibits, a variety of special programs, and a gift shop. Both are situated on West State Street (between Willow and Calhoun streets), which has been designated a state and national historic district. Across from the Capitol complex are some of the city's most beautiful large old homes, an architectural potpourri of a half dozen different styles.

If you're interested in seeing still more old houses, you can visit the **Mill Hill Historic District,** a residential neighborhood that has undergone a renaissance since the "brownstone revival" of the early 1970s, when rehab fever began sweeping many of the nation's older cities. Several city blocks now recapture the charm of the Victorian era, with handsomely restored homes, brick sidewalks, and gaslights.

Any time your appetite alarm sounds, you can head toward the eastern part of the city, not far from Mill Hill. The greatest concentration of fine restaurants, in many price ranges, can be found in the Chambersburg section of town, a maze of dozens of residential streets, with a predominantly Italian population. The restaurants specialize in Italian cooking, although most offer other dishes, too. You can stick your head out a car window to ask directions to "the Burg," as it is commonly known, and once there, roll down the window again and ask, "Where's a good place to eat?" It's hard to go wrong with whatever a local Trentonian might suggest. **Crecco's** is a long-established favorite for Italian food. The pasta is homemade, and fettucini alfredo a particularly savory dish. **Z's** is a very popular relative newcomer, serving a variety of seafood and pasta; for a sample of both, try bay shrimp with angel hair pasta.

On a fine day, you might want to take a picnic lunch to **Washington Crossing State Park,** which is eight miles north of Trenton on SR 29, along the Delaware River. Here is where Washington crossed into New Jersey on Christmas night, 1776, and began the trek south in the cold and snow. The 807-acre park features a ferry house where General Washington discussed strategy for the Colonial Army's attack on the British, and a visitor center museum with an extensive collection of Revolutionary War artifacts.

Cross the Delaware yourself into Bucks County, Pennsylvania, and travel down the river back to Trenton. You'll go through Washington Crossing, Pennsylvania, Yardley, and Morrisville, charming communities, where you can admire the river view and attractive homes, and perhaps stop for some shopping.

Don't miss Cadwalader Park in Trenton. The park was created in 1891, according to the design of the noted landscaped architect Frederick Law Olmstead, designer of New York's Central Park. Its 100 acres were part of the estate of a wealthy Philadelphia family, who built their summer home, Ellarslie, in its center. Today, that Italianate villa, dating to 1850, has been restored and in its new life is the **Trenton City Museum.** On display are a number of the city's other claims to fame, including historical artifacts and products and works by artists from the Trenton area.

Trenton was home to perhaps 100 different ceramic companies from the late 19th through the early 20th centuries, including Lenox, Cybis, and Boehm. The museum displays a large collection of ceramic works. You will also see portraits of the Roeblings, a prominent Trenton family. John A. Roebling, whose Trenton company made wire cable for suspension bridges, and his son, Washington, were responsible for the design of the Brooklyn Bridge in the late 19th century. Naturally, the company owned by the Roebling's supplied the cable for the construction of this famous bridge.

Pottery, cable, and other products were manufactured in such quantity in New Jersey's capital that one bridge crossing Trenton into Pennsylvania has for decades carried the huge sign "Trenton Makes, the World Takes." Trentonians, with a feel for the practical as well as the whimsical, have been known to provide an addendum to this slogan: "And what the world refuses, Trenton uses."

DESTINATIONS

Mercer County Chamber of Commerce, 214 W State St, Trenton, NJ 08608. 609/393-4143. **William Trent House,** 15 Market St, Trenton, NJ 08611. 609/989-3027. Mon-Sat 10 am-4 pm, Sun 1-4 pm. Adults 50 cents, children 25 cents. **Old Barracks,** Barrack St, Trenton, NY 08608. 609/396-1776. Mon-Sat 10 am-5 pm, Sun 1-5 pm. Adults $2, seniors $1, children under 13 50 cents. **State Museum,** 205 W State St, Trenton, NJ 08608. 609/292-6464. Tue-Sat 9 am-4:45 pm, Sun 1-5 pm. **Mill Hill Historic District** is bounded by South Broad St, Front St, US 1, and Greenwood Ave. **Washington Crossing State Park Visitor Center,** Washington Crossing, NJ 08560. 609/737-9303. Wed-Sun 9 am-4:40 pm; summer, daily 9 am-5 pm. **Trenton City Museum,** Cadwalader Park, Trenton, NJ 08618. 609/989-3632. Tue-Sat 11 am-3 pm, Sun 2-4 pm.

RESTAURANTS

Crecco's, 273 Morris Ave, Trenton, NJ 08611. 609/393-6323. Tue-Fri 11:30 am-2:30 pm; daily 4:30 pm-1 am. **Z's,** 419 Hudson St, Trenton, NJ 08611. 609/695-7444. Daily 11 am-2:30 pm, weekdays 5-10 pm, weekends 5-11 pm.

ACCOMMODATIONS

Capitol Plaza Hotel, 240 W State St, Trenton, NJ 08608. 609/989-7100.

40

The Invention Factory

Edison National Historic Site
West Orange, New Jersey

Despite a pitifully scant formal education ending at age 12, when he went to work as a railroad newsboy, Thomas Alva Edison, born in 1847, went on to become one of America's best known and most prolific inventors. In his lifetime, he was granted a remarkable 1,093 patents, nearly half of them taken out at **West Orange, New Jersey** where he lived and worked for more than 40 years. Much of the history of the man and his work can be seen at the **Edison National Historic Site,** which preserves his laboratory complex and his home.

Were it not for the intense activity in West Orange during this period, the world might be minus such pleasure-producing machines as the phonograph and the motion-picture camera, as well as the electric storage battery. At this "invention factory," with its chemistry lab, machine shop, stock room, and library, Edison used his considerable managerial talents to direct a team of 60 scientists and technicians. Though unaware at the time, he was creating the nation's first research and development facility.

Park rangers direct visitors through the laboratory complex (which may be visited only as part of a 90-minute tour), including the library containing Edison's desk, preserved as it was when he died on October 18, 1931. The tour includes demonstrations of early Edison phonographs and records and a visit to a replica of the Black Maria, the tiny tar-paper-covered studio, built at a cost of about $600, where the motion picture was born.

The Visitor Center, located in the laboratory complex, offers a variety of exhibits as well as presentations of an orientation video, *The Invention Factory*, and of an eight-minute, one-reel feature film, *The Great Train Robbery*. This film, produced in 1903 by an Edison-owned company and directed by Edwin S. Porter, contains footage shot on the tracks of the Delaware, Lackawanna, and Western Railroad in New Jersey, and generally is acknowledged to have signalled the beginning of the motion-picture industry.

At the Visitor Center, pick up a pass for a visit to **Glenmont,** Edison's former home, located about a half-mile from the lab complex. The 23-room Queen Anne mansion, built in 1880, contains original furnishings of the Edisons, and sits on a 13.5-acre estate. Edison's interest in horticulture is evident in the gardens surrounding the home. The fruit trees, lawns, and flower beds are maintained by a full-time staff and include exotic planting of trees and shrubs from around the world. The estate contains a poured-cement garage, the product of a building technique Edison was testing when it was constructed in 1907, and a man-made pond where the Edison family ice-skated.

Although many of the best known parts of New Jersey are industrialized and urban, large portions of the state provide a habitat for wildlife. You'll find it represented at **Turtle Back Zoo,** the largest in New Jersey, with an extensive collection of fauna native to the state, past and present. Exhibits include bobcat, cougar, wolves, bear, bison, sea birds, a sea-lion pool, and an eagle flight cage. A miniature train provides rides around the grounds.

For a dress-up dinner, head for the elegant dining rooms of **The Manor,** set on beautiful grounds with waterfalls and fountains. Traditional specialties include lobster, rack of lamb, beef Wellington, and Dover sole.

DESTINATIONS

Edison National Historic Site, Main St & Lakeside Ave, W Orange, NJ 07052. 201/736-5050. Daily 9 am-5 pm. Adults $2, seniors & children free. **Turtle Back Zoo,** 560 Northfield Ave, W Orange, NJ 07052. 201/731-5800. Mar-Oct Mon-Sat 10 am-5 pm, Sun 11 am-6 pm; Nov-Feb daily 10 am-4:30 pm. Adults $4.50, seniors & children $1.50.

RESTAURANTS

The Manor, 111 Prospect Ave, W Orange, NJ 07052. 201/731-2360. Mon-Fri noon-3 pm, 6-11 pm; Sat 6 pm-midnight; Sun 1-8 pm.

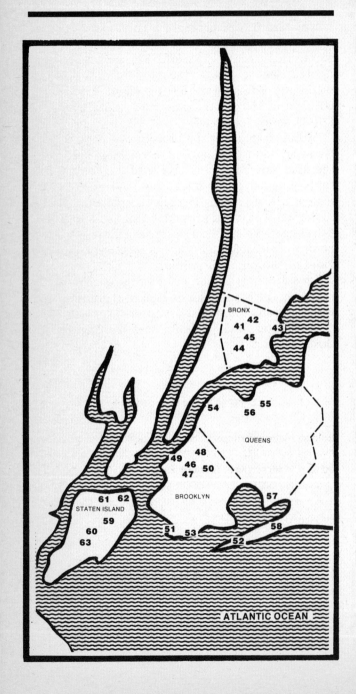

NEW YORK—BOROUGHS

THE BRONX

BROOKLYN

QUEENS

STATEN ISLAND

41

Cheer About The Bronx

Bronx Heritage Trail
Bronx, New York

The Bronx dates back to 1639 when a Swede named
Jonas Bronck bought 500 acres of land from the
Dutch. Little did he know that a borough of the
largest city in the United States would come to bear
a slightly altered version of his name.

The rich history of the Bronx remains much in evidence, as a stroll along the **Bronx Heritage Trail** soon reveals. Along your route you'll visit three historical houses, a museum, a major park, and a revealing slice of neighborhood life.

At the **Bronx Heritage Center,** guides will take you through the **Museum of Bronx History** and the historic **Valentine-Varian House.** The latter is a fieldstone farmhouse that was built in 1758 by a blacksmith named Isaac Valentine. In the following century it was the boyhood home of New York City Mayor Isaac Varian. Its colonial-era craftsmanship survived the Revolutionary War and the ravages of time, and today you can see the original hand-hewn floorboards and hand-forged nails.

The Museum of Bronx History traces the contributions of the Bronx to American life in the areas of government, science, sports, and other fields. The museum periodically hosts crafts demonstrations, outdoor art shows, and musical programs.

The **Edgar Allan Poe Cottage,** built sometime around 1812, was the last house the brooding writer ever inhabited. While living there from 1846 to 1849 Poe wrote *Annabel Lee* and *The Bells.* The brightly-painted house belies the suffering endured by Poe, his wife Virginia, and her mother. Poe was far from a success in his own lifetime and often sold for a pittance works that later became acknowledged masterpieces of the genre. During the years they lived there the family came close to starvation. In 1847, Virginia died there of tuberculosis. A guided tour, audio-visual presentation, exhibits, and period furnishing provide a revealing look at Poe's life and work.

Your last stop along the Bronx Heritage Trail is the **Van Cortlandt Mansion.** It preserves the quintessence of Revolutionary-era elegance, both in its architecture and its furnishings. The Georgian farmhouse was built of stone and brick in 1748, and was reputedly used as a headquarters by George Washington in 1783. Inside, take particular note of the early American dollhouse, the wonderful kitchen and poster beds, and the fine collection of Delftware. **Van Cortland Park,** which surrounds the mansion, is a pleasant spot for rest and contemplation.

Although it's not part of the Heritage Trail, another historic estate worth visiting is the **Wave Hill Conservatory,** site of a well-preserved Georgian mansion built in 1843. Before the city took over ownership in 1960, the estate was owned by a succession of prominent wealthy Americans. Among its illustrious occupants were such diverse gentlemen as Mark Twain, Teddy Roosevelt, and Arturo Toscanini. With sweeping lawns, greenhouses, gardens, and nature trails, the 28-acre estate offers splendid views of the Hudson River. A wide range of flora includes elms, maples, and hemlock, overhanging wisteria, a rose garden and herb garden, and a collection of cacti and tropical plants. Wave Hill offers a varied program of concerts, workshops, exhibits, nature programs, and many events suitable for family outings, such as demonstrations of tapping maple trees to collect syrup.

For another place with a view—this time of Long Island Sound—head for a lunch or dinner at the **Lobster Box** on City Island, where you'll find a number of seafood restaurants including **Johnny's Reef Restaurant** (see trip #43). The Lobster Box has 22 different ways of preparing the tasty crustacean, ranging from Creole and thermidor to au gratin and Cantonese-style, and also serves up a variety of shrimp dishes, as well as mussels, steamed clams, and other seafood selections. As a starter, try the thick and creamy lobster bisque. This popular eatery, with its New England ambience, views over the water, and reliable seafood has been a City Island institution for several decades.

DESTINATIONS

Bronx Heritage Trail, Bronx County Historical Society, 3309 Bainbridge Ave, Bronx, NY 10467. 212/881-8900. Sat 10 am-4 pm, Sun 1-5 pm. **Wave Hill,** Independence Ave at 249 St, Bronx, NY 10467. 212/549-2005. Daily 10 am-4:30 pm. Adults $2, seniors & children $1.

RESTAURANTS

Lobster Box, 34 City Island Ave, Bronx, NY 10464. 212/885-1952.
Late-Mar-Oct noon-11 pm.

42

It's A Jungle In There

The Bronx Zoo
Bronx, New York

Apartment-dwellers know how difficult it can be to
find a place in New York where they can keep a dog
or a cat. But imagine the task of keeping nearly
4,200 animals in the midst of the largest city in the
United States. Well, it takes a pretty large zoo,
which is just what New York City has. The **Bronx
Zoo** is the largest urban zoo in the country, sprawling over 265 acres of parkland and offering a dozen
major exhibits. The zoo claims that you would have
to travel more than 31,000 miles around the world
to see all the animals that you could see there in one
day. Because most of your condensed world tour
will be undertaken on foot, comfortable walking
shoes are prudent, if not an absolute necessity.
(Also, weekends can get very crowded in nice weather—you'll enjoy your visit more if you get there
early.)

The zoo, established in 1899, is in a state of transition. It is gradually changing from a zoo of the past,
with animals in tiny concrete cages in Victorian
buildings, into a modern zoo, with animals in man-
made outdoor environments without bars. The zoo's
major exhibits include several large outdoor habitats
that fit its new mold. **Wild Asia** is transversed by a
monorail from which visitors can see Asian
elephants, tigers, rhinoceri and other species unique
to the world's largest continent. The **African Plains**
is another huge area. There, lions, zebras, gazelle,
antelope, ostriches, cheetahs, and giraffes abound in
an approximation of Africa's vast plains. The

Himalayan Highlands habitat is the home to some of the most beautiful—and rarest—animals in the zoo: snow leopards, tragopan pheasants, red pandas, and white-naped cranes.

The zoo also has many indoor exhibits, and some of these are quite spectacular. **Jungle World** is an enclosed acre that brilliantly recreates a jungle atmosphere. Visitors may feel an urge to don a pith helmet as they wander around viewing such exotic animals as proboscis monkeys, gharials, hornbills, tapirs, and gibbons.

More traditional exhibits include the **Great Ape House** with its lowland gorillas; the **Carter Giraffe Building;** the **Reptile House** with snakes, crocodiles, and a reptile nursery; and the **Mouse House,** home to various types of rodentia.

One special exhibit is the **Children's Zoo** where children become the main attraction as they delight in climbing up a kid-sized spider web, crawling through a prairie dog's tunnel, or flapping their arms while roosting in a giant bird's nest. Kids also can pet porcupines, feed farm animals, and (although this raises more than a few parental vetoes) even find out what a skunk smells like!

The zoo is only blocks away from Bronx's **Little Italy** neighborhood (see trip #44), a perfect spot to dine. **Maria & Joe's** looks a bit unprepossessing, but offers a fine little slice of Sicily in the city. Try the fresh pasta dishes or from among the five varieties of *calzone,* pockets of dough stuffed with goodies such as sausage, eggplant, and cheese.

If your feet have held up after all of this, it's only a short stroll to the adjoining **New York Botanical Garden,** (see trip #45), offering 250 acres of flora to accompany the fauna you've just experienced.

DESTINATIONS

The Bronx Zoo, Bronx River Pkwy at Fordham Rd, Bronx, NY 10460. 212/367-1010. Mar-Oct Mon-Sat 10 am-5 pm, Sun 10 am-5:30 pm. Nov-Feb daily 10 am-4:30 pm. Mar-Oct adults $3.75, children under 12 $1.50; Nov-Feb adults $1.75, children under 12 75 cents. Tue-Thu free. Seniors and children under 2 years old always free. Nearest subway stop: IRT 7th Avenue Express #2—Pelham Parkway station.

RESTAURANTS

Maria & Joe's, 712 E 187th St, Bronx, NY 10458. 212/584-3911.
Mon-Sat 9 am-10 pm.

43

Island In The City

City Island
Bronx, New York

Few tourists think of Manhattan as an island since
the two rivers play such a minor role in the average
visit. But the Bronx's **City Island,** only a half hour
from Manhattan, is *definitely* an island. Surrounded
by Eastchester Bay and Long Island Sound, the island is only about four blocks wide and just a little
over a mile long. And it's definitely a world apart.

City Island is inhabited year-around by a colony
of close-knit families. The many older houses are reminiscent of those found in a New England fishing
village. To the casual tourist, it might seem that City
Island is one long strip of restaurants. There is only
one road straight through the island, aptly named
City Island Avenue, and it's home to all the commercial attractions, including restaurants. Most of
the restaurants are large seafood houses with Italian
overtones. Considering the isolated area, most of
these are surprisingly expensive. But, to get a real—
and reasonably priced—taste of City Island seafood,
try **Johnny's Reef Restaurant.** This large restaurant
is perched on the southern tip of the island and during nice weather patrons can sit on the large deck
and watch the boats. Johnny's is arranged like a
huge cafeteria or fast-food restaurant although all
the seafood is fresh and of top quality. Patrons can
go to the different counters (serving, for example,
steamed scallops, fried shrimp, or raw oysters,
among other types of seafood), order their food and
take it on trays to a table. Even the liquor bar operates in this fashion. Prices, although lower than the
other restaurants on the island, are higher than the
decor might indicate—but the food is excellent.

With all this attention being paid to food on the island, most people simply drive there, eat, and leave without looking around. Though restaurants far outnumber any other businesses on City Island, there are other worthwhile sites to visit.

A number of charter boat outfits take visitors on fishing excursions, day cruises, or romantic moonlight sails. The **New York Sailing School** offers instruction and rentals. Stroll the docks and piers to ogle the beautiful yachts docked at the island's marina. It's said that the boats moored there handily outnumber the island's residents!

There is one museum on the island, the **City Island Nautical and Historical Museum,** housed in an old schoolhouse and run by the North Wind Undersea Institute. The museum offers a glimpse into man's attempts to conquer the sea. There is a mini-submarine, examples of scuba gear, and other new and old equipment. The Institute also trains seals to aid divers. Lucky visitors might see some of the animals being put through their paces.

The parkland leading to the island has its own attractions. Turtle Cove Golf Complex consists of a miniature golf course and a well-maintained driving range. Rodman's Wildlife Area offers birdwatchers and hikers beautiful surroundings. There are nearby picnic tables and ballfields as well as Orchard Beach, one of New York's best kept secrets. Orchard Beach is less crowded than other better-known beaches and it is kept immaculately clean. Even in fall and winter, a walk along the beach can prove invigorating.

DESTINATIONS

New York Sailing School, 560 Minnieford Ave, City Island, NY 10464. 212/885-3103. **City Island Nautical and Historical Museum,** alley between City Island Ave & Fordham St, City Island, NY 10464. 212/885-1616. Sun 2-4 pm and by appointment.

RESTAURANTS

Johnny's Reef Restaurant, 2 City Island Ave, City Island, NY 10464. 212/885-9732. Daily 11 am-9 pm.

44

That's Amore!

Bronx's Little Italy
Bronx, New York

You can take the boy out of the Bronx, but you can't take the Bronx out of the boy. Case in point: When rock 'n' roll crooner and heart-throb Dion, who grew up in the **Bronx's Little Italy,** hit it big in the late 1950s and early 1960s, he did it with a band he called the Belmonts, named after the local designation for the neighborhood.

This ethnic enclave may not be as big or as well-known as its neighbor in Manhattan, but neither is it as glitzy or crowded. The Bronx's Little Italy is in fact only about seven blocks of stores, restaurants, cafes, bakeries, and groceries. The majority of the businesses are on three blocks of Arthur Avenue. The other main street, 187th Street, crosses Arthur Avenue one block below Fordham Road. On these two cross-streets you'll experience an authentic Italian neighborhood. While you may get the impression that its cousin across the river is really just a commercialized tourist mecca, you'll never doubt the credentials of the Bronx's Little Italy. It is a real neighborhood that mainly caters to locals.

Part of the appeal is the authentic Italian foodstuffs at the many groceries. You won't find huge supermarkets, yuppiefied pasta stores, or ersatz Italian pastry shops. Even visitors from outside the neighborhood seem intent on serious shopping. The goods sold in the grocery stores, butchers shops, pasta shops, bakeries, and mom-and-pop delis are authentic. More often than not these are family enterprises where you'll find the proprietors assisted by sons and daughters as well as by grandsons and granddaughters. And these provisions can be as inexpensive as they are authentic. The prices are often half of those charged in Manhattan.

For a concentrated helping of the area's shops, head for the **Arthur Avenue Retail Market,** a European-style indoor market built in the 1940s to house vendors who formerly roamed the neighborhood's streets with pushcarts full of merchandise. There you can find homemade mozzarella and ricotta, sweet cannolis and round loaves of *pane di casa,* spicy sausages and paper-thin-sliced prosciuto, as well as a veritable garden of fresh produce and—of course—a nearly exhaustive selection of pastas. The vendors—some dating back to the pushcart era—are a generally friendly lot, often willing to explain to potential customers what sauce, cheese, or pasta to use for certain recipes.

For an excellent Italian meal for which you *won't* have to shop for ingredients, try **Mario's** or **Dominick's,** across Arthur Street from each other. Mario's offers a large menu of favorites as well as less-well-known entrees. For a change-of-pace, try the deep-fried mozzarella sandwich in anchovy sauce or perhaps the octopus salad. Dining at Dominick's can be a bit of an adventure, because the restaurant has no set menu. You can order your favorite Italian pasta, fish, or meat dish, and the restaurant's inventive kitchen will come up with their tasty version of your request. (Or, if you'd rather, your waiter can suggest a particular dish.)

For an overview of Italian-American culture, stop by the **Enrico Fermi Cultural Center,** the area's local New York Public Library branch. The cultural center features books, artifacts, photographs, and other reference materials relating to Italian-American studies.

DESTINATIONS

Arthur Avenue Retail Market, 2344 Arthur Ave, Bronx, NY 10458. 212/367-5686. **Enrico Fermi Cultural Center,** 610 E 186th St, Bronx, NY 10458. 212/933-6410.

RESTAURANTS

Mario's, 2342 Arthur Ave, Bronx, NY 10458. 212/584-1188. Tue-Sun noon-11 pm. **Dominick's,** 2335 Arthur Ave, Bronx, NY 10458. 212/733-2807. Daily noon-10 pm.

45

Every Blooming Thing

The New York Botanical Garden
Bronx, New York

Want to pore over seed catalogues from the mid-1800s, look at dried and mounted plants collected by famed American explorers Lewis and Clark, and stroll through the only remaining stand of untouched forest in New York City? If so, head for the 250 lush and scenic acres of the **New York Botanical Garden** in the Bronx. Founded in 1891, the botanical garden is a green and pleasant oasis, harking back to the days when most of the Bronx was forests, meadows, and gardens.

An important part of the garden's educational role is the new **Library and Plant Studies Center.** There, visitors may browse through the collection of research materials, seeking answers to botany-related questions. The library contains nearly one million items, including collections of botanical art, handwritten manuscripts dating back to the 13th century, and even old-time seed catalogues. These supplement a vast collection of books and periodicals on botany and horticulture. The unique **Herbarium** houses thousands of dried plant specimens, preserved and mounted for scientific study. This exhaustive collection even includes flora collected by the Lewis and Clark expedition of 1804-06, which explored and reported on the geographical and natural state of the vast section of America northwest of the Mississippi River.

While enriching the mind, the garden also delights the eye with its varied collection of plants, flowers, and trees. Focal point is the **Enid A. Haupt Conservatory,** a crystal palace of a greenhouse, modeled after London's Kew Gardens' Palm House. The conservatory's 11 galleries offer a variety of exhibits: some feature a specific type of plant, such as ferns or violets; others represent different geographical areas of the world or periods of garden design.

At the center of the building is the stunning Palm Court, with examples of more than one-quarter of the different types of palm in the world, some growing almost to the top of the building's 90-foot-high dome!

Among an assortment of outdoor gardens, the Rose Garden contains more than 200 varieties and is in bloom during spring, summer, and even late fall. There is a dramatically landscaped rock garden as well as perennial gardens and native plant gardens. The fragrant Herb Garden is a favorite, as are the many demonstration gardens, which offer ideas on garden design and plant selection for house or apartment.

Picnics are welcomed in the stunning Twin Lakes area. A more formal lunch may be enjoyed at the garden's **Snuff Mill River Terrace Cafe.** Housed in a four-story fieldstone structure built in 1840, the cafe features a light menu of soups, salads, sandwiches, and quiches. Intrepid travelers with sturdy arches and/or comfortable shoes may want to spend a half-day at the botanical garden and then visit the adjacent **Bronx Zoo** (see trip #42).

DESTINATIONS

The New York Botanical Garden, Bronx, New York 10458. 212/220-8700. Apr-Oct daily 8 am-7 pm, Nov-Mar daily 8 am-6 pm. Admission by voluntary donation. Admission for the Enid A. Haupt Conservatory: adults $3.50, seniors and children 6-16 $1.25. Nearest subway stops: IRT Lexington Avenue #4, IND 8th Avenue C, or IND 6th Avenue D—Bedford Park Boulevard stations.

RESTAURANTS

Snuff Mill River Terrace Cafe (see Destination). 212/220-8700. Daily 9 am-4 pm.

46

Theatrical Renaissance

Brooklyn Academy of Music
Brooklyn, New York

Around the turn-of-the-century, Brooklyn had two

lively theater districts and was in the midst of building 20 more theaters. During the borough's lean
years, these theaters became abandoned, torn down,
and, in some instances, converted into churches and
supermarkets. For many years, the only operating
theater in downtown Brooklyn was **The Brooklyn
Academy of Music (BAM).** Then, in 1987, BAM re-
opened the **Majestic Theater** in what Brooklyn patrons of the performing arts hope is the beginning of
a theatrical renaissance.

Located in the Fort Greene neighborhood, known
for its rowhouses and lines of chestnut trees, The
Brooklyn Academy of Music is America's oldest
performing arts center. It was founded in 1859 by
members of the Philharmonic Society of Brooklyn
and rebuilt in 1908 after a fire. In its early days it
brought to Brooklyn such theatrical luminaries as
Sarah Bernhardt, John Drew, and Edwin Booth, and
lecturers Mark Twain, Booker T. Washington, and
Henry Stanley (with his account of meeting Dr.
Livingston). A grand bazaar raised funds for soldiers
wounded in the Civil War; a gala celebrated the
opening of the Brooklyn Bridge in 1883.

Enrico Caruso, Mary Pickford, Gertrude Stein, and
Sherwood Anderson were just a few of the greats
who graced the Academy's stages. Anna Pavlova,
performing in *Swan Lake,* is among the famous who
have danced on its boards.

Today, BAM offers remarkably diverse programs
ranging from top-rated opera and dance to symphony concerts, chamber music, and special performing arts programs for youngsters. Its annual
Next Wave Festival is internationally known as an
avant garde showcase of contemporary performing
arts.

The Academy's main building houses three performance halls: the 2,100-seat Opera House, the
1,011-seat Carey Playhouse, and the Lepercq Space,
an experimental facility with flexible seating. The
Attic Theater and the Hillman Studio are used as re-
hearsal spaces and for small functions.

In 1904 the Majestic Theater (only two blocks
from BAM) opened with a production of *The
Wizard of* Oz, and soon established itself as the

most important "try out" house for Broadway. Many
of the plays that premiered there, including *When
Johnny Comes Marching Home* and Noel Coward's
Home Chat, went on to long Broadway runs. In the
1920s, the Majestic founded its own musical repertory company presenting musicals and light opera,
including Gilbert and Sullivan favorites. In the
1930s, theater-lovers came from afar to see Ethel
Barrymore in *The School For Scandal* and George
Abbott's triumphant *Brown Sugar*. Then, in 1942,
having housed a variety of theater, from vaudeville
to Shakespeare and opera, the Majestic was renovated and re-opened as a first-run movie house by
wealthy Parisian showmen fleeing Nazi occupation.
It closed in the 1960s and lay dormant for nearly
two decades, before opening on October 13, 1987 as
the BAM Majestic Theater with a Peter Brook's production of the Indian epic, *The Mahabharata*, part
of the Next Wave Festival. Radical redesign reduced
the original seating capacity by 50 percent and arranged the remaining 900 seats in two semicircular
tiers around an extensive stage, forging an intimate
connection between audience and actors.

Many BAM patrons follow a show with a visit to
Junior's for a slice of what many claim is the
world's best cheesecake. This garish deli and bakery
also is a full-service restaurant where you'll find
beef goulash, seafood, and steaks along with steaming pastrami sandwiches and other deli items. Go
for the cheesecake, but if you're splurging on dessert
try a slice of cream pie or one of the tall soda-foun-
tain creations which come in great variety. Nearby
Gage & Tollner (see trip #50) is another landmark
eatery that was founded in 1879, only a few years
after BAM.

DESTINATIONS

Brooklyn Academy of Music, 30 Lafayette Ave, Brooklyn, NY
11217. **BAM Majestic Theater,** 250 Fulton St, Brooklyn, NY 11217.
718/636-4100. Nearest subway stop: IND 8th Avenue Express A
or Local C—Lafayette Avenue; or Brooklyn-Queens Crosstown
G—Fulton Street.

RESTAURANTS

Junior's, 386 Flatbush Ave, Brooklyn, NY 11217. 718/852-5257. Sun-Thu 6:30 am-1:30 am, Fri-Sat 6:30 am-3 am. **Gage & Toll-ner,** 372 Fulton St, Brooklyn, NY 11217. 718/875-5181. Mon-Fri noon-9:30 pm, Sat 4-10:30 pm.

47

A Forest Grows In Brooklyn

Brooklyn Botanic Garden
Brooklyn, New York

Brooklyn's residents have long found refuge in an oasis of natural beauty. From humble beginnings in 1910 on city waste land, the **Brooklyn Botanic Garden** has grown into one of the world's great botanic gardens. Today, the 52-acre preserve is an international pacesetter and its acclaimed horticultural handbook series, *Plants & Gardens*, is sold in 55 countries worldwide.

Spring produces massive blooms of fragrant magnolias and a spectacular explosion of pink blossoms on avenues of Japanese cherry trees. Summer brings out the best in the Cranford Rose Garden, started in 1917 and one of the largest and finest in the country. Pink, white, red, yellow, and orange blooms of 6,000 bushes representing nearly 1,000 species of roses add color to walkways and climb over trellises and arbors. Fall is enlivened by flashy displays of multi-colored chrysanthemums and the burnished hues of autumn foliage. Winter is the season of witch-hazels and snowdrops, and of crocuses poking through the snow, followed by sweeping carpets of bright yellow daffodils in early spring.

The Herb Garden contains more than 300 different kinds of medicinal and culinary plants and has as its focus Elizabethan "knots" of foliage of different colors and textures, intricately woven in 16th-century fashion. Raised beds of plants with fragrant flowers, aromatic foliage, and unusual texture are located in the Fragrance Garden where labels also are in Braille. Inviting visitors into the Shakespeare Garden is a charming English cottage garden framed by a serpentine brick wall. The garden is carpeted with violets, rosemary, and chamomile, and showcases more than 100 plants mentioned in the Bard's plays and sonnets.

Popular with artists and photographers is the Japanese Garden, built in 1915 by landscape architect Takeo Shiota and considered the finest of its kind outside of Japan. Providing an island of tranquility in the heart of New York's largest borough are shrines, temples, and pavilions, pines, stone lanterns, a tea garden, and a flower-shaped lake with bridges gracefully curved to reflect in the water and stepping stones that simulate the flight of wild geese.

The newest addition and well worth a visit on its own account, is the $25 million **Steinhardt Conservatory,** where you can savor the Sonoran Desert and enter the lilliputian world of bonsai gardening. Transporting you to the dinosaur era of 200 million years ago is the Trail of Evolution, tracing the history of plants from the Precambrian era to the present, and focusing on their adaptability to almost every environment—submerged in water, soaked by rains, blown by wind, baked by sun. There's an aquatic house with two pools and underwater-viewing windows, a bog, and a gorgeous orchid collection; a notable bonsai museum with exhibits from the garden's world famous collection of 750; and three major pavilions that create environments of the desert (with giant saguaros and other cacti and succulents), the tropics (organized according to fragrances and use as food, medicine, and in industry), and warm temperate regions (with a fern grotto carved out of granite and a limestone cave with a mushroom-growing display).

At this multi-faceted preserve you can sign-up for classes and workshops, attend annual events such as plant sales, philharmonic concerts, and Easter and Christmas shows, rent a video, and walk a celebrity path paved with stones inscribed with the names of famous Brooklynites, such as Danny Kaye, Eli Wallach, and Mary Tyler Moore. The **Terrace**

Cafe provides an idyllic setting for homemade soups, sandwiches, salads, and hot and cold drinks.

The gift shop is great for seeking out unusual presents—perhaps a gardening book, a big jar of pot pouri, ceramic tiles decorated with botanical art, or a canvas bag with the slogan "A tree grows in Brooklyn."

DESTINATIONS

Brooklyn Botanic Garden, 1000 Washington Ave, Brooklyn, NY 11225. 718/622-4433. Apr-Sep Tue-Fri 8 am-6 pm, Sat & Sun 10 am-6 pm; Oct-Mar Tue-Fri 8 am-4:30 pm, Sat & Sun 10 am-4:30 pm. **Steinhardt Conservatory** (same as above). Apr-Sep Tue-Sun 10 am-5:30 pm, Oct-Mar Tue-Sun 10 am-4:30 pm. Adults $2, seniors & children 3-12 $1.

RESTAURANTS

Terrace Cafe (see Destinations). Apr-Oct.

48

Underground High Jinks

Brooklyn Children's Museum
Brooklyn, New York

Hands-on museums for children are a fun idea, although certainly not a new one. Over the last decade, museums of this genre have proliferated almost as fast as golden arches and there now are several hundred throughout the United States. Pioneer of this innovative concept is the **Brooklyn Children's Museum,** the world's first museum designed expressly for children.

Founded in 1899 in a Victorian mansion, the museum offered an alternative to existing museums with exhibits too sophisticated for children. In 1977, the progressive museum went underground—quite literally—moving into new 35,000-square-feet quarters that are mostly below ground, with just an iceberg tip poking up into eight-acre Brower Park. The unique, $3.5 million high-tech structure incorporates into its design objects from urban and rural

American life. Its entrance is a turn-of-the-century subway kiosk, a huge drainage pipe serves as a neon-lighted "people tube" connecting four levels of exhibit space, and an oil tank houses an auditorium.

Although techniques and technology change, the museum's guiding philosophy remains the same—to provide interactive and entertaining learning experiences for children and their families. All museum activity is based on the conviction that children learn best through first-hand experiences. With this in mind, children can play in a model of a diamond crystal, turn a grist mill to grind grain, direct the water flow in an indoor stream, climb through a molecule-shaped tunnel called "curved space," and find out about the working of windmills, a greenhouse, an aquarium, and a steam engine.

At the Boneyard they can compare the size and functions of different bones, shake the Boneyard arm, and learn about objects made from bones. The Early Learners Arena, exclusively for kids five years and younger, enhances motor skills through imaginative play. This territory for tots includes building blocks and an adventure platform that they can climb over, under, and around.

Among the newer exhibits, "The Mystery of Things" invites youngsters to become super sleuths as they use their five senses to unlock the mystery of objects. They press a button to hear sounds made by a cuckoo clock, tea kettle, trolley car, typewriter, and telephone; they identify unknown smells inside squeeze bottles; they use their hands instead of their eyes to find a perfect match of such objects as oil lamps and Indonesian sculptures.

Borrowing from the world of super heroes and prime-time heroines, the "Doctor Dimension and the Rulers of the Universe" exhibit engrosses kids in measuring length, weight, and time. Doctor Dimension is a "hands-on" sculpture character of scales, clocks, rulers, and various measuring devices; a cave is the setting for a lesson on the relationship of size and weight; foam pillars help young visitors explore differences in height.

An immensely popular event is the annual Halloween Monster Mash, when the museum's neon-lighted tube sets an eerie scene for face painting, potato carving, and storytelling with a macabre musical serenade by a trio of witches. The single largest event, however, is the June "Balloooon," a festival for parents and children in the museum and surrounding park that attracts more than 15,000 visitors and includes dance, workshops, a parade led by costumed stilt-walkers, and the museum's signature balloon floating 30 feet overhead.

For another adventure, head with the youngsters to the section of Atlantic Avenue between Court and Henry streets, where it becomes a Middle Eastern bazaar. This is where many of Brooklyn's estimated 50,000 Arabs congregate, many of them patrons of Sahadi Imports, a massive importer of Middle Eastern food. Visit the **Damascus Bakery** for rich filo pastries and *lahem jahne*, a kind of Lebanese pizza featuring spiced lamb. For a sit-down meal, try the **Moroccan Star,** with cucumber salad, shish kebab, couscous, and apricot crepes for dessert.

DESTINATIONS

The Brooklyn Children's Museum, 145 Brooklyn Ave, Brooklyn, NY 11213. 718/735-4400. Mon-Fri 2-5 pm, Sat-Sun & school hols 10 am-5 pm. $2. Nearest subway stop: IRT 7th Avenue Express #3—Kingston Avenue station.

RESTAURANTS

Moroccan Star, 205 Atlantic Ave, Brooklyn, NY 11213. 718/596-1919. Noon-11 pm. **Damascus Bakery,** 195 Atlantic Ave, Brooklyn, NY 11213. 718/855-1456.

49

Cityscapes And Great Escapes

Brooklyn Heights
Brooklyn, New York

For a nearby escape, follow the footsteps of those who have found it in **Brooklyn Heights.** Now a fashionable neighborhood of brownstones and tranquil, tree-lined streets, Brooklyn Heights has provided literary escape for writers such as Thomas Wolfe, Herman Melville, Walt Whitman, and Truman Capote, all of whom once lived and worked there, and for novelist Norman Mailer, who still does. There's a church with tunnels that sheltered runaway slaves escaping to Canada, and docks that provided an escape route for George Washington and his army in retreat from the British. For a romantic escape, there's a promenade with a spectacular view of the Manhattan skyline, and a floating restaurant that serves up sunsets, piano music, and nonpareil harbor vistas.

Built atop a bluff that slopes down to the water's edge, the **Esplanade** is one of the most popular— and romantic—spots for strolling, with benches where you'll find people with brown bags of bagels and coffee leisurely reading the Sunday *Times* or simply enjoying the cityscape. This spectacular view of the Manhattan skyline across the river attracts crews filming television commercials and movies such as *Moonstruck* and *Annie Hall*. You'll get a good view of the Statue of Liberty and, on a clear day, see as far as the Verrazano Bridge to the south. Occasional craft festivals are held on the Promenade, and this is the time to buy a piece of art or pottery or a dried-flower arrangement, and watch chairs being caned at a booth beside a stone marking George Washington's headquarters.

It was during the Continental Army's long retreat in 1776 that Washington led his men under the cover of fog and darkness to safety in Manhattan. This Dunkirk-like evacuation preserved the Army to fight again another day.

In 1814 the ferryboat *Nassau* established a regular route between Fulton Landing and Wall Street. In 1883 the **Brooklyn Bridge** was completed. With its Gothic stone towers, spidery latticework of steel cables, and wooden pedestrian walkway, the bridge is itself an attraction.

Once a bucolic area of orchards and pastures known as Clover Hill, Brooklyn Heights has hundreds of pre-Civil War buildings with many notable examples of Federal and Greek Revival architecture.

Included in a 30-block historic district are an 1824 clapboard house at 24 Middagh Street, and red-brick Plymouth Church, once part of the Underground Railroad, where abolitionist preacher Henry Ward Beecher once "sold" a slave in protest and where the congregation has included Abraham Lincoln, Mark Twain, and Charles Dickens. In a pretty garden surrounded by a wrought-iron fence is a statue of Beecher. Another church, St. Ann and the Holy Trinity, has the first stained-glass windows made in the United States and is the home of a performing arts program of music, dance, and theater. Head here for a classic movie, Texas swing, Delta blues, or Bach cantata.

On the river at the foot of Brooklyn Bridge, the utterly elegant **River Cafe** occupies a former barge. Picture windows capture an ever-changing view of river traffic, an alfresco dining area is decked with bouquets of flowers. Sip champagne and nibble on caviar, or try such specialties as sweetbreads sautéed in white wine and basil, rack of lamb with onion tart and marinated artichoke, and grilled squab with smoked bacon and a pepper salad. Nearby, **The Ferrybank** restaurant is housed in a Victorian bank building with distinctive cast-iron architecture and pillared columns. Specialties include a variety of fresh fish, crab cakes, shrimp, and clams. Dessert features Irish whiskey pie. Another floating attraction is **Bargemusic Ltd.,** a former Erie Lackawanna coffee barge that now is the venue for twice-weekly, year-around chamber-music concerts.

DESTINATIONS

The Fund For The Borough of Brooklyn, Inc, 16 Court St, Brooklyn, NY 11201. 718/643-3480. **Bargemusic Ltd,** Fulton Ferry Landing, Brooklyn, NY 11201. 718/624-4061. Nearest subway stops. IRT Broadway-7th Avenue Express #2 Clark Street station; or IND 8th Avenue Express A—High Street station.

RESTAURANTS

River Cafe, 1 Water St, Brooklyn, New York 11201. 718/522-5200. Mon-Thu noon-2:30 pm, 6:30-11 pm; Fri-Sat noon-2:30 pm, 7-11:30 pm; Sun noon-3 pm, 6:30-11 pm. **Ferrybank,** 1 Front St, Brooklyn, NY 11201. 718/852-3137. Mon-Fri noon-10:30 pm, Sat-Sun 5-10:30 pm.

50

Treasure In Park Slope

Brooklyn Museum
Brooklyn, New York

In the heart of Park Slope, Brooklyn's neighborhood of brownstones, you can visit a charming Dutch Colonial house built in 1675 by Jan Martense Schenck. Originally located in the Flatlands, the historic home has been reconstructed, complete with some of the original siding, and now is preserved for posterity on the fourth floor of the wonderful **Brooklyn Museum.** It is part of the museum's acclaimed collection of decorative arts and one of 28 rooms furnished in varying American styles that range from Colonial through Art Deco.

The Art Deco room is the recreation of a 1928 Park Avenue apartment. With its geometrical design and Parisian-made furnishings, this room symbolizes the Jazz Age and Prohibition (a private bar is tucked unobtrusively into a cubbyhole). This collection of period rooms includes the bedrooms, parlors, and dining rooms of families from various social strata. There's the two-room house of a prosperous miller (note the handsome walnut-and-cherry wardrobe), a room in early-Georgian style from a plantation in the Low Country of South Carolina, and the Moorish room from the Manhattan townhouse of John D. Rockefeller, Sr. Depicting the lifestyle of a gentleman landowner is a room (circa 1730) from the house of Maj. Henry Trippe, Secretary of Maryland. You can walk through the 1853 brownstone from 236 Clairmont Avenue, noting rooms crammed with the heavy rosewood furniture (made in Troy, New York) that was typical of the Victorian period. In contrast is the uncluttered elegance of the Neoclassical parlor, circa 1818, with heavy velvet brocaded purple drapes and a center table set with flowers.

Already one of the world's largest museums, this Neoclassical behemoth, designed in 1893 by the famous firm of McKim, Meade & White, is but one-fifth of its intended size and mega-buck expansion is planned. Despite its high ranking, the museum takes a back seat to its Manhattan counterparts and, consequently, is often uncrowded, sometimes downright empty.

Yet it is a storehouse of treasures. Here, among a collection of two million objects, you'll find oils by Degas, Monet, and Cezanne, prints by Rembrandt and Goya, watercolors by John Singer Sargent and Winslow Homer, and sculptures by Frederic Remington. The spectacular Egyptian collection has been called the best outside of Cairo and London, and collections of African and pre-Columbian art are world famous. Outdoors is a unique collection of architectural ornaments from razed New York City buildings. In this graveyard of demolition you'll find friezework, gargoyles, and statues from old Penn Station, a Coney Island amusement park, and other buildings long gone.

This is a vast museum to enjoy collection-by-collection over a number of visits, perhaps taking advantage of docent-conducted tours specializing on specific collections. One piece of art that many like to point out is the evocative painting "Winter Scene in Brooklyn," circa 1817-20. With a dark, foreboding sky and primitive style, it provides historic documentation of an area of the borough destroyed by the building of Brooklyn Bridge. Also receiving feature treatment from these Brooklyn boosters is Georgia O'Keeffe's 1948 oil painting, "Brooklyn Bridge," that stylizes its latticework of cables.

Don't overlook shopping at the museum. The main giftshop sells books, folk art, handicrafts from around the world, and quality reproductions of artworks. A separate children's shop has art supplies, crafts, toys, storybooks, and games.

Wood paneling, a stamped tin ceiling, and gas lights create a warm atmosphere at another Brooklyn landmark, **Gage & Tollner,** which opened its restaurant doors in 1879. Crabmeat Virginia, lobster Maryland, and a variety of dishes made with fresh clams, bay scallops, shrimps, and oysters are among the noted seafood. Starters include lobster bisque, oyster stew, and clam chowder. For meat eaters, the classic English-style mutton chop is recommended.

DESTINATIONS

The Brooklyn Museum, 200 Eastern Pkwy, Brooklyn, NY 11238. 718/638-5000. Daily 10 am-5 pm. Adults $3, students $1.50, seniors $1. Nearest subway stop: IRT 7th Avenue Express #2 or #3—Eastern Parkway/Brooklyn Museum station.

RESTAURANTS

Gage & Tollner, 372 Fulton St, Brooklyn, NY 11217. 718/875-5181. Mon-Fri noon-9:30 pm, Sat 4-10:30 pm.

51

Boardwalk And Borscht

Coney Island/Brighton Beach
Brooklyn, New York

In Woody Allen's semi-autobiographical comedy *Annie Hall*, he played a character who jokingly re-called (in a hilarious flashback scene) how his family lived at **Coney Island**—under the world-famous Cyclone roller coaster. Although Brooklyn-native Allen actually grew up in Flatbush (and depicted a more realistic view of a 1940s Brooklyn childhood in a later film, *Radio Days*), who could blame him for fantasizing a fun-filled childhood amidst the excitement of Coney Island? The Cyclone, the Parachute Jump, and the Wonder Wheel; hot dogs, popcorn, and cotton candy—these and all the rest of the diversions of the boardwalk captivated the dreams of many a New York child, and represented a wonderfully unique world that was only a subway ride away.

But, like everything else, Coney Island has not been immune to the ravages of time. Many of the rides have been torn down or closed (the forlorn skeleton of the Parachute Jump remains—with some talk of renovation), and the boardwalk has become a bit run-down. However, the bone-rattling Cyclone, **Astroland** amusement park, and **Nathan's Famous** hot dog stand still exist, and are all still worth visiting. The wooden Cyclone has been thrilling visitors for more than 50 years, and is still considered "the King of Roller Coasters." Astroland is the last remaining major amusement park in the city, and offers dozens of thrilling rides, such as the Water Flume and the Astrotower. Nathan's has been serving its famous all-beef hot dogs since 1911, back when both the dog and the subway ride it took to get one cost a nickel. In addition to Nathan's hot dogs, chick-on-a-bun and chow-mein-on-a-bun sandwiches, and fried clams, this joint serves some of the city's best French fries. Finding a little bit of counter space and dunking fat french fries into a big plop of catsup at Nathan's is a *de rigueur* part of a visit to Coney Island.

While the thrills of Coney Island represent the area's past, the recent influx of Russian immigrants to the **Brighton Beach** neighborhood has been a strong influence on its present. Often referred to as "Little Odessa-By-The-Sea," the neighborhood boasts a main street—Brighton Beach Avenue—that is lined with Russian markets, book and gift shops, and restaurants. Stop at **M & I International Foods** for pickled fruits and vegetables, imported caviar, homemade Russian pastries and yogurt, and cold-smoked salmon, sturgeon, and herring.

For an unforgettable evening and an abundant meal, don't miss the **National Restaurant,** which may be familiar to visitors who saw the movie *Moscow on the Hudson*; this is where Robin Williams danced and drank in a scene from that film. Come prepared to eat, drink, and be merry until the wee hours—for a fixed price of approximately $25 per person, you get lively entertainment from an authentic Russian dance band, a bottle of vodka (or wine, if you prefer) for every four people, pitchers of soda, and a panoply of cold and hot appetizers, main entrees, and desserts. Sample smoked fish, baked eggplant, gefilte fish, beef tongue, stewed chicken, borscht, and kebabs of chicken, lamb, and beef. Join the lively dancing between courses or simply relax and enjoy the company of your new-found Russian *tovariches*—friends.

The boardwalk at Coney Island is also home to the **New York Aquarium** (see trip #53.)

DESTINATIONS

Astroland, 1000 Surf Ave & W 10th St, Coney Island, NY 11224. 718/266-1234. Palm Sun-Jun & Sep Sat & Sun noon-midnight; Jun-Sep daily noon-midnight. Individual ride tickets available or $8.65 for unlimited rides. **M & I International Foods,** 249 Brighton Beach Ave, Brooklyn, NY 11235. 718/615-1011. Daily 8 am-10 pm. Nearest subway stop: BMT Broadway Express and Locals B, N, & D, and IND 6th Avenue Local F—Coney Island station.

RESTAURANTS

Nathan's Famous, Surf Avenue at Stillwell, Brooklyn, NY 11224. 718/946-2202. Sun-Thu 8 am-2 am, Fri & Sat 8 am-4 am. **National Restaurant,** 273 Brighton Beach Ave, Brooklyn, NY 11235. 718/646-1225. Fri & Sat 8 pm-3 am, Sun 8 pm-1 am.

52

Gateway To Outdoor Recreation

Gateway National Recreation Area
Brooklyn, New York

Progress, as we all know, can be a rather mixed bag; with added convenience and modernization comes a loss of the past—usually an *irretrievable* loss. But this need not always be so. Take the area along the Rockaway Sand Spit, just south of Brooklyn and Jamaica Bay. Algonquin Indians lived here in more than 100 villages, until supplanted by the farms and forts of settlers from Europe. Later, warehouses and mills sprang up. Next came docks, roads, factories, and airports—and finally pollution. Birds and fish died off or found more agreeable habitats. People stopped swimming because the Atlantic beaches became contaminated. Progress had taken its toll.

But this story doesn't end there. Recognizing the importance of protecting the stretch of shore that falls within the city limits of New York (and, across the Lower Bay, the shore area of New Jersey), the

U.S. government established **Gateway National Recreation Area,** and began a massive clean-up and reclamation effort. Today, the **Breezy Point** unit of the recreation area, on Rockaway, has been returned to a natural state that has begun to bear a closer resemblance to its pre-colonial past.

Recreation has once more become a primary reason to visit—and not just to swim, but to also jog, fish, and once again to count the birds. There are also facilities for soccer, football, softball, and basketball.

Also at Breezy Point is Fort Tilden, a crumbling old fort whose guns have sat ready to defend New York City since the War of 1812. It's the starting point for ranger-led hikes to explore the marine life that flourishes along the ocean and bay beaches.

Gateway's **Staten Island** unit affords recreational opportunities of several kinds. You can fish or swim at Great Kills Park in the usually calm waters of Lower New York and Raritan bays. There are football and baseball fields, as well as tennis at Miller Field. Hikers have a choice of trails through woodlands and grasslands and over dunes. Special programs are designed for bird watchers, butterfly fanciers, stargazers, and rockhounds.

In Gateway's **Jamaica Bay** unit (see trip #57) you can view great flocks of migrating birds as they stop on their semiannual journey along the Atlantic Flyway. And any time of year the refuge offers exceptional hiking. Floyd Bennett Field, New York's first municipal airport is also located there. The airport didn't succeed commercially, but it gained fame nonetheless as the take-off point for several record-breaking airplane flights by aviators such as Howard Hughes, Wrong Way Corrigan, John Glenn, and Wiley Post. Post's flight around the world in 1933 (the first in history) both began and ended here. Today Floyd Bennett Field hosts educational programs for teachers and schoolchildren at its Gateway Environmental Study Center.

Back on the mainland, near Jamaica Bay, stop at **Lenny's Pizza** for lunch or dinner. This neighborhood favorite offers the ubiquitous thin-crust, extra-cheesy New York-style pizza pie.

DESTINATIONS

Gateway National Recreation Area, Breezy Point Unit, Fort Tilden, New York, NY 11695. 212/474-4600. **Jamaica Bay Unit,** Floyd Bennett Field, Brooklyn, NY 11234. 212/630-0126. **Staten Island Unit,** PO Box 37, Staten Island, NY 10306. 212/351-8700.

RESTAURANTS

Lenny's Pizza, 159-49 Cross Bay Blvd, Howard Beach, NY 11414. 718/738-3500. Mon-Thu 11 am-11 pm, Fri & Sat 11 am-1 am, Sun noon-10 pm.

53

Sealed With A Kiss

New York Aquarium
Brooklyn, New York

Gigi was behaving badly. Maybe it was the natural contrariness of a Californian transplanted to New York, but she was certainly causing a scene at the **New York Aquarium.** Firmly, one of the aquarium personnel asked the young lady to leave the sea-mammal performing area. Gigi looked at the trainer, and slowly began heading for the exit. But just before she got there, she dashed away, and dived over the barricade into a pool of dolphins readying themselves for a performance! As the trainer blew her whistle in vain, Gigi swam and cavorted with the dolphins, much to the delight of the crowd. It looked spontaneous, but the whole scene had been planned—and Gigi the California sea lion had played her mischievous starring role to the hilt. With a nuzzle for her trainer, Gigi's version of a kiss, she waddled off.

Located in the Coney Island section of Brooklyn, adjacent to Brighton Beach and Astroland (see trip #51), the New York Aquarium seems to fit solidly in its decidedly urban surroundings. It's no SeaWorld, to be sure; no slick, razzle-dazzle sea-mammal shows, no technicolor exhibits with four-part harmony. But you will find a wide variety of marine life there, ranging from colorful tropical fish to huge whales.

The aquarium was opened in Manhattan in 1896 as the first public aquarium in the United States; it moved to its present site in 1957. The 14-acre facility is run by the progressive and influential New York Zoological Society, which also operates the acclaimed **Bronx Zoo** (see trip #42).

The aquarium has more than 22,000 aquatic animals, representing more than 225 species of vertebrates and invertebrates. Among the favorites are the penguins, an exhibit of sand tiger and nurse sharks, the only Pacific walrus in any New York City zoo or aquarium, the talented seals (who moonwalk and stand on their front flippers in performance), the dolphins, and the sea lions. The aquarium was a pioneer in the study and exhibition of whales. In 1897, it was the first aquarium to exhibit beluga whales, and in 1981, the first beluga ever bred in captivity was born at the aquarium. Today, two belugas dance and swim together in what one fancies a very romantic *pas-de-deux*. In addition, there are large tanks filled with fish from the world's habitats.

The animal shows, such as Gigi's *tour de force*, are presented only during good weather. But the daily feedings—of the whales, sharks, seals, sea lions, and dolphins—provide an opportunity to learn about these creatures and to see them do some of their fancier tricks. A list of feeding times is posted daily in the aquarium.

Nearby is **Pier 28,** one of the Coney Island-Sheepshead Bay area's largest restaurants. The specialty there, of course, is seafood, with an ever-changing menu offering whatever's fresh and/or in season. Try the grilled tuna, the massive lobsters, or the delicate salmon with dill sauce.

DESTINATIONS

New York Aquarium, Boardwalk and W 8th St, Brooklyn, NY 11224. 718/265-3474. Daily 10 am-4:45 pm; Mem Day-Lab Day, weekends, and holidays 10 am-5:45 pm. Adults $3.75, children 2-12 $1.50; seniors free after 2 pm. Nearest subway stop: IND 6th Avenue Local F or BMT Broadway Express D—West 8th Street station.

RESTAURANTS

Pier 28, 2801 Emmons Ave, Brooklyn, NY 11235. 718/769-7100.
Mon-Thu noon-10:30 pm, Fri-Sun noon-1 am.

54 🍎

A Day At The Movies

American Museum of the Moving Image
Queens, New York

You step up to the box office of the garish neo-Egyptian movie palace, and purchase your tickets—from sultry silent film star Theda Bara. Mae West leers over the candy counter, Orson Welles takes tickets, and Mickey Rooney stands ready to show you to your seat. Of course, these famous persons are merely represented by whimsical sculptures, but the movie theater *does* exist and it shows typical serial adventures of the silent era. This is "Tut's Fever," one of the fascinating and entertaining exhibits at the **American Museum of the Moving Image,** which adjoins the Astoria Studios in **Astoria, Queens.** Only minutes from Manhattan, the museum offers a glimpse into the past, present, and future of the motion picture and television.

The movie industry in America began just across the Hudson River from Manhattan in New Jersey where Edison had his laboratories at West Orange (see trip #40). There in the Black Maria (the first studio) he perfected the moving picture camera. Soon a burgeoning industry grew in Manhattan and the silent-film industry was born. The Astoria Studios were mainly used by Paramount Pictures to film Broadway stars in their greatest hits. The early films of the Marx Brothers, W. C. Fields, and the Barrymores were among the features filmed at the studios.

Soon after World War I, the movies went to California in search of better weather and to escape Edison's Patent Trust, which dictated which studios could make movies and which theaters could show them. The Astoria Studios continued to operate into the sound era, but, as time went by, fewer pictures were made there. When the United States entered World War II, the studios were turned over to the War Department and used for its propaganda and training films. In the 1950s and 1960s, television came into its own and the huge sound stages became the home to many of the TV series that were produced in Manhattan.

After television also deserted Manhattan, Astoria declined. In the 1970s, productions began using Manhattan as a backdrop again and Astoria enjoyed a new lease on life. Now, with New York a major film location, the Astoria Studios have been refurbished and modernized in an ambitious program.

Part of this renovation has been the founding of the American Museum of the Moving Image. The museum has constantly changing exhibits as well as several permanent installations showing and telling how movies and television affected and influenced our culture. There is also a pair of theaters (besides the Egyptian fantasy) whose programs rival those of the great *cinematheques*.

The museum concentrates on the "hardware" of the moving image—the cameras, projectors, sound equipment, settings, costumes, and receivers of motion pictures and television. Exhibits range from full stage sets to fan magazines chronicling the history of the 20th century's most important media.

The museum also has educational and interpretive programs in addition to its exhibits and film and video screenings. Actors, directors, screenwriters, and television personalities often introduce their work, give lectures, and lead discussions. These figures have included Sidney Poitier, Nestor Almendros (cinematographer of such films as *Kramer vs. Kramer* and *Places in the Heart*), and a number of leading independent film-makers.

Astoria is also a renowned Greek neighborhood. (Some claim its large Greek population makes it third after the Grecian cities of Athens and Salonika for Greek population in the world!). Many inexpensive Greek restaurants are within walking distance of the museum. Most notable of these is **Roumeli Taverna,** offering Greek standards such as lemon chicken and stuffed grape leaves, as well as a variety of lamb specialties.

DESTINATIONS

American Museum of the Moving Image, 35th Ave at 36th St, Astoria, NY 11106. 718/784-0077. Wed & Thu 1-5 pm, Fri 1-7:30 pm, Sat 11 am-7:30 pm, Sun 11 am-6 pm. Nearest subway stop: Brooklyn-Queens Crosstown G or BMT Broadway Local R— Steinway Street station.

RESTAURANTS

Roumeli Taverna, 33-14 Broadway, Astoria, NY 11106. 718/278-7533. Mon-Thu 11 am-10 pm, Fri & Sat 11 am-midnight, Sun 1-9 pm.

55

Hard Won Freedom

Bowne House
Queens, New York

If any part of the U.S. Constitution has come to symbolize freedom in America it is the first 10 amendments to the U.S. Constitution, better known as the Bill of Rights. And one of those rights—freedom of religion—got a major boost from a man named John Bowne.

Bowne was an English merchant and landowner in the Flushing section of Queens—a settlement originally known by the Flemish name of Vlissingen, after a city in the Netherlands. Bowne was also a devout Quaker. When the governor of New Netherlands, Peter Stuyvesant, sought to outlaw the Quaker Faith, Bowne invited his fellow Quakers to hold their religious services in his kitchen.

Bowne paid for his defiance with imprisonment and exile to Europe in 1662. But he was later vindicated by the Dutch West India Company and allowed to return in 1664. Although the First Amendment to the Constitution wasn't adopted until more than 100 years later, Bowne's courageous act is often cited as one of the reasons for its existence.

Built in 1661, the **Bowne House** stands today not

only as a symbol of religious freedom, but as a splendid example of the vernacular Dutch-English architecture in the United States. The original "salt-box" style house that Bowne built consisted of a kitchen, two adjoining rear rooms, and an upstairs bedroom. The most unusual features of the kitchen are the oversized fireplace and the beehive oven.

In 1680 Bowne added a parlor next to the kitchen. Now called the dining room, it retains its 17th-century authenticity with hand-hewn beams and pegged floors. Bowne's son Samuel added the present entryway and living room in 1696. The last additions to the house were made in the 1830s. The house remained in the family for nine generations, until 1946. A plaque commemorates the role it played in advancing the cause of religious freedom.

Today Bowne House contains 17th- and 18th-century furniture—including a Chippendale secretary—plus pewter, family portraits and documents, and old maps. There are kitchen implements and such items as hot-water bottles and foot warmers.

Once the Quakers had won their religious freedom and clandestine meetings were no longer necessary, they built their own house of worship. The **Friends Meeting House,** built from 1694 to 1719, is just a few blocks from the Bowne House and is a fine example of American colonial architecture. Inside you'll find simple plastered walls, heavy wooden beams, and plain wooden benches. It remains the oldest religious building in New York City in continuous use. Visitors are welcome to attend Sunday meetings.

For a more contemporary look at Flushing's ethnic patchwork quilt, head along Northern Boulevard to the neighborhood known as "Little Asia." These newest arrivals from Asia—largely Chinese and Koreans, but with some Japanese and Indians—now comprise about half the population of Flushing. For the adventurous, an interesting dining spot is the **Stony Wok,** where the custom is to order a number of dishes and create your own casserole prepared in a tableside wok. Choose from mutton, oysters, venison, and a variety of fish. More exotic offerings include cuttlefish, squid roll with ginger sauce, and dried lily flower.

DESTINATIONS

Bowne House Historical Society, 37-01 Bowne St, Flushing, NY 11354. 718/359-0528. Tue, Sat, Sun 2:30-4:30 pm. Adults $1, children 25 cents. **Friends Meeting House,** 137-16 Northern Blvd, Flushing, NY 11354. 718/358-9636.

RESTAURANTS

Stony Wok, 137-140 Northern Blvd, Flushing, NY 11354. 718/445-8535. Daily 11:30 am-3 am.

56

World's Fair To World Series

Flushing Meadows/Corona Park
Queens, New York

Flushing Meadows Park was created in the late 1930s from a huge swampland to accommodate the World's Fair of 1939-40. Almost 25 years later the Park served as the site of the New York World's Fair of 1964-65 and was the first home of the United Nations. Several buildings remain from both fairs, the most spectacular of this century. After most of the last World's Fair's buildings were demolished, the New York City Parks Department resodded over 6,000 cubic yards of concrete and asphalt to create huge lawns.

But the park is much more than just a leafy greensward. The general layout of the past fairs remains and many of the surviving buildings house new exhibits. A leisurely stroll around the grounds with a stop here and there for the museums and other attractions can be invigorating, informative, and enjoyable.

The focal point of the park is the Unisphere, the symbol of the 1964-65 World's Fair. The Unisphere, a huge balancing globe, serves as a landmark as you wander around. Another remnant of that fair is the **Hall of Science,** right across Grand Central Parkway

NEW YORK — BOROUGHS **161**

(by pedestrian bridge) from the Unisphere. The Hall of Science is New York's first public science-technology center since the city's Museum of Science and Industry closed in the 1940s. Visitors are urged to explore the various worlds of science and technology represented in the hall by pushing buttons, pulling levers, and conducting experiments.

Permanent exhibits at the hall include "Seeing the Light," which introduces the visitor to theories of color, light, and perception; "Feedback," an exhibit of self-sensing machines that visitors interact with; "Realm of the Atom," the first major museum effort to present quantum theory and its application to the layman; "Structures," an exploration of the science and mathematics of building things; and "Hidden Kingdoms," an interactive exhibition about microorganisms.

The **Queens Museum** is a relic from the 1939-40 World's Fair. Today it exists partially to celebrate the two great fairs. The Queens Museum New York World's Fair Association sponsors film screenings, seminars, lectures, and walking tours, all focusing on the two historic fairs and what they meant to New York and the United States. The museum also houses art galleries, photography exhibits, special film series, and the magnificent Panorama of the City of New York. The Panorama, the largest scale model in the world, is an exact duplicate of all five boroughs of New York City.

After exercising their brains at the museums, visitors to Flushing Meadows/Corona Park can find physical activity just by stepping back outside. The 1,255-acre park (second largest in the city, after Central Park) offers many recreational diversions. From May through October, bicycles can be rented ($4/hour) from a concession adjacent to the Tennis Center. Thee is a five-acre, 18-hole Pitch and Putt Golf Course (with rental clubs available) near the Passarelle entrance to the park. Golf season begins in March and generally runs through October.

If you prefer spectator sports, Flushing Meadows is also the site of **Shea Stadium,** home of the New York Mets, and the **National Tennis Center,** host of the U.S. Open Championship each September.

Children enjoy the newly refurbished **Queens Zoo,** operated by the New York Zoological Society. The zoo concentrates on animals native to North America, emphasizing humanely designed exhibits with large open areas. Next to the zoo is a beautiful carousel, a combination of two Coney Island carousels, the Feltman Carousel, circa 1903, and the Stubbman Carousel, circa 1908. They were combined in 1964 for the World's Fair. The carousel, equipped with a magnificent Ruth Band Organ, has another special feature, jumper's poles that enable the horses to swing outward when the carousel is in motion.

Flushing has a large concentration of oriental restaurants, particularly those featuring Korean cuisine. Try **Seven Seas,** offering seafood such as eel, abalone, and herring, as well as Korean-style pork ribs, noodle dishes, and soups.

DESTINATIONS

New York Hall of Science, 47-01 111th St, Corona, NY 11368. 718/699-0005. Wed-Sun 10 am-5 pm. Adults $2.50, children 17 and under & senior citizens $1.50. **The Queens Museum,** New York City Bldg, Flushing, NY 11368. 718/592-5555. Tue-Sat 10 am-5 pm, Sun 1-5 pm. Adults $1, students & seniors 50 cents. **Shea Stadium,** Flushing Meadows, Flushing, NY 11368. 718/507-8499. **U.S. Tennis Association/National Tennis Center,** Flushing Meadows, Flushing, NY 11368. 718/592-8000. Nearest subway stop: IRT Lexington Avenue Subway, Flushing Local #7—111th Street station.

RESTAURANTS

Seven Seas, 42-05 Main St, Flushing, NY 11368. 718/762-7214. Daily 24 hours.

57

Yellowstone, New York

Jamaica Bay Wildlife Refuge
Queens, New York

A scant 12 miles from the concrete canyons of Wall

Street and within plain sight of the runways of Kennedy Airport, there's a pristine expanse of grassy marshlands that's part of a National Recreation Area administered by the National Park Service. That means that this wildlife refuge—the largest in any city in the world—is run by the same agency that administers the Grand Canyon and Yellowstone. And just like those national parks, it's teaming with wildlife—raccoons, rabbits, squirrels, chipmunks, mink, turtles, frogs, bats, birds, bees, and butterflies. Which comes as a nice surprise to city dwellers under the impression that just about all of the wildlife in New York is of the two-legged variety.

Not only does the **Jamaica Bay Wildlife Refuge** support a variety of wildlife, it is considered one of the most important urban wildlife refuges in the United States. Its more than 9,000 acres include saltwater marshes, upland fields and woods, several fresh and brackish water ponds, and an open expanse of bay and islands—all within the city limits of New York.

Here's a spot where you'll see osprey and hawks circling overhead, alert for potential prey, and observe a variety of flora that includes cattails, black pine, brambles, yucca, bayberry, and a variety of wildflowers. And here's where you can participate in such fun and educational programs as "moon prowls," astronomy nights, and photography and craft workshops—and where you can watch nature films and attend a naturalist lecture series.

The refuge is part of the **Gateway National Recreation Area** (see trips #36, #52, and #58), which includes Riis Park, Fort Tilden and the Breezy Point tip in the Rockaways; Great Kills and Miller Field in Staten Island; Floyd Bennett Field, Plumb Beach, Dead Horse Bay and Canarsie Pier in Brooklyn; and Sandy Hook, New Jersey. Altogether, these areas cover 26,000 acres.

Strategically located on the Atlantic Flyway, this wildlife refuge is known as a prime birding spot. During migration periods in spring and fall, thousands of water, land, and shore birds stop here. More than 325 species have been recorded. Included are egrets, ibises, and herons.

The best way to appreciate the refuge is by hiking one of the trails. You can take a self-guided tour or join a ranger-led walk. Informative maps and brochures are available at the visitor center on Crossbay Boulevard, Queens. When hiking, keep an eye out for poison ivy, and remember to check yourself for tiny deer ticks (carriers of Lyme disease) after leaving grassy and wooded areas.

There's no snack bar or any other kind of eatery here, so you might want to pack a picnic lunch (there are tables outside the visitor center). Along Cross Bay Boulevard in the nearby Howard Beach neighborhood, you'll find **Lenny's Pizza,** a locally popular spot.

Another option is to provision a picnic (and do a bit of urban sightseeing) on a side trip to another area of Queens—the old German neighborhood of **Ridgewood,** which straddles the line between Queens and Brooklyn. This is a neighborhood of handsome brick rowhouses and one of the largest Federal Historic Districts in the country with authentic restorations that made it the choice for filming scenes for the movie *Brighton Beach Memoirs*. Head for Seneca Avenue and **Jobst & Ebbinghaus** for a variety of cold meats and sausages. For dessert, pick up a flaky, fruit-filled cherry or apple strudel at **Rudy's Pastry Shop,** a popular neighborhood bakery that has had more than 50 years in which to perfect the art of strudel-making.

DESTINATIONS

Jamaica Bay Wildlife Refuge, Gateway National Recreation Area, Floyd Bennett Field, Brooklyn, NY 11234. 718/474-0613.

RESTAURANTS

Jobst & Ebbinghaus, 676 Seneca Ave, Queens, NY 11385. 718/821-5747. **Rudy's Pastry Shop,** 905 Seneca Ave, Queens, NY 11385. 718/821-5890. **Lenny's Pizza,** 159-49 Cross Bay Blvd., Howard Beach, NY 11414. 718/738-3500.

58

Sandy Shore At Manhattan's Back Door

Rockaway Beach
Queens, New York

Not many real estate bargains can compare to the one that Peter Minuit got in 1626 when he bought Manhattan from the Brooklyn Indians for $24 worth of trinkets. But one comes close: the deal struck in 1685 by one Capt. John Palmer, an Englishman, when he bought **Rockaway** from the Rek-ka-wanes Indians for $52. (Even then, real estate was appreciating nicely.)

Palmer's purchase was approved by New York Governor Thomas Dongan in the name of James II, King of England, and the deed was entered into the official record on November 3, 1685. So if you've ever spent a languid weekend at the Rockaways—or if you ever plan to—don't forget to raise a toast to John Palmer.

The Rockaway Peninsula pokes a finger across the Atlantic at Staten Island, helping to protect the entrance to New York Harbor. In the 1600s it was known as Rek-ka-wanes, after the tribe that sold this prime piece of real estate to John Palmer. The translation of the name is "a sandy place."

The Rockaways claim to have some of the finest ocean beaches anywhere in the world. A strand of sandy beach more than seven miles long stretches alongside the pounding surf of the Atlantic Ocean, paralleled for most of its length by a boardwalk. Here, you'll find people pursuing most of the traditional oceanside activities, including enjoying outdoor art fairs and concerts, surf fishing, beachcombing, building sand castles, tossing frisbees, and seeking the amusement-park thrills of Rockaways Playland.

In the 1800s the upper classes used the beaches as their exclusive playground. One long-forgotten writer described these sandy shores as "the brightest jewel within the diadem of imperial Manhattan.''

Most of the permanent residents left around the turn of the century, but a new wave replaced them during the decades of the 1930s, 1940s, and 1950s. Ocean-front apartments began appearing in the 1960s. One of the most popular of a string of beaches here, is the Atlantic shore of Jacob Riis park, named for the crusading journalist who battled for better housing and recreation facilities around the turn of the century.

There are many stands along the beach where you can buy hot dogs, hamburgers, tacos, and other snack foods. For something more substantial, try the **Snug Harbor** restaurant, just a block from the beach. You can't get much more nautical than the ambiance of this locally popular eatery. They took apart a pair of New Jersey tug boats to create it. Expectedly, seafood is a major component of a 50-item menu. You can start with shrimp bisque or New England or Manhattan clam chowder and follow with shrimp scampi, scallops, or lobster. Cream of broccoli and pea soup are recommended and the restaurant also has built a reputation on prime-cut steaks (with surf 'n' turf a reliable compromise).

Rockaway is part of the Breezy Point unit of the Gateway National Recreation Area, which is administered by the National Park Service. You can take ranger-led tours to learn about marine life, go on photo safaris, and indulge in a variety of recreational activities, such as softball, baseball, football, rugby, paddle ball, handball, tennis, and miniature golf.

DESTINATIONS

Rockaway Beach, Community Board #14, 1931 Mott Ave, Far Rockaway, NY 11691. 212/471-7300.

RESTAURANTS

Snug Harbor, 108-02 Rockaway Beach Blvd, Queens, NY 11694. 718/634-4384. Mon-Fri noon-10:30 pm; Sat-Sun 5-10:30 pm.

59

Treasures Of Tibet

Jacques Marchais Center of Tibetan Art
Staten Island, New York

Leaving behind the busy hum of commerce of central Staten Island, you ease your car up the steep incline of Lighthouse Hill, past sleek new condos, to a quiet retreat that looks as though it might belong on a mountain plateau of central Asia. Clinging to the hillside are two stone buildings and terraced gardens, serene with a meditation arbor and a lotus pond with goldfish. Designed in Tibetan architectural style, with thick walls, tiny windows, and overhanging cedar rafters, the buildings resemble a Buddhist mountain temple.

In this unlikely setting is the **Jacques Marchais Center of Tibetan Art,** a small but active museum that is one of the unexpected treasures of Staten Island. Founded in 1946, the museum contains the largest private collection of Tibetan art in the Western Hemisphere. Included within its monastery-like buildings are displays of Tibetan bronze images, paintings, and ritual artifacts as well as representative forms of art from Japan, Nepal, China, India, and Southeast Asia.

The museum was founded by the late Mrs. Jacqueline Norman Klauber, a Manhattan art dealer who used "Jacques Marchais" as a professional name. Curiously, she never was in Tibet (or even the Orient). The genesis of the collection were 12 small bronzed sculptures of Tibetan deities brought from Darjooling by her great grandfather. As a result of this childhood gift, she developed a life-long interest in the culture and arts of Tibet and spent her adult years acquiring art objects from the Orient. Major pieces came from Sven Hedin, eminent Swedish explorer and collector of Oriental artifacts, part of a display at the Chicago World's Fair of 1933.

Separate showcases focus on the geography and people of Tibet, deities, ceremonial masks and statues (many of which contain rolled-up prayer papers), monks and monasteries, and clothing, dolls, and children. A sacred three-tier Buddhist altar, with its prayer wheels and offering urns, is occasionally used by visitors, including some of the estimated 60 or so Tibetans who live in the New York area. Rich in brass, bronze, and copper figurines of deities and Buddhas, as well as a large number of *thanka* paintings (depictions of images to aid in ritual meditation), the collection also includes notable examples of jewel-encrusted Nepalese metalwork, a set of silver ceremonial implements belonging to the spiritual advisor to the Dalai Lama, Tibetan miniature paintings and jewelry, dance masks, and decorative Chinese cloisonné work.

Wide-ranging programs are held on Sunday afternoons, most free with admission to the museum. These include such diverse subjects as the art of paper folding, lhasa apso dogs, Japanese love poems, and Peking Opera. A popular annual event is the Tibetan Harvest Festival (late October), where visitors can sample authentic Tibetan food and tea, shop at an outdoor bazaar, see puppet performances and calligraphy demonstrations, attend tarot-card readings and Tibetan divinations by a lama, and listen to chanting monks. A gift shop has an unusual stock including Nepalese jackets, Tibetan shirts, Oriental jewelry, incense, and tapes (including a recording of a lecture given by the Dalai Lama during a visit to the United States).

For dining, it's worth a trip to Victory Boulevard and the **Tokyo Japanese Restaurant,** which serves excellent sushi and sashimi. Other choices include tempura shrimp, chicken, and vegetables and broiled salmon or shrimp with teriyaki or butter sauce served with soup, salad, and steamed rice. Starters include hamaguri (clam soup with scallions); dessert selections include fresh fruit and fried ice cream. Beverages include wines, sake, and Japanese beer.

DESTINATIONS

The Jacques Marchais Center of Tibetan Art, 338 Light-

house Ave, Staten Island, NY 10306. 718/987-3478. May-Sep
Wed-Sun 1-5 pm, Apr, Oct, Nov Fri-Sun. Adults $2.50 children $1.

RESTAURANTS

Tokyo Japanese Restaurant, 1710 Victory Blvd, Staten Island,
NY 10314. 718/727-1771.

60

New York's Country Village

Richmondtown Restoration
Staten Island, New York

It's a middle-of-winter deep freeze and the village
mill pond is frozen solid. It's cold enough to see
your breath and you're glad of a visit to the general
store, circa 1837, with its wooden post office, chec-
kers game, and the comforting warmth of an ornate
coal stove. Well-stocked shelves display goods that
would have been sold in the 19th century. Today,
you can buy freshly ground coffee and bread baked
at an adjoining farmhouse. Providing this realistic
slice of early Americana is the **Richmondtown Restoration,** a historic village, located on 96 acres of
Staten Island greenbelt, that depicts three centuries
of the history and culture.

Originally known as "Cocclestown," the town of
Richmond began in the 1690s as a minor crossroads
settlement among scattered farms and estates. By
1730, it had become Staten Island's principal village, its political center, and the seat of Kings
County. Today, the restoration features 25 historic
buildings, 10 of which are at their original locations,
and many important historic sites dating from the
late-17th century. More than half the buildings are
open to the public, with interpreters to re-enact the
daily tasks of early Staten Island householders,
farmers, merchants, and tradesmen and their apprentices Among the buildings are a Greek Revival
courthouse, Queen Anne-style railroad depot,
Gothic Revival Dutch parsonage, the modest house

of a Dutch basketmaker, a 19th-century sawmill, a carriage-and-wagon works, and the oldest surviving elementary school in the United States, circa 1695. Among the skills demonstrated are traditional country carpentry, the production of red earthenware pottery, tinsmithing, basketry, and hearthside cooking.

Richmondtown is a great place to learn a new craft, discover a new hobby, gain fresh insights into heritage and history, and find pure entertainment. Workshops teach quilting, needlepoint, 19th-century contra dancing, and (as a parent-child project) creating Victorian valentines. Lectures focus on such subjects as early settlers, colonial cooking, and historic architecture.

At a popular weekend concert series in a re-created 19th-century tavern you can sip a mug of beer or cider by the wood stove and sit back as songs are sung and tales are told. Featured are folk and traditional music—1920s tunes played on ukulele and banjo, Scottish and Irish airs and ballads, a zany jug band, sea chanteys, old-time country fiddle music, English Music Hall ditties, and bawdy British ballads. Combine a concert with dinner at **M. Bennett Refreshments,** a 19th-century building adjacent to the tavern that offers such fare as Yankee pot roast and apple pie. After each performance M. Bennett is open for homemade soup, chili, barbecue beef, hot sandwiches, and dessert. The cellar bakery offers traditional home-baked goods to take home. Above the restaurant is a marvelous museum of dolls, games, and toys.

Selected summer weekends feature early 19th-century dinners prepared and eaten outdoors with special entertainment. Annual events include: Spring in Richmondtown (May, June) with outdoor craft demonstrations and turn-of-the-century music and theater; antiques and crafts markets (May, June, September); Militia Day (3rd Sunday, May), with mock battles and re-enactments of drills and camp life; Richmond County Fair (Labor Day weekend), the only county fair in New York City, with contests, music, food, entertainment, and games; Old Home

Day (3rd Sunday, October), with dozens of traditional craftspeople demonstrating 18th- and 19th-century trades and domestic activities; Christmas in Richmondtown (early December) with tours of festively decorated buildings; and Candlelight Tours (mid-December evenings) with music, merriment, holiday activities, and seasonal tours.

DESTINATIONS

Richmondtown Restoration, Staten Island Historical Society, 441 Clarke Ave, Staten Island, NY 10306. 718/351-1617. Mon-Fri 10 am-5 pm Sat-Sun 1-5 pm. Adults $4, Students, seniors, youths (6-18) $2.50.

RESTAURANTS

M. Bennett Refreshments (see Destinations). 718/979-5258.

61

Snug Harbor For Arts

Snug Harbor Cultural Center
Staten Island, New York

In the early 19th century it provided a snug harbor for sailors retiring from the rigors of life at sea. Today, the **Snug Harbor Cultural Center,** is a lively center of discovery, a rambling, shirt-sleeves sort of place where the performing and visual arts flourish, where fresh talent is nurtured, and where minds, young and old, are expanded. It offers a stimulating variety of attractions and events for innumerable outings. In fact, with contemporary art, theater, outdoor sculpture, and concerts presented in landmark settings, it's easy for Snug Harbor to become a habit—particularly when you add to the mix a children's museum and botanical garden. And, with a new trolley shuttle from the ferry dock, it's now possible to reach Snug Harbor via public transportation.

Overlooking the bay, the center includes 28 historic buildings on a nationally landmarked historic district, among them examples of Greek Revival architecture considered to be some of the finest in the country. Founded in 1801, Sailor's Snug Harbor was the first maritime hospital and home for retired sailors in the United States.

Visit the changing exhibits of contemporary art in the Newhouse Gallery. Or take a class in fine arts, crafts, or photography at the Art Lab, where the Atelier Gallery also presents a number of annual exhibitions. Head for Veterans Memorial Hall, formerly the sailors' chapel (the original pews remain), now an intimate recital hall, and attend a silent-film festival or concerts featuring jazz, classical, chamber, and folk music. You'll see such performers as the Gary Burton Quintet, the Boys Choir of Harlem, or the New York Light Opera Company.

On summer weekends head for an outdoor concert in the meadow. You may see the Tommy Dorsey Orchestra, the New York Philharmonic, a Metropolitan Opera performance of "La Boheme," or perhaps Chuck Mangione or Joan Baez supplemented by such special events as a Fifties' Hop, Italian Festival, and a stand-up comedy competition. An annual sculpture festival helps decorate the 80-acre grounds during summer.

The **Staten Island Botanical Garden,** has a formal English perennial border, a Victorian rose garden, and greenhouse collections of tropical and temperate plants. A lake and stream bordered by willows and a lawn provide a pastoral setting for strolling and sitting; a tranquil pond attracts migrating ducks and geese. Special events include a bird-seed sale (January), an Easter greenhouse display, spring plant sale (May), fall plant and bulb sale (September), an annual flower show and harvest festival (October) with spectacular displays of chrysanthemums, and a Winter Fair and Christmas greenhouse display (November/December), with poinsettias, amaryllis, and Christmas cactus.

The award-winning **Staten Island Children's Museum** has interactive exhibits such as "It's News To Me" that shows how the print and electronic media function and enables youngsters to try reporting and TV newscasting and features an abbreviated version of Orson Welles' *War of the Worlds* broadcast. Free programs include puppet shows, storytelling, mime, and dance.

In early December, get a jump on holiday shopping with a visit to Snug Harbor. The "Gift Gathering" features merchandise from 10 different museum shops.

Across from Snug Harbor, **R.H. Tugs,** with a high tin ceiling, shiny black tables, and framed watercolors of tugboats, is a handsome reclamation of a dilapidated waterfront building. It is noted for its bar pies—mozzarella and tomato, pepperoni pizza, crab pizza, and broccoli, garlic, and oil. Windows and a small patio area overlook the busy harbor—after dark, the unsightly storage tanks of oil refineries on the Jersey shore are transformed by twinkling lights. For starters, there is chowder made with shrimp, crab, and fish, and fried seafood dumplings. Entrees include seafood fettucini and shrimp sautéed in a spicy sauce and served over rice.

DESTINATIONS

Snug Harbor Cultural Center, 914 Richmond Terrace, Staten Island, NY 10301. 718/448-2500. Hours and admission charges vary according to event or attraction. Admission to grounds free. Trolley schedule: Wed & Thu 1-5 pm, Fri-Sun noon-8 pm (later for special events); the trolley runs every half-hour. $1.

RESTAURANTS

R.H. Tugs, 1115 Richmond Terrace, Staten Island, NY 10301. 815/447-6369. Sun-Thu noon-12pm, Fri-Sat noon-1 am.

62

Ship To Shore

Staten Island Ferry
Staten Island, New York

It's the beginning of an adventure. The excitement of the impending departure heightens as you wait in the large, bright waiting hall, your senses piqued by the aroma of freshly-brewed coffee and the rustle of the early editions of the morning newspapers. The waiting passengers are a mix of bored commuters and expectant tourists. The latter include Europeans taking advantage of the weakened dollar, camera-toting Japanese, and video-toting Midwesterners. A lighted sign announcing, simply, "NEXT BOAT," whets tourists' appetites for the odyssey ahead.

Certainly, a ride on the **Staten Island Ferry**—at 25 cents, one of New York's greatest travel bargains—can't be compared to plying Mediterranean ports on *Sea Goddess II*. But it is fun. And, combined with some sightseeing on the island within easy walking distance of the ferry dock, it makes an entertaining and economical excursion.

A fellow passenger, a young man wearing sturdy hiking boots, a "Hard Rock" T-shirt, and a backpack, put it succinctly: "For 25 cents, and in 25 minutes, I can be in the country."

Claim a place at the bow, and as the ferry pulls away, you'll find the commerce of the busy harbor played out before you. Coast Guard cutters skim across the water, while Circle Line tour boats carry complements of tourists to the Statue of Liberty. Strident horns clamor for attention as the ferry passes grimy wharves, bristling with derricks, that conjure the scene from *On The Waterfront* where union boss Johnny Friendly is confronted by work-hungry longshoremen.

Soon, the ferry has left behind the grove of trees of Battery Park and the famous steel latticework of the Brooklyn Bridge, and you pass Lady Liberty, her torch bright even in the strong morning sunlight. Halfway across, you pass a Manhattan-bound sister ferry—stubby, but somehow liner-like with her yellow paint job and red and white insignia on her elongated stack. In the open harbor, a freshening breeze brushes away the cobwebs of the city and the Verrazano Narrows Bridge (an alternative route onto Staten Island) slips out of the haze and you can pick out autos crawling across it like ants on a fence rail. Nearing shore, you pass green-painted buoy No. 27, its chiming bell a welcoming carillon. Then, with barely a discernible bump, the ferry noses into her berth and you're ready to explore Staten Island.

Walk uphill to Stuyvesant Place (look back for spectacular views of the Manhattan skyline) and visit the galleries of the **Staten Island Museum**. Usually, there are exhibits of the work of local artists as well as important traveling shows, such as the Smithsonian's traveling photo exhibit, Vietnam Veterans Memorial. On Sundays, the works of important filmmakers are screened, such as films by D.W. Griffith and Carl Foreman (bargain movie-going at $2). For a unique child's birthday celebration, ask the museum about a Dinosaur Party, complete with "dig up" fossils and a dinosaur skeleton to assemble. The museum shop has a small, but nice, selection of gifts ranging from 75-cent rocks, to please children, to an $80 elegant hand-quilted vest from Peru.

On the next block, **Lil's Eatery** is a 50s-style diner with James Dean and Elvis posters, booths with their original individual juke boxes, and terrific home cooking. Simply because the owners like to cook, they provide special Friday dinners that elevate this eatery way above the diner level. These festive, four-course dinners (a bargain at $7.95 to $14.95) are popular with in-the-know locals and feature such dishes as leek soup, broccoli and cheddar soup, escargot, mussels marinara, veal chop with port wine, and beef Wellington.

DESTINATIONS

Staten Island Ferry, Dept of Transportation, 40 Worth St, New York, NY 10013. 718/390-5253. Daily 9:30-11 pm. Nearest Subway Stop: IRT Broadway-7th Avenue Subway; South Ferry Station.
Staten Island Museum: Staten Island Institute of Arts & Sciences, 75 Stuyvesant Pl, Staten Island, NY 10301. 718/727-1135. Tue-Sat 10 am-5 pm, Sun 2-5 pm. Free.

RESTAURANTS

Lil's Eatery, 95 Stuyvesant Pl, Staten Island, NY 10301. 718/273-9555. Mon-Thu 8 am-7 pm, Fri 8 am-3 pm, 6-9 pm, Sat 8 am-2 pm, Sun 11 am-2 pm.

63

Staten Island Sampler

Staten Island, New York

Pointing across the choppy waters of Upper Bay to the distinctive New York skyline, a native New Yorker said: "I grew up in Manhattan and was 24 years old before I knew much about Staten Island. You rarely hear what's happening here. Even weather forecasters forget about it. And that makes **Staten Island** a great place to discover."

Indeed! And it's a big island to explore. New York City's most rural borough is a patchwork of country lanes, spiny hills, valleys, beaches, grand seascapes, wide swathes of parkland, wildlife preserves, Victorian neighborhoods, and a lot of history. If you use public transportation, getting there is half the fun with a breezy, 30-minute ferry ride (see trip #62). If you travel by car, you'll have lots of exploration to do on this island that is twice the size of Manhattan.

Although not as large as its more famous counterparts, the 8-1/2-acre **Staten Island Zoo** has a children's zoo with a miniature farm and a noted reptile collection with the most complete collection extant of North American rattlesnakes. Recent additions include an animal hospital with a nursery viewing area, and a state-of-the-art aquarium. Ongoing modernization and expansion includes the creation of a tropical-rain-forest habitat. Among popular children's programs are Saturday morning "Breakfast with the Beasts," where youngsters learn about animal diets and help feed animals. (Another terrific spot for kids when visiting Staten Island is the **Staten Island Children's Museum**—see trip #61.)

In a quiet backwater where you can enjoy fresh breezes off the bay and a spectacular view of Manhattan, is the **Alice Austen House,** at the water's edge almost in the shadow of the Verrazano-Narrows Bridge (the longest suspension bridge in the country). With sweeping lawns and a huge rustic gate, this Victorian cottage was the home of Staten Island's pioneer woman photographer. It exhibits Austen photographs from the 1880s and 1890s and a motion picture about her life, *Alice' World*, narrated by Helen Hayes.

One of the island's premier natural preserves is **High Rock Conservation Center,** covering 87 acres of deciduous woodland, swamps, ponds, and streams. It has six walking trails, native wildflower and fern gardens, and a sensory garden with fragrant and textured herbs that is marked with Braille.

Another major landmark is **The Conference House,** the scene, on September 11, 1776, of the only peace conference held in an attempt to stave off the Revolutionary War. In attendance was Benjamin Franklin, John Adams, Edward Rutledge, and the British commander, Lord Howe. Built in the 1680s, the stone manor house remains intact with period furnishings, a 17th-century working kitchen, and rolling lawns extending to the waterfront—an ideal picnic setting. On the first Sunday of each month, there are demonstrations of open-hearth cooking and spinning and weaving.

For the island's best hamburgers, insiders point to the **Kopper Cettle** (try a burger with bacon, cheese, and cherry peppers served on Italian bread). Notwithstanding its spelling, this eatery offers a solid menu of soups, sandwiches (crab cake with melted cheese on a bun is popular), appetizers (such as baked clams and artichokes au gratin), and such pasta favorites as baked ziti Bolognese and baked ravioli parmagiana.

DESTINATIONS

Staten Island Zoo, 614 Broadway, Staten Island, NY 10310. 718/442-3100. Daily 10 am-4:45 pm. Adults $1, children 75 cents, seniors free. **High Rock Park Conservation Center,** 200 Nevada Ave, Staten Island, NY 10306. 718/987-6233. Visitor center daily 9 am-5 pm. **Alice Austen Home,** 2 Hylan Blvd, Staten Island, NY 10305. 718/390-5100. May-Nov 15 Thu-Sun 10 am-5 pm. **The Conference House,** 7455 Hyland Blvd, Staten Island, NY 10305. 718/984-2086.

RESTAURANTS

Kopper Cettle, 680 Cary Ave, Staten Island, NY 10305. 718/447-9554. Mon 11:30 am-3 pm, Wed-Fri 11:30 am-3 pm 5-11 pm, Sat 5-11 pm, Sun 2-10 pm.

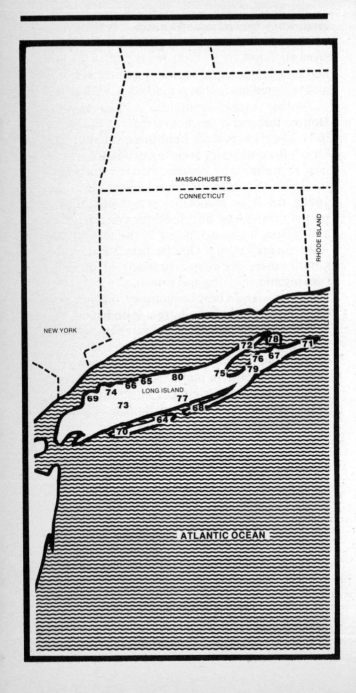

NEW YORK— LONG ISLAND

64 🍎

Gone Fishin'

Captree State Park
Babylon, New York

Along the railing on both sides of the 68-foot twin-diesel-engine boat, would-be fishermen (and women) stand ready, their poles pointed skyward like so many shouldered rifles on a parade ground. They wait with baited hooks and bated breath, reels set, minds sharp, ready to do battle with the wily flounder, fluke, bluefish, or any other fish tempted to hit their lines. As the boat's whistle sounds a strident blast, the rod tips dip almost as one and sinkers drag hooks under the waves with a kerplunking splash. It won't be long until the first cries of "I've got one!" are heard on deck.

Such is the scene every day aboard the *Captain Whittaker,* the *Miss Captree,* the *Anna M,* and any of a dozen other open party boats that operate in the fish-rich waters of the Great South Bay off the shore of **Captree State Park,** on the south coast of Long Island.

The splendid fishing that has developed in the bay came, in part, due to the misfortune of earlier sailors. Since Colonial times, ships have sought sanctuary from ocean storms in the bay. However, many ships limped into the bay only to sink anyway. These so-called "Fire Island Wrecks" act as breeding grounds for fish, ensuring a large population to challenge fishermen. To provide bayside recreation and to take advantage of the fine bay and ocean fishing in the area, the state of New York created Captree State Park, on the eastern edge of Jones Island, the same barrier island that is home to **Jones Beach State Park** (see trip #70).

Head for Captree Boat Basin to get in on the bay's fishing action. Passengers can board any of the open party boats on a first come, first served basis for a half- or full-day fishing excursion. Poles, hooks, lines, sinker, and bait are included in the price (approximately $17 for four hours, $25 for two sessions of four hours with a lunch break), and the helpful crew will even bait your hook and offer free fishing advice as needed. In fact, there's no need to worry about being a beginner. The water is clear and calm. "It's perfect for families or the unseasoned fisherman," notes Captain Richie Abrams, who has been living around and fishing these waters since he was 12. And if the fish aren't biting where you're docked, the captain will sound the whistle—poles up, please—and head for another spot where, with any luck, the fishing will be better.

There is always some species of fish running in

the bay or in the ocean. Flounder and fluke, highly popular with party-boat fishermen, each have separate, successive seasons. Other species include weakfish, porgies, blackfish, sea bass, mackerel, and codfish; the menu is varied and delicious.

Besides the fishing cruises, many of these boats are available for moonlight dinner and party cruises, as well as daytime luncheon and sightseeing jaunts. It is estimated that these fishing boats, plus the charter, sightseeing, and scuba diving boats that ply the bay, carry more than 250,000 tourists each year. The prime season runs from March to November. Each year, a fishing contest is held for various varieties of fish caught in the bay between May 1 and November 30; ask your captain or crew members for details.

For dining once you return to shore, try the **La Grange Inn Restaurant** in West Islip. This popular restaurant is known for its German specialties, such as weiner schnitzel, sauerbraten, and a variety of roast-goose dishes.

DESTINATIONS

Captree State Park, Babylon, NY 11702. 516/669-0449. Fishing boat information: 516/669-6464.

RESTAURANTS

La Grange Inn Restaurant, Montauk Hwy & Higbee Ln, West Islip, NY 11795. 516/669-0765. Wed-Fri, Sun & Mon noon-11 pm; Sat noon-midnight.

65

The House That Vanderbilt

The Vanderbilt Museum
Centerport, New York

Around the turn of the century, wealthy families built elaborate homes on the hilly woodland of secluded coves on Long Island's legendary "Gold Coast." Here, you can visit a millionaire's mansion, frozen in time, and enjoy a picnic and a concert under the summer sky, perhaps a string recital of Bach, Haydn, and Gershwin performed in a Spanish courtyard. And you can study the heavens through a powerful, 16-inch reflecting telescope, trace "The Mysterious Death of the Dinosaurs," and touch the surface of a meteorite that is 4.5 billion years old.

Once known as "Eagle's Nest," the former home of William Kissam Vanderbilt II (1878-1944) is an opulent 24-room mansion on 43 acres of woods and gardens, with terraced lawns sweeping down to Northport Bay and a medieval French-style boathouse where Vanderbilt entertained afternoon yachting guests. The Spanish Revival-style mansion—resplendent with heavily carved wood doors and ornate wrought-iron windows—the beautifully landscaped grounds, a museum filled with marine specimens collected during Vanderbilt's around-the-world voyages, and an adjoining planetarium are collectively known as **The Vanderbilt Museum.**

From the moment you enter this waterfront estate, through gates flanked with massive black iron eagles rescued from New York's old Grand Central Station, demolished in 1910, you're unquestionably aware that the Vanderbilts knew how to live in high style. In the dining room, 17th-century chairs of carved walnut match a refectory table from the same period. The master bedroom has Napoleonic Empire furniture (including a copy of Napoleon's bed, embossed with his seal) and rare Oriental rugs. Fireplaces are carved of marble and wood; the dining room has a Dutch country fireplace with tiles depicting seasonal labors; a Portuguese mantel dating from 1494 adorns the sitting-room fireplace. Tapestry from the 18th century conceals a 2,000-pipe 1918 Aeolian Duo-Art pipe organ. French windows open onto stone terraces with spectacular views of Long Island Sound and the distant Connecticut shore.

Vanderbilt, who traveled to far-flung corners of the globe in a 265-foot yacht that carried a crew of 36 and its own seaplane, was a passionate collector. On display in the Hall of Fishes are mounted fish and reptiles such as a devil ray and an anaconda, and case-upon-case of colorful tropical fish, shells, and other marine specimens. Other displays include wildlife habitat dioramas with mounted birds and animals, naturalist watercolor paintings, ship models, and yachting memorabilia.

The planetarium, one of the largest and best equipped in the country, was completely renovated in 1987 and is a complete production house—like a mini-movie studio—right down to composing its own music and working with such well-known narrators as Vincent Price and William Shatner. In addition to a calendar of varied shows in the 238-seat Sky Theater, the planetarium has a gallery where visitors can see an astronaut's hammock, touch a meteorite that crashed down in Texas in 1927, operate a touch-screen video that answers such questions as "What is the sun?" and check out what they would weigh on the moon, Mars, Jupiter, and other planets. If you're a boat-owner, you might wish to sign up for a course in celestial navigation taught by the Merchant Marine Academy.

Nearby, at the **Mill Pond Inn,** you can find a table overlooking the water. The menu, however, is largely Italian with good renditions of such standards as fettucini Alfredo, linguine pesto, and a variety of veal dishes, as well as such innovative offerings as *capelli di Angeli* (crabmeat marinara over fine pasta). Popular selections include lobster bisque, crocks of cioppino, and "Francese-style" dishes—veal, chicken, or sole coated with an egg batter and prepared with sherry, lemon, and butter.

DESTINATIONS

The Vanderbilt Museum, 180 Little Neck Rd, Centerport, NY 11721. 516/262-7888. Tue-Sat 10 am-4 pm, Sun & hols. noon-5 pm. Adults $4, students & seniors $3, children $2.

RESTAURANTS

Mill Pond Inn, Main St, Centerport, NY 11721. 516/261-5353. Mon-Thu 4-10 pm, Fri-Sat 4 pm-midnight, Sun 1-10 pm.

66

Whale Of A Time

Cold Spring Harbor, New York

Take a class in scrimshaw, attend a sea-chantey concert, learn how to make a ship-in-a-bottle. Create a very special Valentine in the style of the 19th century sailors who fashioned elaborate mosaics of colorful tropical shells for sweethearts left behind. As a Christmas treat, take a youngster to see *Willy, The Operatic Whale*, the story of a whale with the ambition to sing at the Met. For a family outing, sign up for a walking tour of a historic whaling village. These enticing programs are offered by **The Whaling Museum** at **Cold Spring Harbor,** which houses a fully equipped whaleboat and many whaling implements, marine paintings, scrimshaw, and models of whaling ships. The town was the last port of registered whale ships on Long Island.

In the middle of the last century, the town of Cold Spring Harbor supported a fleet of nine whaling vessels. Their voyages in search of whales lasted between one and five years, sometimes taking them as far as the Pacific Arctic. Their prize was the oil that kept American homes illuminated and her industrial machinery running smoothly. In those days, a colorful mixture of languages was heard around the harbor, since whaling crews included many Portuguese, South Sea islanders, and American ethnic minorities.

The museum's collection includes a fully equipped, 30-foot-long wooden whaleboat, a sturdy open boat that held a crew of six and was last used on a 1912-13 voyage out of New Bedford of the brig *Daisy*. A diorama depicts Cold Spring Harbor as a whaling port in 1850, and a permanent exhibition chronicles Long Island's whaling industry. A standout exhibit is a collection of 700 scrimshaw items produced in the 19th century. Also on display are tools used by whalemen to render this folk art, including samples of wood ash and tobacco used for inking. Youngsters love the ship's wheel that faces a painting of a raging sea where they can imagine themselves on the deck of a whaler riding out a fierce Atlantic storm.

For another piece of local history, visit the **Cold Spring Harbor Fish Hatchery & Aquarium.** On February 12, 1883, the first brown trout imported into the United States arrived at the hatchery. More than 100 years later the landmark facility is still around—as a demonstration hatchery that raises thousands of brook, brown, and rainbow trout to stock private ponds. It also offers tours, fishing festivals, and numerous educational programs.

Pick up a brochure for a self-guided tour and wander around the outdoor rearing ponds, habitat house, main aquarium, and exhibit building. Among nine species of freshwater turtles, you'll easily spot the bright yellow markings of painted turtles sunning themselves on logs; occasionally, you'll see a trout break the surface of a pond as it rises to a fly. The hatchery houses the state's largest collection of native freshwater fish, reptiles, and amphibians, with 20 aquariums housing more than 50 species of fish. The hatchery will sell you fresh trout to take home.

If you'd rather someone else do the cooking, head for the **Whaler's Inn.** Choices include daily fish selections, shrimp stuffed with crab meat, and lobster from a tank. Starters include Manhattan-style clam chowder, lobster bisque, baked clams, and Cajun-style shrimp with linguine. The menu offers a number of beef selections, including steak Diane. Mississippi mud pie is a popular dessert. There's live entertainment on Friday and Saturday evenings.

DESTINATIONS

The Whaling Museum, Main St, Cold Spring Harbor, NY 11724. 516/367-3418. Tue-Sun 11 am-5 pm. Adults $1.50, students $1, seniors 75 cents. **Cold Spring Harbor Fish Hatchery & Aquarium,** PO Box 535, Cold Spring Harbor, NY 11724. 516/692-6768. Daily 10 am-5 pm. Adults $1.50, children 5-12 & seniors 75 cents.

RESTAURANTS

Whaler's Inn, 105 Harbor Rd, Cold Spring Harbor, NY 11724. 516/692-5655. Sun-Thu noon-3:30 pm, 5-10 pm; Fri-Sat noon-3:30 pm, 5-11 pm.

67

Windmill Wonderland

East Hampton, New York

Long Island claims to have more 18th-century windmills standing than any other section of the country. Three of them are in **East Hampton;** one of them, the cedar-shingled Hook Mill, is a landmark on the Montauk Highway on the east edge of this immaculate town. (The working, wind-powered gristmill is open for tours.)

As with neighboring Southampton (see trip #79), East Hampton is full of fine boutiques and restaurants and quality antique shops. Founded in 1648 by English settlers who bought the land from the Shinnecock Indians, it is a textbook of 17th- and 18th-century architecture, full of charming colonial saltbox houses as well as grand mansions. Broad, manicured Main Street, nationally known for its beauty, once was a grazing pasture. Despite its popularity as a quintessential summer place, the town has managed to preserve its provincial quality, with its windmills, stately elms, a pastoral village green, and even the obligatory duck pond.

Across from the village green is the **Home Sweet Home Museum,** the boyhood home of playwright, actor, and poet John Howard Payne (1791-1852). Named for the famous song written by Payne while homesick in Paris, the house has period furniture and an exhibit about Payne. On the grounds are an herb garden and another of East Hampton's operating windmills.

Adjacent to the Payne residence is the **Mulford Farm House,** built in 1680 and filled with early American furnishings dating back to 1770. It is maintained by the East Hampton Historical Society along with two other properties (combined admissions available). The Clinton Academy, built in 1784, is New York's first prep school and now a museum of eastern Long Island; the Osborne-Jackson House dates to 1775, and is an original colonial saltbox modified by a later wing addition, displaying 18th- and 19th-century decorative arts in period rooms.

The cultural center for East Hampton is the **Guild Hall** on Main Street. Head to its art museum to see the work of regional artists, with about 20 changing exhibits during the year. It also has an art library and a museum shop. Adjoining the art galleries is the 400-seat **John Drew Theater,** which offers a year-around schedule of plays, films, concerts, lectures, and special shows for children.

One of the Hamptons' most intimate restaurants is the **1770 House,** with candlelight dining at a dozen tables, antique furnishings that include clocks and stained glass, and an innovative prix-fixe menu. Entrees include roast duck with lingonberry glaze, rack of lamb, swordfish steaks, sweet and sour chicken with walnuts, calves liver Dijonnaise, Cajun veal, and paella. Freshly-made soups such as broccoli with barley draw rave notices.

New Yorkers may feel at home with a visit to the **Huntting Inn** and a local outpost of **The Palm,** albeit with a turn-of-the-century decor. Patrons of Manhattan's upscale steakhouse will find the expected prime cuts of beef along with king-size lobsters and such accompaniments as cottage fries. Also popular with exurbanites is **Sapore di Mare** ("taste of the sea"), an offshoot of Il Cantinori, a highly-regarded Village restaurant that specializes in the food of Tuscany. Located in Wainscott, about halfway between East Hampton and Southampton, it is decorated Italian-country style and produces innovative cuisine, including fresh fish, creative variations of rissoto, and classic pasta dishes.

If you decide to extend your stay in East Hampton, accommodations are available at the Huntting Inn. Another lodging choice is **The Maidstone Arms,** a 19th-century inn located in the village's historic district, across from the village green.

DESTINATIONS

Chamber of Commerce, 4 Main St, East Hampton, NY 11937. 516/324-0362. **Home Sweet Home Museum,** 14 James Ln, East Hampton, NY 11937. 516/3240713. Jul 1-Lab Day Mon-Sat 10 am-4 pm, Sun 2-4 pm; Lab Day-Jul 1 Thu-Mon 10 am-4 pm. Adults $1, children 50 cents. **Guild Hall Museum,** 158 Main St, East Hampton, NY 11937. Tue-Sat 10 am-5 pm, Sun 2-5 pm. **East Hampton Historical Society** properties: Mulford Farm House, James Ln; Clinton Academy, 151 Main St; The Osborne-Jackson House, 101 Main St; Jul 1-Lab Day Wed-Mon 1-5pm, rest yr by apptmt. Combined admission: Adults $2.50, seniors $2, children $1, family rate $5.

RESTAURANTS

1770 House, 143 Main St, East Hampton, NY 11937. 516/324-1770. Jul 1-Lab Day Thu-Sun, rest yr Fri-Sat 2 sittings 6-7 pm & 9:15-9:45 pm. **The Palm,** Huntting Inn, 94 Main St, East Hampton, NY 11937. 516/324-0411. Late-Mar-Lab Day daily, Lab Day-Dec Sat-Sun 5-10:30 pm. **Sapore di Mare,** Montauk Hwy & Wainscott Rd, Wainscott, NY 11975. 516/537-2764. Mon-Thu 6-11 pm; Fri-Sun noon-3 pm, 6 pm-midnight.

ACCOMMODATIONS

Huntting Inn, 94 Main St, East Hampton, NY 11937. 516/324-0411. **The Maidstone Arms,** 207 Main St, East Hampton, NY 11937. 516/324-5006.

68

A Day At The Beach

Fire Island National Seashore
Fire Island, New York

Within sight of Manhattan's skyscapers, booming Atlantic surf assaults the miles of white sandy beach of **Fire Island National Seashore.** Fringing the nation's most densely populated region, this narrow barrier island stretches for 32 miles off Long Island's south shore. It provides a great natural playground where you can swim, sunbathe, play volleyball, or beachcomb for shells and driftwood. Fishermen cast into the surf for striped bass, bluefish, mackerel, and weakfish—and into the sheltered waters of the Great South Bay for bluefish, striped bass, winter flounder, and other species. The island is rich in marine life, waterfowl, and other wildlife. Rafts of migrating waterfowl bob on the bay. There are common terns, sapsuckers, chickadees, peewees, and many varieties of mallard ducks. Wild geese and brant fly over the salt marshes, long-legged herons stalk stiffly through grassy wetlands. The island has a population of about 400 deer, a common sight in the thickets and pine groves. More rare is the wily red fox. Migrating monarch butterflies stop off on their long journey to California, clustering on the fragile vegetation of the dunes that flank the beach.

It is possible to drive across to Fire Island. But once you get there, you won't be able to travel very far by auto. Near its westerly tip, the island is connected with the mainland by the Robert Moses Causeway, which terminates at a state park. To the east, a shorter causeway links the island to Long Island. For the most part, visitors and residents reach the island's beaches and 17 communities by ferry or private boat.

Ferries operate between May and November and leave three mainland terminals to serve eight island docks. One of the more popular ferry routes is between Sayville (see trip #77) and Sailors Haven on the island. This makes a pleasant days' outing where you can enjoy a breezy boat ride, relax on a long, wide expanse of sugar-white beach, and explore an ecological preserve.

The **Sailors Haven Visitor Center** has showers, a bathhouse, restrooms, a snack bar, groceries, ice, and umbrella rentals. A small museum has a whaling exhibit, photographs of early life-saving drills, and a well-stocked "touch table" where you'll find such items as clam shells and the shell of a horseshoe crab. Explore a 1.5-mile trail through the Sunken Forest, where gnarled holly, sassafras, tupelo, and shadblow form a canopy and vines of catbrier and wild grape climb from the forest floor. Follow

the wooden boardwalk behind the dunes past cattails and reeds that grow up to 15 feet tall, and
through a freshwater bog with ferns and cranberries.
At a scenic overlook you can stand on a bench and
see most of the island, the ocean, the bay, the causeway, and the landmark Robert Moses lighthouse.

There are two blemishes on this idyllic scene.
Poison ivy grows abundantly and it is prudent to
learn to identify it. Be wary also of deer ticks, which
can transmit Lyme Disease; stay on boardwalks, use
a repellant, and inspect yourself if you walk through
grass or brush.

Near the Sayville ferry dock, the **Land's End** restaurant has well-tended lawns and gardens and a
gazebo. Picture windows offer views of the bay and
boat slips on the river. Appetizers include clams
casino, oysters Rockefeller, and angel hair pasta
with mussels marinara; entrees feature beef, veal,
lamb, and seafood, including broiled filet of salmon
with herbed lime butter. Baked French onion soup
and seafood bisque, a creamy, cognac-accented
blend of shrimp, scallops, and crabmeat, are offered
at lunch and dinner.

DESTINATIONS

Fire Island National Seashore, 120 Laurel St, Patchogue, NY
11772. 516/289-4810. **Sunken Forest Ferry Co.** River Rd, PO
Box 626, Sayville, NY 11782. 516/589-8980. Adults $3.75 one-
way, children $2.

RESTAURANTS

Land's End, 80 Brown's River Rd, Sayville, NY 11782. 516/589-
1888. Wed-Sat noon-9 pm; Sun 11:30 am-3, 3:30-9 pm.

69

Gatsby's Golden Glories

The Gold Coast of Long Island
Nassau County, New York

Against the backdrop of a Jazz Age summer on Long
Island's **Gold Coast,** author F. Scott Fitzgerald set

his masterpiece novel, *The Great Gatsby*. The book's tale of romantic longing and looming tragedy is counterpointed by the giddy affluence of its protagonists and their mansions, parties, and generally reckless spirits.

Times have changed dramatically since the "Roaring Twenties" of Fitzgerald's heyday, and the Gold Coast has lost some of its 14-carat luster. During the Depression, many of the ornate castles and manor houses constructed during more prosperous times were torn down, converted to industrial use, or allowed to fall into decay. But several typical Gold Coast estates have passed into the public hands of preservation societies or local governments, allowing visitors to experience the glamor and grandeur of this now-distant period of American aristocracy.

The town of Westbury is a good place to start absorbing the flavor of the Gold Coast. **Old Westbury Gardens,** once the stately home of Mr. and Mrs. John S. Phipps, was built in the early part of the 20th century. Since 1959, its 100 acres of formal gardens and the lavish, antique- and art-filled house have been open to the public. Both the house and gardens were designed by noted London architect George A. Crawley to resemble the house and grounds of an English country estate. The Charles II-style mansion contains mainly 18th-century English furnishings and decorations, as well as paintings by noted artists Joshua Reynolds, Thomas Gainsborough, and John Singer Sargent. Surrounding the house are eight formal gardens, including the Boxwood Gardens, with giant boxwoods that are nearly 200 years old; the Cottage Garden, where colorful flowering shrubs surround a thatched-roof cottage; and an official All American Rose test garden. Just west of Westbury is **Clark Garden,** 12 acres of flowers, bushes, and trees on the grounds of another former residential estate.

Perhaps the grandest vision of Gold Coast opulence and style belonged to railroad heir Howard Gould, original master of **Sands Point Preserve.** Visitors approaching this turn-of-the-century estate first encounter Castlegould, a massive, turreted building

modeled after Ireland's Kilkenny Castle. Its grandeur seems even more awesome when you realize
that this castle served only as the stables! Today,
Castlegould is a visitor center and art gallery, which
displays works from the collection of the Nassau
County Museum. The estate's main house,
Hempstead House, incorporates elements of a
Tudor-period castle, and is also open for tours. Also
on the grounds of the preserve is **Falaise,** a Nor-
mandy-style manor house built in 1923 by Harry F.
Guggenheim. Falaise is furnished lavishly with antique pieces, and also includes artifacts relating to
various stages of Guggenheim's career—military, aviation, political, and publishing—and to his philan-
thropic interests.

In nearby Centerport is the **Vanderbilt Museum**
(see trip #65). Known as "Eagle's Nest," the former
home of William Vanderbilt II is an elegant 24-room
mansion on 43 acres of woods and gardens. The site
includes a museum filled with marine specimens
collected during Vanderbilt's around-the-world voyages, and an adjoining planetarium.

To continue in the lavish style of the Gold Coast,
dine at **Westbury Manor,** an elegant restaurant located in an 1880s mansion. Its continental specialties include Dover sole, veal Francese, chateaubriand, and roast duckling.

DESTINATIONS

Old Westbury Gardens, Old Westbury Rd, PO Box 430, Old
Westbury, NY 11568. 516/333-0048. Apr-Oct Wed-Sun 10 am-5
pm; also open various other times, depending on season and
weather. Gardens: adults $4.50, children 6-12 $1. House: adults
$3, children 6-12 $1.50. **Sands Point Preserve,** Middleneck Rd,
Port Washington, NY 11050. 516/883-1612. May-Nov Sat-Wed 10
am-5 pm. Vehicle admission: $1, Jul 4-Lab Day $2; Falaise tour
$2.

RESTAURANTS

Westbury Manor, Jericho Turnpike, Westbury, NY 11590. 516/
333-7117. Mon-Thu noon-3 pm, 5-10:30 pm; Fri & Sat noon-3 pm, 5
pm-midnight; Sun 2:30-10:30 pm.

70

New York's Backyard Pool

Jones Beach State Park, New York

Miles of deserted sandy beaches, towering sand dunes swept by the wind, a bay littered with a maze of shoals and sandbars, and worlds-apart silence broken only by the sound of waves rolling in...

Such was the scene a little more than 60 years ago on the southwestern shore of Long Island, at a secluded area known as the outer beach or, in deference to a 17th-century soldier, privateer, and whaler who settled nearby, **Jones Beach.** Today, those beaches are dotted with the colorful umbrellas, beach towels, and swimsuits of its tens of thousands of daily visitors; those dunes are hiked for the scenic view they afford, and rolled down just for fun; the bay is plied by a variety of pleasure boats; and the sound of the surf is joined by the pleasant cacophony of people at play.

Development of the beach began in the late 1920s, under the auspices of the Long Island State Park Commission and its president, Robert Moses (for whom the state park at the western tip of Fire Island is named—see trip #68). The beach was officially opened on August 4, 1929, but the opening-day festivities were hampered by a howling sandstorm, giving more fuel to the project's long-time critics, who objected to development of the beach as a waste of time and money. However, the beach was soon a popular success—in 1930, the first full year of operation, the beach tallied more than 1.5 million visitors.

Today, Jones Beach is a summertime staple of the metropolitan area, offering more than 2,400 acres of recreation, and that yearly attendance figure has soared to approximately *ten million* visitors. They come (and keep coming back) for the eight Atlantic Ocean swimming areas at Jones Beach, another beach at Zach's Bay, and an Olympic-size pool with both diving and wading areas. The state park also offers a 1.5-mile boardwalk with entertainment and games, miniature and pitch-and-putt golf, softball and baseball diamonds, roller skating, and even a surfing area. Another major attraction at the beach is the **Jones Beach Theatre,** a 10,000-seat outdoor stadium where the stands are on the edge of Zach's Bay and the stage is on a manmade island approximately 75 feet into the bay. The summer concert season at the theater features such performers as Elton John, Neil Diamond, and the Beach Boys (no word on whether any of the Boys have tried out the surfing area).

There are refreshment and snack stands located throughout the park. For a more formal meal, journey to Merrick, located back on mainland Long Island, near Meadowbrook State Parkway, for Hunan, Szechuan, and Cantonese dishes at **Hunan Gourmet East.**

DESTINATIONS

Jones Beach State Park, Ocean Dr, Wantagh, NY 11793 516/785-1600. **Jones Beach Theatre,** PO Box 1000, Wantagh, NY 11793. 516/221-1000.

RESTAURANTS

Hunan Gourmet East, 2035 Merrick Rd, Merrick, NY 11566. 516/378-2323. Mon-Thu noon-10 pm, Fri noon-11 pm, Sat 1 pm-midnight, Sun 1-10 pm.

71

Tip Of The Tine

Montauk, New York

Should you feel a strong call to the sea, you might head for **Montauk,** where you'll find yourself practically surrounded by it. This is where Long Island runs out of land, at the most easterly point of the South Fork—the tip of the tine, so to speak.

Montauk also is the spot where you can go out to sea, with a big fleet of ships ready to take you sportfishing, whale watching, or sailing. You also can take a 75-minute ferry ride to New London, Connecticut, and an excursion to Block Island, Rhode Island. And you can *look* far out to sea (bring binoculars!) from the tip of land at Montauk Point in **Montauk Point State Park,** at Long Island's easternmost point. There you can visit the landmark 100-foot-high **Montauk Lighthouse,** commissioned in 1790 by George Washington and built of red Connecticut sandstone. It has a small museum, and offers tours enabling you to climb a spiral staircase to an antechamber below the light.

Montauk is the antithesis of the upscale Hamptons. During the peak season it is a busy fishing port and the kind of resort with wild dunes and boundless beaches where young families settle in efficiency motel units clustered near the beach. In the off-season, when the frenetic summer pace of the Hamptons slows to a mere jog, tourist activity at Montauk slows to barely a crawl. And what better reason could there be for a visit?

There's usually more action around the docks and marinas of Montauk than in town. Rows of gleaming boats stretch seemingly to infinity, ready to transport you to prime fishing waters. More world-class fishing records have been set off Long Island shores than anywhere else in the world, and the waters around Montauk have accounted for more than 30 current world-record fish. If you've an unfulfilled Hemingway fantasy—and some bucks to spend— you can get together a few similarly minded companions, charter a $650-a-day boat, buckle yourself into a fighting chair, and hope that a 200-pound tuna, marlin, or mako shark will start your reel singing and lock you in a battle that will set your muscles aching. Or you can spend $20-$50 and join other hopeful fishermen (and women) at the rails of a party boat on a half- or full-day trip bottom fishing for flounder or out to the famous "cod ledge." Boats such as those of the **Viking Fishing Fleet** have sun and observation decks, full-menu galleys, free instruction, and all of the bait and tackle you'll need. They fill wheelbarrows with porgies hauled aboard by patrons, and will take you night fishing for fighting blues, and help you land tackle-straining blackfish and fluke and halibut so large as to take two fishermen to hold up the prize for the camera. Other inshore species include pollock, striped bass, sea bass, weakfish, green bonito, and mackerel. Among offshore big game are sharks, marlin, swordfish, giant bluefin, albacore, and yellowfin tuna.

Many Montauk visitors are content to get a vicarious thrill from fishing, congregating at the docks when fishing boats unload their catch. No species generates more awe than the shark, particularly since Hollywood began sensationalizing the killer instincts of this sleek predator. A local celebrity is Frank Mundus, a legendary shark hunter who once harpooned a 17-foot great white shark weighing 4,500 pounds. Based upon his exploits is the character Quint, the obsessed bounty-hunter of *Jaws*. Mundus also helped a local fisherman land a 3,450-pound shark, the largest ever caught on rod and reel. Excitement heightens during the annual shark-fishing tournament, held mid-July.

Head for **Gosman's Dock,** usually around 5-6 pm, to witness the bustle and excitement of the day's haul being brought ashore to the accompaniment of much bragging, picture-taking, and the squawking of hungry gulls expecting a free meal. There's special excitement when a trophy-sized mako shark is hauled ashore or when a 300-plus-pound yellowfin tuna attracts Japanese buyers eager to appraise the fish as potential for sushi or sashimi (with a single giant tuna commanding a price of several thousand dollars).

At this busy dock, **Gosman's Restaurant & Bar,** is *the* acknowledged spot for enjoying fresh seafood as you observe the busy harbor traffic and dockside activity. There are open-air covered dining patios, a rooftop deck, a topside clam bar, a fish store, a take-out counter with steamers and lobster rolls, and an assortment of shops. Prime attractions are legendary large lobsters and an array of fresh-from-the-boat fish. You'll also find oysters, scallops, and soft-shelled crabs.

Whale-watching trips are scheduled May through September by the **Okeanos Ocean Research Foundation, Inc.** aboard **Finback II,** a 90-foot vessel specially designed for whale watching and research. It's equipped with an upper observation deck, a heated cabin seating 90, and a full galley/gift shop that provides breakfast, lunch, snacks, souvenirs, and film. Cruises last about 4-1/2 hours, but can vary in length since they are research- and education-oriented. You'll study fin, minke, and humpback whales as they feed in the rich waters off eastern Long Island. Naturalists lecture on these and other marine species such as dolphins, porpoises, and sea turtles, and point out seabirds such as petrels, gannets, and shearwaters.

Not all of Montauk's 300-plus-year history is so strongly tied to the sea. In 1686, America's first cattle ranch was established at Montauk, with 15,000 acres used as summer pasture for horses, cows, and sheep, and spring and fall cattle drives to and from points west. In 1898, Teddy Roosevelt selected Montauk to provide R&R for 30,000 "Rough Riders" returning from the Spanish-American War. During World War I, dirigibles were housed at Montauk, and during Word War II, torpedoes were tested there.

In the tradition of TR, horseback riding is a popular pastime and several stables provide rides along the dunes and along the bridle paths in **Montauk County Park.** West of town, **Hither Hills State Park** is popular with campers—so popular, in fact, that a lottery is held in January to determine which applicants will be allocated campsites during prime times. In fall, however, this oceanside park is uncrowded and beautiful.

Another popular dining spot is **Gurney's Inn,** with dining rooms overlooking the ocean specializing in fresh seafood, pasta, and a sumptuous Sunday brunch. **Gurney's Inn Resort & Spa** also provides top-rated accommodations and a full range of amenities, including a 1,000-foot private beachfront. Also providing deluxe, upscale accommodations is the **Montauk Yacht Club.**

DESTINATIONS

Montauk Chamber of Commerce, Box CC, Montauk, NY 11954. 516/668-2428. **Okeanos Ocean Research Foundation, Inc,** 216 E Montauk Hwy, PO Box 776, Montauk, NY 11954. 516/728-4522. May-Sep. Adults $25, children $15. **Viking Fishing Fleet,** West Lake Dr, PO Box 730, Montauk, NY 11954. 516/668-5700.

RESTAURANTS

Gosman's Restaurant & Bar, Westlake Dr, Montauk, NY 11954. 516/668-5330. Daily noon-10 pm (closed Tue off season). **Gurney's Inn** (see Accommodations). Mon-Sat 7:30-10 am, noon-3 pm, 6-10 pm; Sun 7:30-10 am, 1-10 pm.

ACCOMMODATIONS

Gurney's Inn Resort & Spa, Old Montauk Hwy, Montauk, NY 11954. 516/668-2345. **Montauk Yacht Club & Inn,** Star Island, Montauk, NY 11954. 516/688-3100, 800/832-4200.

72

Pleasant Peninsula

North Fork of Long Island, New York

As Long Island gently tapers eastward, it thrusts two skinny fingers into the Atlantic Ocean. The larger South Fork boasts the chic and popular attractions of Southampton (see trip #79), East Hampton (see trip #67), Montauk (see trip #71), and Sag Harbor (see trip #76), and has long been a favored getaway of New Yorkers. More rural and less "discovered" is Long Island's **North Fork,** with such communities as Mattituck, Cutchogue, and Southold. Some 70 miles (at the fork's base near Riverhead) to 115 miles (at the fork's tip near Orient Point) east of New York City, the North Fork offers an easily accessible getaway to an area of pastoral beauty and historic attractions, and may well be Long Island's best-kept secret. Among its charms are more than two dozen wineries and vineyards and a clutch of charming inns and bed-and-breakfast establishments.

Most of the North Fork is in the curiously named township of Southold, so-called by settlers who crossed the Long Island Sound from Connecticut, and established the colony as the "southernmost holding" of New England. Accordingly, much of the early architecture and culture of the North Fork reflects the influences of New England, rather than New York.

The scenic and historic town of **Riverhead** (see trip #75) is located just west of the terminus of the Long Island Expressway, and is gateway to the North Fork.

Heading east from Riverhead along Route 25 (the North Fork's main east-west artery), the first major town is **Mattituck.** Offering the only Long Island Sound harbor east of Port Jefferson, as well as a beach and port area on Peconic Bay, Mattituck is a popular destination for boaters, fishermen, and swimmers. Historic buildings include the 1715 **Presbyterian Church** on Main Street, the unique eight-sided 1856 **Octagon House** (now home to a general store), and the **North Fork Theater,** located in a former 19th-century church. Mattituck is also in the heart of the North Fork's berry country, and is surrounded by farms where visitors can buy or pick their own strawberries, raspberries, blackberries, and other varieties. Each June, the town holds a Strawberry Festival, offering games, rides, craft exhibits, cooking contests, and the crowning of a local Strawberry Queen.

The next village east is **Cutchogue,** centered around the 17th-century **Village Green** (a National Landmark). On the green, you'll find the **Old House,** a shingled framehouse that dates from 1649; the **Old Schoolhouse,** built in 1847, and now a museum of the town; and the 1740 **Wickham Farm House.** All three are open to the public. Southeast of the Green, forming the eastern barrier of Cutchogue Harbor, is Little Hog Neck peninsula. Now the site of Nassau Point, an upscale waterside residential area, it earned its name as a communal pig pen: In the 18th and 19th centuries, the peninsula was fenced off, and all the town's hogs (after being distinctively earmarked by their owners) were allowed to run wild there.

Southold is where the first settlers of the North Fork landed, reaching shore at Founder's Landing in 1640. Southold is also the location of a number of historic sites, including the 1660 **Lt. John Budd House,** the 1653 Cape Cod-style **Joseph Horton House,** and the 17th-century **Burying Ground** (adjacent to the **Old First Church,** which was founded in 1640; the current church building dates from 1803). The town is also known for its **Archaeological Museum,** which houses one of the most extensive collections of American Indian artifacts on Long Island; and the **Historical Society Museum,** which displays a typical 18th-century house and barn of the area, complete with tools, costumes, furniture, toys, and other day-to-day items.

The North Fork's New England flavor is especially strong in **Greenport,** a fishing village that was once a major rail/boat link between New York and Boston. Wander down the narrow streets of this seaside village, filled with antique shops, art galleries, and historic homes. At the harbor, you'll find ancient wooden fishing schooners next to sleek yachts; there, you'll also find the ferry to unspoiled **Shelter Island** (see trip #78). Other highlights of Greenport include the **Museum of Childhood,** with an extensive collection of antique dolls and an intricately hand-carved Swiss Village; the **Stirling Historical Museum,** focusing on all things nautical; and the tall ships, most notably the **Ebenezer** and the **Rachel,** open to the public (and available for charter) when they are in port.

At the tip of the North Fork are the villages of **Orient** and **Orient Point.** Originally known as Oysterponds, these twin villages boast a number of pre-Revolutionary houses, and were said to be where traitor Benedict Arnold headquartered the British force he commanded against patriots in Connecticut. Orient and Orient Point are surrounded by Long Island Sound and Gardiners Bay, making shoreline activities a major attraction. On the bay side, at **Orient Beach State Park,** visitors can enjoy acres of scenic beachfront for swimming, fishing, picnicking, and birdwatching. Just off Route 25 on the Sound side are the **Indian Memorial Carvings**— more than 20 contemporary rock carvings commemorating the area's Poquatuck Indians. At the Orient-By-the-Sea Marina, at the tip of the North Fork, you can catch the daily ferry between Orient Point and New London, Connecticut (see trip #6).

The North Fork is gaining increasing recognition as a wine producer, and now has more than two dozen wineries and vineyards. These sites are open to the public for tours and tastings, and produce acclaimed Long Island Chardonnays, Rieslings, and Cabernet Sauvignons, among others. Notable among these are **Hargrave Vineyard** and **Bedell Cellars,** in Cutchogue, and **Pindar Vineyards** and **Lenz Winery,** in Peconic, west of Southold.

As you might guess, with water all around it, dining on the North Fork focuses on fish. One of the best restaurants for seafood on all of Long Island is **Armando's Seafood Barge,** in Southold. You may be put off by the kitschy 20-foot-tall picture of a grinning Armando Cappa clutching a giant lobster that adorns the front of the restaurant, but rest assured, all the tackiness went into the decor, not the cuisine. In an atmosphere of nautical memorabilia, Armando's serves up softshell crabs, various grilled fish, broiled eels, and a massive four-pound lobster dinner for two. In Greenport, **Claudio's** has been serving fresh fish and shellfish specialties since 1870. Try the scallops, shrimp, or clam entrees, or perhaps enjoy one of the restaurant's acclaimed steaks.

For bed-and-breakfast accommodations, try the **Goose Creek Guesthouse,** in Southold (located in a Civil War-era home on six acres of forestland), or the **Mattituck Bed & Breakfast,** in Mattituck (in a Victorian manor house and convenient to a number of beach areas). Comfortable conventional accommodations on a private beach are available at **Aliano's Beachcomber** in Cutchogue.

DESTINATIONS

Long Island Tourism and Convention Commission, 213 Carleton Ave, Central Islip, NY 11722. 516/234-4959. **Greenport-Southold Chamber of Commerce,** Southold, NY 11971. 516/477-1383. **Southold Town Promotion Committee,** Box 66, Greenport, NY 11944. **Hargrave Vineyard,** Rte 48, Cutchogue, NY 11935. 516/734-5158. **Bedell Cellars,** Rte 25, Cutchogue, NY 11935. 516/734-7537. **Pindar Vineyards,** Rte 25, Peconic, NY 11958. 516/734-6200. **Lenz Winery,** Rte 25, Peconic, NY 11958. 516/734-6010.

RESTAURANTS

Armando's Seafood Barge, Rte 25, Southold, NY 11971. 516/765-3010. Apr-Oct daily noon-10 pm. **Claudio's,** 111 Main St, Greenport, NY 11944. 516/477-0627. Apr-Nov daily 11:30 am-11 pm.

ACCOMMODATIONS

Goose Creek Guesthouse, 1475 Waterview Dr, Southold, NY 11971. 516/765-3356. **Mattituck Bed & Breakfast,** 795 Pike St, Mattituck, NY 11952. 516/298-8785. **Aliano's Beachcomber,** Depot Ln, Cutchogue, NY 11935. 516/734-6370.

73

A Fair Village

Old Bethpage Village Restoration
Old Bethpage, New York

Like some Ichabod Crane come to life, the stern-faced teacher grabbed the hand of the errant student and raised his cane. The small boy was unafraid, knowing it was make-believe and that the hickory "discipline stick" wouldn't fall. The teacher smiled and went on to describe to visitors jammed into tiny desks in the one-room schoolhouse at **Old Bethpage Village Restoration** conditions during the middle of the 19th century. At that time this building was located at Manhasset, New York, and a teacher who toiled there earned $15 a month—only $7.50 if the teacher was a woman.

Nestled on 200 acres in a hidden valley amid

sprawling suburbia, Old Bethpage Village offers a taste of life in a typical rural Long Island village of the generation before the Civil War. Wandering its quiet lanes, you see villagers performing agricultural and domestic tasks and working at handicrafts. Standing on a hillock you hear the faint ring of the blacksmith's anvil, the tolling of church bells, and the rattle of horsedrawn wagons, the cluck of a chicken, the snort of a pig, and the neigh of a horse. There are more than 45 historic buildings, most of them relocated from elsewhere. Many are open to the public, others still undergoing restoration as the village continues to grow. Restored buildings include a church, farmhouses and barns, various other dwellings, the schoolhouse, a hat shop, tailor's, and several other stores, an inn, and blacksmith and carpenter's shops.

Costumed interpreters breathe life into the village. You'll find farmers tending livestock, the storekeeper reviewing accounts in a thick ledger, and tradesmen fashioning shoes and barrels. Kids love the dusty roads, the farm animals, and the old-time stores where they can buy a penny candy or a mug of ersatz birch beer.

Marking the changing seasons at the village is a full calendar of events. Flickering candles, whale-oil lamps, and magic-lantern shows brighten dark January afternoons, while in February villagers and visitors fashion valentines and celebrate Washington's birthday. In March, you'll find bonneted village ladies at a quilting bee in the ballroom of the Noon Inn or demonstrating rug hooking, embroidery, and other decorative needlework. April brings gardening, house cleaning, town meetings, outdoor games, and an 1860 wedding. Village sheep are sheared during a festive Memorial Day weekend and June brings a Civil War encampment and a horticultural exhibition with flower and vegetable varieties popular more than a century ago.

Summer brings weekend concerts of 19th-century music and such events as a summer social and 1860-rules baseball. Labor Day festivities include traditional food cooked up by the Chowder Society, while October brings the Long Island Fair, perhaps the year's busiest event, when the fairgrounds bustle with exhibitions of livestock, needlework, and crafts, old-fashioned contests, music, and entertainment. Stock up from huge boxes of different varieties of apples, tuck into a slice of pie or carrot cake, or wash down some fresh donuts with cider. Admire prize-winning dahlias of every imaginable hue and shiny purple eggplants, listen to a marching brass band in Union blue, buy a wedge of New York state muenster or a loaf of soda bread to take home.

November brings political campaigning for a 19th-century election, an old-fashioned recipe contest, Thanksgiving feasts, and a target shoot. In December there is seasonal music, decorations, mulled cider, and candlelight evenings.

In nearby Huntington, **The Petite Gourmet** is a take-out shop that also serves lunch, with homemade soups, such as oxtail barley and black bean, Mexican and scallion-and-potato omelettes, and imaginative salads. A dessert favorite is strawberry/rhubarb pie.

DESTINATIONS

Old Bethpage Village Restoration, Round Swamp Rd, Old Bethpage, NY 11804. 516/420-5280. Tue-Sun Mar-Nov 10 am-5 pm, Dec-Feb 10 am-4 pm. Adults $4, children & seniors $2.

RESTAURANTS

The Petite Gourmet, 328 Main St, Huntington, NY 11743. Mon-Sat 9 am-5 pm. 516/271-3311.

74

A Bully Outing

Oyster Bay, New York

Adventurer, soldier, sportsman, conservationist, and state, national, and world leader—Theodore Roosevelt, the 26th president, earned all of these labels. But he also was a devoted family man, father of six. He cherished his home in the hamlet of Oyster Bay, now preserved as the **Sagamore Hill National Historic Site.** "There could be no healthier and pleasanter place in which to bring up children," he said, "than in the nook of old-time America around Sagamore Hill."

Roosevelt built the rambling, 23-room frame-and-brick house in 1885 and it remained his permanent home. During two terms as president it served as the "Summer White House," when famous statesmen and politicians joined him on the spacious piazza overlooking the harbor and Long Island Sound. In 1919, at age 60, he died there, peacefully in his sleep. His widow, Edith, continued to live at Sagamore until her death in 1948 at age 87.

The parlor, where Edith worked at embroidery and received guests, is bright and airy, decorated in soft colors, and displays a silver tea service. In contrast, the library, used by TR as a study, is dark and masculine, with animal sculptures, mounted trophies, and portraits of his heroes, including George Washington and Roosevelt's father, "the best man I ever knew." Upstairs is the gun room with TR's weapon collection, the hideaway where he went to write, clean guns, or entertain friends. The book-lined room has an ancient Remington Standard typewriter, drawings of Indians and western scenes, and a shaggy buffalo head mounted above the fireplace.

The North Room, finished in handsome woods—mahogany, black walnut, swamp cypress, and hazel—is filled with hunting trophies, books, paintings, flags, and furniture. Dominated by huge elephant tusks, it is a room which Theodore Roosevelt, Jr. eloquently recalled: "The North Room, to me, always means evening, a great fire blazing on the hearth, its flickering light dancing on the flags in the gloom of the ceiling, Father, a book under one arm, poking it with a long iron trident, Mother sitting sewing in a corner of the sofa by a lamp." You can almost see them there.

The Georgian house built in 1938 by TR, Jr. on an adjoining apple orchard, now is a museum relating to Theodore Roosevelt's political and family life. Films and videos are shown on a regular schedule all year.

A delightful stop is the adjacent **Theodore Roosevelt Memorial Bird Sanctuary,** the oldest National Audubon songbird sanctuary, founded in 1923. On its 12 wooded, hilly acres, 124 bird species have been seen. There are hiking trails, bird hikes, a small museum with a picture window overlooking a bird-feeding station, and events such as tapping trees for maple syrup.

Also nearby is **Planting Fields Arboretum,** with 409 acres and one of the finest rhododendron and azalea collections in the east. Also notable are a large camellia collection, a wildflower walk, displays of orchids and cacti, and thousands of bulbs. A concert program features chamber and orchestral music, dance, and internationally renowned artists.

Celebrate the town's namesake mollusk at **Canterbury Ales,** a pleasantly pseudo-English pub with bare brick walls, a dartboard, and light streaming in through a stained-glass skylight. Oysters are prepared in more than a dozen different ways, including Cajun-style, alfredo, Portuguese-style (sautéed with fresh vegetables in a tomato cream sauce), and as fritters. You can order Angels on Horseback (oysters wrapped in bacon and baked in garlic butter, white wine, pepper, and pimentos), and baked oysters served over angel-hair pasta. If you prefer clams, steamers are served as they should be—piled high on a platter and accompanied by steaming hot clam broth, melted butter, a wedge of lemon, and garlic bread coated with melted mozzarella.

DESTINATIONS

Sagamore Hill National Historic Site, Cove Neck Rd, Oyster Bay, NY 11771. 516/922-4447. May-Sep daily 9:30 am-5 pm, Oct-Apr Tue-Sun 9:30 am-4:30 pm. Adults $1. **Theodore Roosevelt Memorial Bird Sanctuary,** 134 Cove Rd, Oyster Bay, NY 11771. 516/922-3200. Daily 9 am-5 pm. **Planting Fields Arboretum,** Box 58, Oyster Bay, NY 11771. 516/922-9200. Mid-Apr-Oct 10 am-5 pm, Nov-mid-Apr 10 am-4:30 pm. Adults $1.50.

RESTAURANTS

Canterbury Ales, 46 Audrey Ave, Oyster Bay, NY 11771. 516/
922-3614. Sun-Thu 11:30 am-midnight, Fri-Sat 11:30 am-2 am.

75 🍎

Iowa On The Peconic?

Riverhead, New York

Where can you find cornfields reminiscent of Iowa,
historic pre-Revolutionary sites that wouldn't seem
out of place in Tidewater Virginia, and a waterfront
with a New England flavor? This mystery spot is the
town of **Riverhead, New York,** nestled at the
juncture of the North and South Forks of Long Island, at the head of the Peconic River. Offering an
entertaining mix of rural, historic, and waterside attractions within easy access of New York City and
urban Long Island, Riverhead is just west of the terminus of the Long Island Expressway, and is the
seat of Suffolk County (which encompasses nearly
two-thirds of Long Island).

Settled in 1690, Riverhead, became county seat in
1727. While the town *was* centrally located, it
wasn't exactly booming: Two years later, a courthouse was erected, and for several years was the
only building in the area. The population grew
slowly, with farmers settling on the rich, arable land
that lined the river. More than two centuries later,
Riverhead is still known for its agriculture. Its farms
are among the major producers of cauliflower on the
East Coast, and Long Island ducklings, shipped and
served around the world, are raised in this region.

The **Suffolk County Historical Museum,** traces
the full 300 years of the area's history. Exhibits
focus on three groups that left major marks on the
county and town: the Indians, the colonists, and the
fishermen and whalers. Artifacts, tools, clothing,
photographs, and recreated dioramas are displayed.

The rural background of Riverhead is also explored at the **Hallockville Museum Farm,** a group of

historic buildings on the site of an 18th-century homestead and farm. Costumed interpreters demonstrate farm chores, crafts, cooking, and other day-to-day activities. Children are especially encouraged to join in, helping to bake bread or operate a weaving loom. A popular time to visit the farm is in October, for the Annual Fall Festival. This harvest-time celebration includes games, dramatic presentations, and demonstrations and sales of locally produced goods, such as food, clothing, and decorative items.

Riverhead is also home to a thriving Polish community, situated, appropriately enough, around Pulaski Street, named for the famed Polish general who fought on the patriot side of the American Revolution. **Polish Town** resembles a typical Polish country village, and boasts friendly shops which reflect the residents' heritage. Stop here for some fresh *pirogen* (dumplings filled with meat, cheese, or potato) or spicy Polish sausage. Each August, the neighborhood holds a Polish Town Fair, offering music, games, food, and other diversions from the Old Country.

Nearby Upton is home to **Brookhaven National Laboratory,** the world's first nuclear reactor designed to carry out research on the beneficial aspects of nuclear energy. Tours of public areas of the laboratories are conducted on summer weekends.

For dining in town, try the **Main Street Cafe,** serving steaks, burgers, fried fish, and other American favorites. Just outside of Riverhead, in Aquebogue, is the **Modern Snack Bar** (so proclaimed by its garish, 1950s-style neon sign). This restaurant is more of a find than it appears: the menu offers a fine selection, including fresh seafood, Long Island duckling, primo rib, sauorbraton, and homemade desserts.

DESTINATIONS

Riverhead Chamber of Commerce, 140 Main St, Riverhead, NY 11901. 516/727-7600. **Suffolk County Historical Museum,** 300 W Main St, Riverhead, NY 11901. 516/727-2881. Mon-Sat 9 am-5 pm. **Hallockville Museum Farm,** PO Box 765, Riverhead,

NY 11901. 516/298-5292. Wed-Sun 10 am-4 pm. **Brookhaven National Laboratory,** Upton, NY 11973. 516/282-2345.

RESTAURANTS

Main Street Cafe, 33 E Main St, Riverhead, NY 11901. 516/727-8668. Mon-Thu 7 am-7:30 pm, Fri 7 am-8 pm, Sat 7 am-7 pm.
Modern Snack Bar, Rte 25, Aquebogue, NY 11931. 516/722-3655. Mar-Nov Sun-Thu 11:30 am-8 pm, Fri-Sat 11:30 am-10 pm.

76

Comely Colonial Cove

Sag Harbor, New York

Nestled in a sheltered bay on Long Island's South Fork, **Sag Harbor** is both a comely, stylish village perfect for weekending, and the roll-up-your-sleeves kind of working town that it was before a number of major industries moved away. It's the kind of place where you could spend a fulfilling day, or linger for a full weekend—combined perhaps with a ferry ride to neighboring Shelter Island (see trip #78). A number of writers and artists have settled here, following the literary heritage of James Fenimore Cooper, who lived here between 1819 and 1823, married a local girl, and used a local seafarer as the model for his famous fictional hero, Natty Bumppo. And of Herman Melville, who wrote of Sag Harbor in *Moby Dick,* and of John Steinbeck, who also wrote about the town.

Whaling played an important role in Sag Harbor's history. At one time it was the fourth largest whaling port in the world. During its peak year of 1847, when 32 whaling ships docked here with their cargoes of bone and oil, the industry in Sag Harbor generated $1 million.

At the **Sag Harbor Whaling Museum,** step through the jawbones of a whale into an age when whalers hunted the seas for months, even years, on end in search of riches in whale oil. Exhibits portraying the lore and legend of whaling range from huge try-pots used shipboard to boil down the oil-producing blubber, to delicate examples of scrimshaw in one of the finest collections extant of this ancient seaman's craft. You'll find oars, harpoons, ship models, logs of whaling voyages, paintings, and collections of guns and children's toys—all housed in a fine temple-front Greek Revival mansion built by a ship owner who made a fortune from whaling. Features of the interior include a beautiful oval stairway and a stained glass skylight.

Sag Harbor, which has been called "the most historic village on Long Island," was used as a harbor by settlers as early as the 1640s. In 1789, President George Washington signed an Act of Congress designating Sag Harbor a Port of Entry—making it and New York two major ports serving the young country. Dating back to this period is **The Old Custom House,** which you will find restored to appear as it did when it was occupied by revenue collector Henry Packer Dering, who also was appointed by Benjamin Franklin as the local postmaster—Long Island's first.

Sag Harbor's tree-lined streets, where you'll see bluish-gray curbstones that were ballast on whaling ships, are a textbook of architectural styles. From saltbox cottages to gingerbread gothic mansions of the Victorian era, you'll find fine examples of Colonial, Federal Italianate, and Greek Revival styles. Temple Adas Israel, Long Island's oldest Jewish congregation, dates to 1898 and features Gothic stained glass windows and a locally-carved altar piece with Lions of Judah flanking the Tablets of the Law. The First Presbyterian Church—the "Whaler's Church"—built in 1844 in Egyptian Revival style, features a cornice with a whaling motif of harpoons and blubber spades.

You'll find waterside dining at the **Chart Inn at Barons Cove,** with steaks, chops, chicken, and ribs and a selection of seafood offerings such as shellfish bisque, clam chowder, fish chowder, softshell crabs, and a shellfish platter consisting of steamed lobster, shrimp, clams, and mussels served with broth and drawn butter. Popular desserts include cheese cake and chocolate cake accompanied by berries and fresh whipped cream.

DESTINATIONS

Sag Harbor Chamber of Commerce, The Windmill, PO Box 116, Sag Harbor, NY 11963. 516/725-0011. **Sag Harbor Whaling Museum,** Main St, Sag Harbor, NY 11963. 516/725-0770. May 15-Sep 30 Mon-Sat 10 am-5 pm Sun 1-5 pm. Adults $1, seniors 75 cents, children 50 cents. **Custom House,** Main & Garden Sts, Sag Harbor, NY 11963. 516/941-9444. Jun 1-mid-Oct Tue-Sun 10 am-5 pm. Adults $1 children 25 cents.

RESTAURANTS

Chart Inn at Barons Cove, W Water St, Sag Harbor, NY 11963. 516/725-3332. Daily noon-11 pm.

77

Oysters Rockefeller

Sayville, New York

This once was oyster country! Rich beds of bluepoint oysters flourished in the shallow waters of Great South Bay, which is protected by the 30-mile length of Fire Island (see trip #68). At its peak, at the beginning of the century, oyster production was counted in the millions of bushels, and the famous bluepoints were shipped around the country and to Europe. Now, the oysters are gone, succumbing in the 1950s to pollution and changing water conditions. Today, baymen work these waters operating clam dredgers or using small boats and bull rakes. But it is a minor industry compared with the glory days of the multi-million-dollar oyster harvests.

That era is recalled at **The Suffolk Marine Museum,** which has a restored oyster house, circa 1907, with a comprehensive collection of shellfishing equipment, and a collection of the beautiful wooden boats of oystermen. Pride of the fleet of nearly three dozen historic small craft is the *Pris-*

cilla, a restored, 60-foot schooner that was built in 1888, is now seaworthy again and a frequent participant in regattas. Another survivor from the oystering trade is the sloop *Modesty,* built in 1923. The museum is on the grounds of the pretty Suffolk County Golf Course (open to the public), housed in a white stucco building with a weathered green roof. Exhibits showcase seamen's crafts, shipwreck artifacts, and maritime activities such as yachting, racing, model building, and the life-saving service. A special display chronicles the impact of Dutch immigrants on the region and on the oyster industry, with retirees from the Dutch community acting as interpreters.

Allow at least a couple of hours to enjoy the natural beauty of nearby **Bayard Cutting Arboretum,** a 690-acre estate formerly owned by the New York financier for whom it is named. In May and June extensive plantings of azaleas, rhododendron, and mountain laurel are at their showy best, while mid-May brings out the colorful blossoms of dogwoods and lilacs. December through May are peak birdwatching months. Follow the Bird Watcher's Walk along the Connetquot River to spot migrating shorebirds and resident geese, ducks, and swans. Spring and summer wildflowers abound throughout the arboretum, while daffodils add a bright splash of color to native woodland areas.

The arboretum has a spectacular collection of fir, spruce, pine, cypress, hemlock, yew, and lesser-known conifers. Several trees are the largest of their species found in the region, including a pitch pine with a circumference of almost eight feet. The former Cutting Tudor mansion, built in 1886, features magnificent fireplaces and woodwork, stained glass windows, and a small natural history museum with an extensive collection of mounted birds. Summer concerts, horticultural programs, and classes are held at the arboretum.

Local seafood fanciers may point you to **Stevie Ray's,** a storefront restaurant landlocked in a tiny shopping center off Sunrise Highway. Specialties are shrimp, scallops, and catfish sautéed in a choice of four sauces: pesto, smoked salmon, lemon and dill, and Mediterranean, which combines scallions, peppers, tomatoes, mushrooms, and feta cheese. Blackboard selections include a wide variety of fish such as mako shark, mahi-mahi, grouper, swordfish, and tuna; appetizers include steamed mussels in a garlicky white-wine sauce, steamers, and clams baked with crispy bacon.

DESTINATIONS

Suffolk Marine Museum, Montauk Hwy, W Sayville, NY 11796. 516/567-1733. Mon-Sat 10 am-3 pm, Sun noon-4 pm. **Bayard Cutting Arboretum,** Montauk Hwy, Oakdale, NY 11769. 516/581-1002. Wed-Sun 10 am-5 pm. Adults $1.50, under 12 free.

RESTAURANTS

Stevie Ray's Seafood Restaurant, 299 Raft Ave, Sayville, NY 11782. 516/589-0600. Mon-Thu 11:30 am-3:30 pm, 4-10 pm; Fri 11:30 am-3:30 pm, 4-11 pm; Sat 4-11 pm; Sun 3-10 pm.

78

Easy Island Escape

Shelter Island, New York

Without doubt, **Shelter Island** seems aptly named. Sprawled between Long Island's north and south forks in the sheltered waters of Gardiners Bay, the 12-square-mile island is a tranquil, insular spot, with no bridges or causeways to connect it to the mainland. It has given shelter to Quakers seeking escape from religious persecution by New England Puritans, to an English royalist who sought deliverance from political strife during the reign of Charles I, and, according to popular local legend, to pirate Captain Kidd who is said to have buried treasure at Sachem's Neck, near Sunset Rock in Dering Harbor. During Prohibition the island provided shelter for the bootleggers who supposedly stored their illicit hooch in isolated barns and houses. Wildlife, including the once-endangered osprey, is sheltered in the forests, beaches, and saltwater marshes of its 2,000-acre Mashomack preserve. Today, with a permanent population of less than 2,000, the tiny island provides a serene retreat for weekenders seeking a remote, yet accessible, rural retreat.

Besides the seclusion itself, the appeal of Shelter Island is apparent. There's a delightfully slow-paced New England kind of atmosphere about the hilly, wooded island that you start to feel as soon as you step off the ferry—even though it is no more than a 10-minute boat ride from the mainland. Nightlife is scant—savoring a leisurely meal and watching the sunset and the stars from a chaise longue on a veranda or from the deck of a boat are de rigueur. There are miles of white beaches, and a network of rural backroads that are perfect to explore by bicycle. Pick up a rental bicycle at The Island Boatyard & Marina or at Coecles Harbor Marina & Boatyard. The latter also rents sailboats. With its irregular coastline, Shelter Island is perfect for boating, offering fine harbors, protected moorings, and waters deep enough for seagoing yachts. The local yacht club is located on Dering Harbor and you'll find sailboat racing on its breezy waters.

Hikers and nature lovers head for the Mashomack Nature Preserve, which sprawls over about one-third of the island and has trails and guided walks. Here is where you can spot, perched atop poles, the huge nests of the osprey—or you might see these large, long-winged hawks diving into the bountiful waters around the island to seize fish in their talons. If golf is your game, you'll find both a 9-hole and an 18-hole course on the island.

Fishing is a popular pastime on and around the island. There is no closed season on salt water fish and no license is needed. Flounder fishing starts in early spring; porgies are plentiful on sandy bottoms from June to October, when anglers also hit the bluefish run. Sea bass are caught on rocky bottoms from May through October and, perhaps the most popular of local sportfishing, the weakfish season in Peconic Bay runs from May 15th to October 15th.

The island's major annual event is the chicken

barbecue sponsored in mid-August by the Shelter Island Heights firemen. Toward the end of August is an annual arts and crafts show and an annual country fair.

There is ferry access to Shelter Island from both the north and south forks of Long Island. The former is from Greenport, about a 10-minute crossing. The latter is from the tip of a peninsula north of Sag Harbor (see trip #76), a five-minute ferry ride.

In season, you'll find entertainment and dancing at the **Pridwin,** a 40-room resort hotel, a rambling place with a big porch and white wicker chairs in the lobby. Off-season, when the hotel is closed, you can stay in an efficiency cottage. There are eight cottages, all but one with a view of the water, some with fireplaces. Recreational amenities include 735 feet of crescent beach, water skiing, Sunfish sailing boats, rowboats, and three tennis courts.

The Pridwin dining room, open to non-guests, is the spot to head for fresh fish. Two days a week the hotel sends out its own fishing boat, and you'll find bass, bluefish, and whatever else is in season grilled on an outdoor barbecue. Grilled marinated tuna is a specialty. If you happen to visit midweek, a Wednesday evening barbecue features beef and pork spareribs, clams, mussels, and shrimp.

Another popular dining spot, also open in season, is **Cogan's Country Restaurant,** where chicken cordon bleu and swordfish are popular menu items. Steaks hang off the side of plates and are big enough to be at home on the dining table of an NFL training camp. The restaurant is owned and operated by a graduate of the Culinary Institute of America and its cozy country atmosphere lives up its name. Meals open with complimentary corn fritters accompanied by apple sauce in mason jars.

For a romantic hideaway, the **Ram's Head Inn** is hard to beat. With shingles and green shutters, the 17-room inn is set on a hill overlooking Coecles Harbor on a peninsula that is almost an island-within-an-island. The inn sits on four acres and offers tennis, swimming at a private beach, sailboat rentals, and plenty of hammocks and lounge chairs. You can

take your meals outdoors on a pleasant terrace overlooking a lawn and prettily landscaped gardens
with rose bushes and big shade trees.

DESTINATIONS

Shelter Island Chamber of Commerce, Box 598, Shelter Island, NY 11964. 516/749-0399. **North Ferry Inc,** Greenport, NY
11944. 516/749-0139. **South Ferry Inc,** Sag Harbor, NY 11963.
516/749-1200.

RESTAURANTS

Pridwin Hotel dining room (see Accommodations). Jul 4-Lab
Day daily 8:30-10 am, 12:30-2 pm, 6:30-9:30 pm. **Cogan's Country Restaurant,** Rte 114 & Duvall Rd, Shelter Island, NY 11964.
516/749-2129. Mon-Sat noon-3 pm, 6-10 pm; Sun 9 am-1 pm, 6-10
pm.

ACCOMMODATIONS

Pridwin Hotel, Box J, Shelter Island, NY 11964. 516/749-0476.
Ram's Head Inn, Ram Island, NY 11964. 516/749-0811.

79 🍎

Sophisticated Lady

Southampton, New York

Unquestionably upscale, **Southampton** is the fashionable summer place of socialites and celebrities,
with elegant inns and chic restaurants where advance reservations are essential on summer
weekends. But it also can be a down-to-earth destination with historic sites, three nearby wildlife refuges, long stretches of dune-sheltered beach, the
Shinnecock Indian Reservation with a big annual
Labor Day weekend Pow-wow, and a wide enough
choice of eateries that you can dine well without
busting the budget. And if you go off-season—especially when the town is bathed in the golden light of
fall—you'll not only avoid the crowds and grid-
locked traffic, but you'll have the bonus of stretches
of duneland and rural acres burnished with crimson
and gold.

First settled in 1640 by colonists from Lynn, Massachusetts, Southampton remained a rural farming community for two centuries until its "discovery" as a vacation destination in the mid-1800s. The arrival of the railroad brought a flood of summer visitors who built cottages and huge estates and Southampton was on its way to becoming a prominent resort of the rich and famous.

Evidence of its affluence is seen in the fashionable shops and galleries along Job's Lane. Here you'll also find the **Parrish Art Museum,** known for its collection of 19th- and 20th-century paintings and prints, for a large collection of the work of William Merritt Chase, and for its lovely arboretum and garden concert series. Main Street has more shops including the quaint **Elias Pelletrau Silversmith Shop,** opened about 1750 by the colonial silversmith and Revolutionary War patriot for whom it is named. Now restored, it offers collectors 200-year-old pieces of early American silver.

More history awaits at the **Old Halsey Homestead,** built in 1648 and the oldest English frame house in New York State, featuring 17th- and 18th-century furnishings and a colonial herb garden and border garden. At the **Southampton Historical Museum,** in the 1843 house of a whaling captain, you'll find a sea captain's living room and bedroom, a colonial bedroom, and collections of toys, costumes, china, glass, quilts, and Indian artifacts. On the grounds are a one-room schoolhouse, a pre-Revolutionary barn (where the British stabled their horses during the war) housing a country store and post office, a blacksmith shop, a carpenter's shop, an old-fashioned drugstore, and a village street of 100 years ago.

Stop at the nearby **Water Mill Museum** to admire an operating 1644 gristmill and perhaps to buy a bag of fresh-ground cornmeal, local crafts or paintings, or a chance to win a beautiful quilt. Each year, the ladies auxiliary creates a handsome quilt and raffles it off to raise funds for ongoing restoration. It also sponsors an annual quilt show and craft fair. A special exhibit shows the history of milling, with emphasis on participation—you may use a mortar and pestle, turn wooden gears, and try your hand at dressing a millstone. Also on display are tools of the cooper, carpenter, joiner, weaver, spinner, leather-worker, ice harvester, and blacksmith. Visitors may try out an 1820 loom, a quilting frame, and a shingle-maker. The mill grinds wheat, rye, and corn.

Among the wide range of Southampton eateries, a modest choice is **The Driver's Seat,** where you can dine in the bar, decorated with redwood paneling and horse-racing prints, or in the bright, airy back dining room with light streaming in through French windows that look out onto a patio where geraniums spill from tubs and window boxes. Daily specials include watercress salad, seafood chowder, broccoli-with-cheese soup, flounder amandine, blackened Cajun-style tuna, dilled salmon tortellini with alfredo sauce, and chicken picata with lin-guine. Popular desserts are raspberry pie, pumpkin pie, and carrot cake.

DESTINATIONS

Chamber of Commerce, 76 Main St, Southampton, NY 11968. 516/283-0402. **Old Halsey Homestead,** S Main St, South-ampton, NY 11968. 516/283-0605 or -1612. Jun-Sep Tue-Sun 11 am-4:30 pm. Adults $2, children 50 cents. **Parrish Art Museum,** 25 Job's Lane, Southampton, NY 11968. 516/283-2118. **Southampton Historical Museum,** Meeting House Ln, South-ampton, NY 11968. 516/283-0605 or -1612. Jun-Sep Tue-Sun 11 am-4:30 pm. Adults $2, children 50 cents. **Water Mill Museum,** Old Mill Rd, Water Mill, NY 11976. 516/726-9685. Early-Jun-late-Sep Mon & Thu-Sat 11 am-5 pm, Sun 1-5 pm. Spring & fall weekends by apptmt.

RESTAURANTS

The Driver's Seat, 62 Job's Lane, Southampton, NY 11968. 516/283-6606. Mon-Sat 11:30 am-11 pm, Sun noon 11 pm.

80

Pages Of The Past

The Museums At Stony Brook
Stony Brook, New York

Life along the north shore of Long Island can be exceedingly tranquil, amid historic houses, pictures-que harbors, misty seascapes, and placid mill ponds. In such a setting is a group of museums that portray life as it was, on Long Island and elsewhere in America, 100 years or so ago. **The Museums at Stony Brook** not only are first-rate museums with internationally regarded collections, they also are fun. One look at the rapt expressions of children on field trips will tell you that these museums make learning pleasurable.

There's diversity, too—certainly enough to prompt return visits. There's a museum of costumes and textiles, a stunning collection of 15 exquisitely-furnished miniature rooms, a major exhibit of nearly 300 decoys, a transportation museum with a dozen galleries filled with carriages plain and fancy, and a museum of Long Island art. Also on the museum's nine-acre site is a 19th-century schoolhouse and blacksmith shop, an historic barn and carriage shed, and a combination granite drinking fountain-horse trough that once quenched thirsty New Yorkers and their animals at Madison Avenue and 23rd Street.

So true-to-life are the miniature rooms that in photographs they look real. All 15 of the fully fur-nished rooms are the work of one man—Frederick Hicks, who did the work between 1936 and 1942. They are made on a one-inch-equals-one-foot scale and feature tiny books with printed pages, drawers that open, and even a suit of armor with hinged joints. The authentically decorated rooms vary from an Elizabethan room with tiny needlework "tapes-tries," to rooms in the Colonial, Georgian, and Fed-eral styles. A delightful antique-shop-in-miniature is stocked with 300 tiny collectibles. From mid-November to early-January the miniature rooms are decorated for the holidays, with tiny trees, wreathes, garlands, centerpieces, and gaily wrapped gifts for Christmas or Hanukkah. The nursery is shown on Christmas morning full of toys; another room has overturned glasses and discarded stream-ers as the aftermath of a New Year's party.

With miles of bays and inlets to attract waterfowl, Long Island once was a "gunners' paradise" for hunters in search of sport and market gunners seeking profit. A legacy from that era are the decoys used to lure birds within muzzle range. Decoys have become a popular art form and desirable collectibles and this collection includes historic examples of the work of well-known Eastern carvers. Displays include grainy, historic photographs of early craftsmen, and exhibits such as a push-button x-ray that reveals the hardware inside a decoy. Among works on display are a trio of black-bellied plovers, circa 1870-1890, their heads bent in search of food. The work of Long Island carver, Obediah Verity, they have a primitive, folk-art quality.

Displays of close to 80 vehicles in the Carriage Museum transport you back to the horse-drawn era. Included are farm and delivery wagons, sleighs, firefighting equipment, children's carriages, and elegant coaches. Featured are the ornate *Grace Darling* omnibus, circa 1880, a garishly-painted gypsy wagon of the same period that has etched glass windows, and the sturdy Conestoga covered wagon that helped win the west.

The Art Museum exhibits the paintings and drawings of William Sydney Mounth. The evocative scenes of everyday life brought this 19th-century artist and native of Stony Brook fame is his own lifetime as one of America's first "genre" painters.

The **Country House** is a good nearby dining choice. Selections include lemon sole sautéed with green apples, bay scallops served Portuguese style, and baked stuffed Virginia ham with rum raisin sauce. The eclectic decor includes an antique, handcrafted, hand-painted carousel horse.

DESTINATIONS

The Museums, 1208 Rte 25A, Stony Brook, NY 11790. 516/751-0066. Wed-Sat 10 am-5 pm, Sun noon-5 pm. Adults $4, seniors $3, students $2.75, children $2, families $10.

RESTAURANTS

Country House, Stony Brook, NY 11790. 516/751-3332. Sun-Fri 11:30 am-3 pm, 5-11 pm; Sat 5-11 pm.

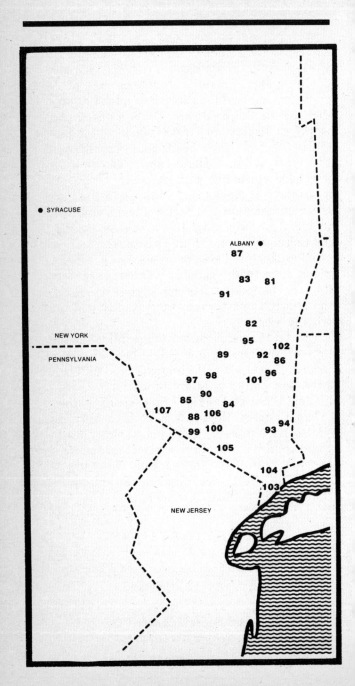

NEW YORK—UPSTATE

81 🍎 🍎

A Little Bit Of Ironweed

Athens, New York

If you saw the movie *Ironweed*, the story of an alcoholic couple set in the early 1900s, you have already seen a little bit of **Athens, New York.** Several scenes from the movie version of Pulitzer-prize winning author William Kennedy's novel were shot here in 1987, as the tiny Hudson River village (along with the town of Hudson, across the river) doubled for turn-of-the-century Albany, the supposed setting of the story. Reminders of stars Meryl Streep and Jack Nicholson linger on. In the **Stewart House** hotel, for example, you'll find props from the movie, although it is a myth that the hotel has a plaque with the inscription, "Meryl Streep died here." Meryl didn't, of course, but her character did, and the hotel *did* use this inscription on commemorative T-shirts (now collectors' items). Keep the Stewart House in mind as you explore the town. It's being restored to its original Victorian splendor, and ranks one of the best places in town to eat and sleep. Another lodging option is **Belnest Bed-and-Breakfast Inn,** also in a handsome Victorian building.

Located on the banks of the Hudson, Athens enjoys a natural setting that has attracted notice dating back to the times when Indians occupied the area. Henry Hudson and his crew were also struck by the beauty of the area, then called Caniskek. So were the first settlers, who purchased the site from the Indians in 1665.

Settled in 1665 and incorporated in 1805, Athens is the third oldest village in the state of New York, and once came close to being chosen as the state capital. It has done a commendable job of preserving its heritage—good enough to receive a citation for architectural integrity from the New York State Division for Historical Preservation.

Among the best-known historic structures in Athens are the three **Van Loan houses,** built in the early 1700s by the first Dutch settlers, and the former **Athens Opera House,** where Teddy Roosevelt once delivered a fiery campaign speech. Another beautiful building you'll want to seek out is the **Hudson-Athens Lighthouse.** The lighthouse was completed in 1874 to help ships negotiate their way around the Middle Ground Flats in the Hudson River, and was attended until the 1950s. The Hudson/Athens Lighthouse Preservation Committee has leased it from the Coast Guard and plans to convert it to a museum depicting the lifestyle of lighthouse keepers—when funding allows.

For a town with a population of less than 2,000, Athens has more than its share of artists and artisans. You can admire their work at several places around town, including the Athens Community Gallery, the Printmakers Workshop, the Arts and Crafts Guild Gallery, the Athens Photographic Workshop, and the Village Craft Center.

Located in the community center, the **Athens Museum** (tours by appointment) recalls the town's early history when it was a center for shipbuilding, brickmaking, pottery, and harvesting ice on the Hudson River. Displays include old postcards, historic photographs of steamboats and paddlewheelers that came off the slips at Athens' shipyards, samples of early bricks, and tools from the ice-harvesting industry.

The Stewart House has a starkly simple wooden facade and an ornate Victorian crown. The elegant downstairs area has been fully restored; completion of the four upstairs guestrooms is a gradual and ongoing project. Meanwhile, each of the rooms (in their unfinished state) is available at the bargain price of $25 a night. This includes No.8, Meryl Streep's room from *Ironweed*, which has been left as it appeared in the movie, with the props still in place, so that it is like sleeping on a movie set. It's a corner room, with a spectacular view of the river and the lighthouse.

Food at the Stewart House is eclectic and features a frequently changing menu with emphasis on grilled dishes. Popular selections are crispy quail, shrimp with peanut sauce, and Lamb Sudan (lamb with yogurt, curry, and mint, served with a hot red-pepper jelly). Made-from-scratch soups include cream of zucchini and lamb with white beans. Dessert favorites are lemon tart, pear tart, and bittersweet mocha torte.

DESTINATIONS

Village of Athens, 2 First St, Athens, NY 12015. 518/945-1551. **Greene County Promotion Dept,** Box 527, Catskill, NY 12414. 518/943-3223. **Athens Museum,** 2 First St, Athens, NY 12015. 518/945-1012. By apptmt.

RESTAURANTS

Stewart House (see Accommodations). Tue-Sat 6-10 pm, Sun 3-10 p.m.

ACCOMMODATIONS

Stewart House, 2 N Water St, Athens, NY 12015. 518/945-9959.
Belnest Bed-and-Breakfast Inn, Rte 385, Athens, NY 12015. 518/731-2519.

82

More Than Borscht

Catskill Forest Preserve
Catskill, New York

Mention the Catskills, and most people think of the famed resorts and Jewish comedians of the so-called "Borscht Belt." But the Catskills are much more than this. While the southern Catskills are home to a number of famous resorts, the northern portion remains an unspoiled region of natural beauty and quiet, quaint towns; this is where you'll find the massive **Catskill Forest Preserve.**

The northern Catskills are first and foremost a lovely range of wooded mountains teeming with wildlife and abounding in recreational opportunities. The forested slopes are especially beautiful in June, when the laurel is in bloom, and again in October, when the leaves of the hardwoods turn glorious shades of red, orange, amber, and gold. **Catskill Park,** with its 688,660 acres, is the largest part of the forest preserve. More than 200 miles of trails wind through its heavily wooded topography, making it a prime destination for hikers and backpackers. Fishermen cast for trout in the Beaverkill, Neverskink, and Willowemoc rivers, three of the best fishing streams in the state of New York. Campers have their pick of eight state-owned campgrounds within Catskill Park, as well as many private ones.

Other activities that draw visitors to the northern

Catskills include golf, tennis, boating, sailing, canoeing, kayaking, rafting, tubing, water skiing, cross country and downhill skiing, soaring, hang gliding, bird watching, antiquing, theater, music, arts, crafts, and, without exaggeration, practically anything else you can do outdoors.

Surrounding the preserve, and, in some cases, within its boundaries, are a number of charming and interesting towns. **Shandaken,** from an Iroquois word meaning "rapid waters," is known for the ski areas of Belleayre Mountain and Highmount. It is also the home of Slide Mountain, the Catskills' highest peak, and Esopus Creek, noted for its trout fishing and tubing. A fine dining choice there is the **Auberge des 4 Saisons,** specializing in fine French cuisine. Chalet-style accommodations are also available at this establishment.

Nearby is the small town of **Cairo,** known for downhill skiing at Ski Windham and 15 miles of cross-country skiing trails at the White Birches Ski Touring Center. Other attractions in and around Cairo include the Catskill Game Farm (see trip #83), which exhibits such exotic beasts as miniature Przewalski horses, white rhinos, and llamas; Carson City, a re-created wild west town with a saloon, general store, trading post, and daily staged shootouts; the Catskill Reptile Institute, with its fascinating and eerie displays of snakes, lizards, and other cold-blooded creatures; and the Zoom Flume Amusement Park.

The town of **Woodstock** is best known as the scene of the world-famous 1969 "happening" called the Woodstock Music Festival. Today, the town continues to enjoy a reputation as a center for the visual and performing arts. A relaxing stroll of the town's Mill Hill Road and Tinker Street reveals an eclectic and charming collection of craft shops, art galleries, and antique stores. A nice dining spot in Woodstock is **Deanie's Towne Tavern,** which offers prime rib, roast duckling, and fresh seafood specialties in the setting of an historic 1863 tavern.

This part of the Catskills is also famous as Rip Van Winkle territory, who reputedly nodded off for

20 years somewhere near here. Also in the vicinity is **Kingston,** the first capital of New York, containing many beautifully restored old buildings (see trip #95).

DESTINATIONS

Catskill Forest Preserve, Department of Environmental Conservation, 50 Wolf Rd, Albany, NY 12233. 518/457-3521. **Greene County Promotion Department,** Box 467, Catskill, NY 12414. 518/943-3223.

RESTAURANTS

Auberge des 4 Saisons (see Accommodations). 914/688-2223. Fri-Sun 6-10 pm (nightly Dec 24-Jan 2). **Deanie's Town Tavern,** NY 212, Woodstock, NY 12498. 914/679-6508. Wed-Mon 4 pm-2 am.

ACCOMMODATIONS

Augerge des 4 Saisons, Rte 42, Shandaken, NY 12480. 914/688-2223. **Pleasant View Lodge,** Gayhead Road, Freehold, NY 12332. 518/634-2523.

83

Best Game In Town

Catskill Game Farm
Catskill, New York

On a bright autumn Sunday, an energetic, white-haired gentleman trundles about the **Catskill Game Farm** in a motorized cart. He is watching the animals and watching the people, and smiling. Roland Lindemann is in his eighties. He came to America from Germany and became a successful banker, but his father was a zoologist and he always loved animals. So he founded the Catskill Game Farm in **Catskill, New York,** more than half a century ago. His first residents were some native deer and a couple of squirrels. Now he is host to such exotic species as Vietnamese potbellied pigs, Przewalski miniature horses, white rhinos, and Java banteng antelopes, among others.

"I love it just as much now as I did then," he says, and the little kid who always loved animals comes out in his smile.

Perhaps it was the little kid in him that caused Lindemann to arrange his game farm—as opposed to zoo—in a very child-friendly way. You can buy snacks for the animals when you purchase your ticket, and all the feeding by visitors has conditioned the animals to be so friendly as to trot, waddle, flap, or hop right to the front of their enclosures for a scratch and a snack. Even the shy Grevy zebra will come by if you've got something good for him to eat. The Catskill Game Farm offers an extensive petting zoo, with fairly patient sheep, goats, llamas, deer, even that potbellied pig, which looks a lot like a cross between a regular pig and an overfed Shar-pei puppy.

More than 2,000 animals make their home in the park, which is organized into several sections: the equine section with zebras, burros, horses, ponies, and other four-hoofed creatures; the African section, with cheetahs, antelopes, and rhino; and a bird area that also features a train ride. There are bears, baboons, kangaroos, and fat little prairie dogs just a little too timid to be touched (but be sure to bring your camera for some great shots). There's also a large playground with rides, a sandbox, swings, and other good kid stuff.

There is so much to see at the Catskill Game Farm that if you perform an assiduous exploration of the entire grounds, especially in hot weather, chances are that your family may find it tiring. Take it slowly, and bring snacks, or plan to stop at the cafeteria on the premises. And if you happen to see an elderly gentleman looking very proud, you may just want to pause and say "thank you" to Mr. Lindemann.

This area of the Catskills is kid heaven. Two miles farther north on Route 32 is **Carson City,** a re-created wild west town with, of course, a Last Chance Saloon, General Store, Gun Shop, and Trading Post where you can buy genuine Indian merchandise. Into this dusty ambiance swagger cowpokes, outlaws, and sheriffs who stage shootouts every day. Also in the area is the **Catskill Reptile Institute,** which displays a variety of snakes, lizards and other cold-blooded species.

Rip Van Winkle lore abounds in this part of New York; many folks claim this is where Rip fell asleep! The countryside is certainly peaceful. Follow any of a number of winding roads and it'll take you into areas of pastoral beauty. One recommended drive is along Route 23A, the road to Hunter Mountain (see trip #91), with cliffs and waterfalls along the way. It's especially beautiful in the fall when the leaves are brilliantly colored. Off this road is Elka Park and the **Redcoat's Return** restaurant, a rustic farmhouse-turned-inn. As the name implies, the fare is British—steak and kidney pie, fish and chips, and such—and the atmosphere is that of a cozy and antique-filled country inn. A little Victorian inn, the **Greenville Arms** in Greenville is also recommended for accommodations.

Another fine restaurant is **Rudy's Harbor Lights,** in the quaint, verging-on-ramshackle town of Catskill, about nine miles from the Game Farm, along Route 32 North and Route 23 East. The restaurant sits on a pretty marina, but the food upstages the view. It is absolutely delicious: fresh seafood, prepared with care. The memorable seafood chowder is thick, creamy, and loaded with fish. Dinners run about $20; lunches are less. Rudy's serves salads, soups, appetizers, and sandwiches for lunch. From Rudy's, head across the Rip Van Winkle Bridge up to **Olana,** the gorgeous, Persian-style villa that was the home of Hudson River artist Frederic Church. The mansion is beautiful and fanciful—a tribute to the artist who helped design it in the 1870s. The house is only part of the story: Church, who appreciated the beauty of the area, contrived the grounds to emphasize the valley's natural charms. He composed numerous scenes: sweeping pastoral views, dark forests, and tranquil waters. Some of the grass remains cut long, as Church planned, creating a windswept and wild effect. But best of all, Olana sits on a hilltop that commands a view of the valley, the encircling hills, and the glorious, wide-open sky, sometimes bright blue, sometimes peppered with clouds, and at night sprinkled with starlight.

DESTINATIONS

Catskill Game Farm, Catskill, NY 12414. 518/678-9595. Apr 15-Oct daily 9 am-6 pm. Adults $8.75, children 4-11 $5, children under 4 free. **Carson City,** Box 109, Route 32, Catskill, NY 12414. 518/678-5518. Mid-May-mid-Jun, Sep & Oct weekends only, hours vary. Mid-Jun-Lab Day daily, hours vary. Adults $7.99, children $4.49. **Catskill Reptile Institute,** Route 32, PO Box 684, Catskill, NY 12414. 518/678-5590. May 15-Sep 15 daily 10 am-6 pm. Other times weekends only, noon-5 pm; weekdays by appointment. Adults $3, children under 12 $2.50. **Olana State Historic Site,** RD 2, Hudson, NY 12534. 518/828-0135. May-Lab Day Wed-Sat 10 am-5 pm, Sun 1-5 pm. Lab Day-last Sun in Oct Wed-Sat noon-4 pm, Sun 1-4 pm. Admission charged for tour of house; grounds open daily 8 am-sunset year-around.

RESTAURANTS

Redcoat's Return (see Accommodations). 518/589-6379. Thanksgiving-Apr 1 & Mem Day-Oct 31 Thu-Mon 6-10:30 pm. **Rudy's Harbor Lights,** Greene St, Catskill, NY 12414. 518/943-5500. Tue-Fri 11:30 am-2:30 pm, 5 pm-closing; Sat 5 pm-closing; Sun noon-closing.

ACCOMMODATIONS

Redcoat's Return, Dale Ln, Elka Park, NY 12427. 518/589-6379. **Greenville Arms,** South St, Greenville, NY 12083. 518/966-5219. Closed Nov 1-May 1.

84

Hello, Hudson

Cold Spring/Garrison, New York

Visitors to the old-fashioned Hudson River hamlets of **Cold Spring** and **Garrison** may find bits and pieces of the scenery familiar. That's because it was this area—most notably the town of Garrison—that stood in for turn-of-the-century Yonkers, New York, in the movie version of *Hello, Dolly.* Even if you don't remember the movie, it's easy to see why this area would appeal to Hollywood's sense of scenic nostalgia: streets of neat 19th-century houses, entire blocks of *real* antique shops (rather than the touristy ones often found in "historic" towns), charming anachronisms such as the weathered bandstand that offers striking vistas of the river and the highlands above, as well as a general feeling of being hundreds of miles from the hustle and bustle of Manhattan, rather than the convenient 50 miles that is the actual distance. Today, these neighboring towns, located across the Hudson from the U.S. Military Academy at West Point (see trip #106), offer a delightful mix of historic sites, natural beauty, and fine dining, and are fast becoming a very popular weekend getaway spot for weary urbanites.

Cold Spring got its name (legend has it) from George Washington himself, who is said to have remarked about the pleasantness of the spring water he found here while traveling during the Revolution. The town's heyday came when President James Madison chose the village as the site of one of the country's primary weapons and ammunition foundries. For nearly a century, the foundry prospered, producing items as disparate as delicately wrought iron furniture and massive railroad locomotives.

After the foundry became obsolete in the early 20th century, the area slipped into a state of repose—not actually decline—just enough to preserve its charms. Chief among these are two exquisite restorations, **Boscobel** and the **Chapel of Our Lady.** Garrison's Boscobel (from *bosco bello*—"beautiful woods" in Italian) dates from 1804. In 1955 it was saved from demolition, and was moved 15 miles north to its present site. Painstaking research and acquisition resulted in the house being restored and furnished to a style believed to be very close to its original state. Currently, it is regarded as *the* outstanding example of New York Federal architecture and decoration. The Greek Revival-style Chapel of Our Lady was built in Cold Spring in 1834 as the first Catholic church in the valley. The one-room chapel has been restored to its dignified 19th century simplicity, and affords a panoramic view of the river. This Doric-columned church (now ecumenical, and still serving the area population) is very popular for weddings.

Cold Spring's Main Street is known for its antique stores. Try **The Sampler** for Hudson Valley handicrafts or **Mycroft Holmes Antiques** for a special collection of Sherlock Holmes memorabilia (in Conan Doyle's books, Mycroft was Sherlock's brother).

Cold Spring is becoming known for its well-regarded restaurants. The fine dining favorite in town is **Plumbush,** the owners of which trained under the original chef at New York's renowned Four Seasons restaurant. Specialties include duck with plum sauce, medallions of pork with chestnuts and apples, and trout fresh from the restaurant's tank. Plumbush also offers a fine dessert menu, highlighted by the excellent Swiss-style apple fritters. A moderately-priced alternative is the **Hudson House Restaurant,** located in an 1832 building on the river, and serving such specialties as rack of lamb, country-style pork chops, and Yankee pot roast.

Should you decide to extend your trip to this area, the **Olde Post Inn** is a fine choice for lodgings. This stone, brick, and wood-beamed structure was built in 1820 and is listed on the National Register of Historic Houses.

DESTINATIONS

Cold Spring Area Chamber of Commerce, PO Box 71, Cold Spring, NY 10516. 914/265-9060. **Boscobel,** Rte 9-D, Garrison, NY 10524. 914/265-3638. Apr-Oct daily 9:30 am-5 pm; Nov, Dec, Mar daily 9:30 am-4 pm. **Chapel of Our Lady,** Market St, Cold Spring, NY 10516. 914/265-2781. Daily 9 am-5 pm.

RESTAURANTS

Plumbush, Rte 9-D, Cold Spring, NY 10516. 914/265-3904. Mon, Wed-Fri noon-2:30 pm, 5:30-9:30 pm; Sat noon-2:30 pm, 5:30-10:30 pm; Sun noon-8 pm. **Hudson House Restaurant,** 2 Main St, Cold Spring, NY 10516. 914/265-9355. Mon-Thu noon-2:30 pm, 6-9 pm; Fri & Sat noon-2:30 pm, 6-10 pm; Sun 5-9 pm.

ACCOMMODATIONS

Olde Post Inn, 43 Main St, Cold Spring, NY 10516. 914/265-2510.

85

An Icy Aerie

Ice Caves Mountain
Cragsmoor, New York

At the top of **Ice Caves Mountain,** near Cragsmoor, New York, south of Ellenville, all is peace. Early on a weekend morning, you can find yourself on what seems like the top of the world, sharing the whistling wind with hawks and eagles, watching hang gliders silently soaring on the upward-spiralling thermals.

The view from the top of the mountain is glorious—from Sam's Point, 2,255 feet above sea level, you can see five states on a good day. And there is considerably more to this special little mountain in the heart of the Catskills, which has been designated a registered national landmark.

To get a full view of what the mountain has to offer, take the tape-recorded guided tour, which includes a three-mile drive and a half-mile walking tour of the cave. The tape and player are free; leave your driver's license as security. Along the way, educational signs explain a little about the geology of the land, noting some of the towering rock formations and illustrating how they came to be. You'll also notice a colony of falling-down shacks, once used by transients, who came up in the summer to pick blueberries.

Near midpoint in the tour is peaceful **Lake Maratanza,** Ellenville's reservoir. Visitors can stop and look, but swimming and picnicking aren't allowed. It's a beautiful little spot, however, for reflecting and enjoying the view.

The primary attraction is the ice cave, carved and colored by water and ice, and, in some places, frozen even in summer. The path through the cave is sometimes steep and icy, and is wet and treacherous in places. Comfortable walking shoes with good treads are imperative, and you should be in fairly good shape if you're going to commit yourself to this part of the tour. The trek is worth its rigors, however. You'll see wild-looking rock formations, odd mineral deposits, towering rock walls, and, as you finish, a spectacular vista of the countryside—as well as a bench to rest on.

Route 52, the road up to Ice Caves Mountain, affords additional sweeping scenic views. The hang gliders that frequent the mountain are usually visible from this road; sometimes they start their flights right from it. Also visible are the **Nevele** and **Fallsview** resorts, two of the Catskills' venerable hotels. Other grand old resorts include Granite Hotel and Country Club, Brown's Resort Hotel, Kutscher's Country Club, Villa Roma Country Club, and the large and elegant Concord Resort Hotel. This is the legendary area that was once widely known as the "Borscht Belt" because of its popularity with mainly Jewish clientele from New York. These large hotels have long histories as family vacation centers. During their heyday, from the early 1930s through the early 1960s, city dwellers came to "the mountains" for a whole summer of rest and rejuvenation. But with the advent of air conditioning, airplanes, and accessibility, as well as the trend toward shorter vacations, the resorts are currently primarily catering to weekenders. Among the facilities at the resorts are tennis courts, golf courses, swimming pools, and spas. Many offer special weekend packages, which include large rooms, all meals, and entertainment.

For dining on a smaller, cozier scale, there are two pleasant little restaurants near Ice Caves Mountain. **Mont Cassino** is a warm northern Italian restaurant in Kerhonkson. The decor is plain—paneled walls reminiscent of a basement den—but most of the employees speak Italian, the menu is written in Italian with sparse English translations, and the food is, predictably, genuine Italian, too, leaning heavily toward country-style food. Among the offerings is *risotto*, a northern Italian rice dish; *spinaci agnolotti* with cream sauce; *linguini caprese*; and a variety of delicious dessert offerings. All the pasta is homemade; prices are reasonable.

The **County Line,** in Spring Glen, is a warm place with imaginative dishes and friendly serving staff. The menu runs the gamut from sautéed kosher calves liver and duckling Montmorency to fried coconut shrimp tempura. On Sundays the County Line offers an extensive smorgasbord, with boiled shrimp, crab legs, clams, fresh salad fixings, and a variety of hot dishes, plus a selection of desserts.

Ice Caves Mountain, in the center of the Catskill resort region, is also strategically located for picturesque drives. Taking Route 42 north, you can visit the charming, rural town of **Grahamsville.** You can continue further north to **Mount Tremper** and the charming little **La Duchesse Anne,** a small, rustic inn serving delicious French food. La Duchesse is one of the coziest bed-and-breakfast inns in the area, not to mention one of the best bargains, and the surrounding countryside is gorgeous. Here you can go fishing, bicycling, hiking, or you can simply lounge around on the inn's lovely porch and chat with the colorful family that runs the establishment. The friendly dogs and stand-offish geese who roam the inn's lawn round out the crew.

To the east of Ice Caves Mountain is Kerhonkson, site of the impressive **Merriman Dam** and **Rondout Reservoir,** an important part of the New York City reservoir system. A little farther east and you're within a shout of the beautiful, Victorian **Mohonk Mountain House,** recommended for a hike, a meal, or a weekend stay (see trip #97). Perched atop the Shawangunk Mountains, it affords breathtaking views of the surrounding valleys, and is widely recognized as one of the most atmospheric hotels in the region.

DESTINATIONS

Ice Caves Mountain, Sam's Point Rd, Cragsmoor, NY 12420. 914/647-7989. Jul-Aug 8:30 am-8 pm; last tickets sold at 6:30 pm. Mid-Apr-Nov hours vary. Adults $6, children 6-12 $4.

RESTAURANTS

Mont Cassino, Rte 209, RR 1, Box 172A, Kerhonkson, NY 12446. 914/626-7375 or -9879. Mon-Fri 4-10 pm, Sat 2-10 pm, Sun 2-9 pm. **County Line,** Rte 209, Spring Glen, NY 12483. 914/647-3310. Mon-Sat 4:30 pm-closing. Sun 1-8 pm.

ACCOMMODATIONS

Nevele Hotel, Ellenville NY 12428. 914/647-6000. **Fallsview Hotel,** Ellenville, NY 12428. 914/647-5100. **La Duchesse Anne,** 4 Miller Rd, Mount Tremper, NY 12457. 914/688-5260. **Mohonk Mountain House,** Lake Mohonk, New Paltz, NY 12561. 914/255-1000 or 212/233-2244.

86

A Day In The Country

Dutchess County, New York

The "simple pleasures" of the country are within easy reach in the southern portion of **Dutchess County,** approximately an hour-and-a-half's drive north of New York City. There you can visit scenic country farms and pick your own fruit and vegetables or purchase a jar of tasty homemade preserves; browse the cluttered aisles of unpretentious rural antique stores, perhaps finding a delicately carved wooden table or a set of 18th-century china; or simply wander the bucolic splendor of the countryside, stopping to sample a chardonnay or cabernet at a family-run winery. Stretching east from the Hudson River to the Connecticut border, Dutchess County is a perfect spot for a leisurely and revitalizing weekend getaway.

The rolling landscape of the county is dotted with farms and orchards. Many of these offer a wide variety of fruits and vegetables for sale, often allowing you to pick your own. **Cross Orchards Roadside Market,** in LaGrangeville, is a great spot for apples by the dozen or the bushel. After you've picked your fill, you'll be greeted with a glass of fresh-pressed apple cider and a still-warm homemade donut. **Secor Strawberries,** in Wappingers Falls, offers its namesake fruit and more. Pick their sweet and tart strawberries in the early summer, or visit in autumn for pumpkins and hayrides. Fishkill's **Lawrence Farms** is a full farm market, and offers a greater selection of items than many of the other area farms. There you can buy fresh fruits and vegetables, custom-cut meat, homemade cheeses, plants, and crafts such as hand-dipped candles, woven wall-hangings, and other decorative items.

Dutchess County is also well-known as a mecca for antiquers. The town of **Millbrook** (see trip #96), in the center of the county, has long been heralded for its concentration of antique stores, but the southern half of the county also boasts some worthwhile shopping stops. At **The Country Thistle,** in Pleasant Valley, the accent is on handmade crafts and gifts, such as braided rugs, antique wooden toys and decorative items, country-scene prints and paintings, and kitchen knickknacks. Pawling's **Antique Center,** a central shop serving a number of area dealers, is a good place to find restored 18th- and 19th-century furniture, fine artwork, glassware, and clothing. Also in Pawling is **Hob Nail Antiques,** which specializes in brass beds and accessories. **Wiccopee Antiques** in Hopewell Junction offers furniture (with a specialty in appraising, buying, selling, and repairing wicker furniture), china, glassware, and a variety of collectibles.

After touring local sights, relax with a glass of fine wine at the **Amberleaf Vineyards** in Chelsea, just south of Wappingers Falls. This family-run winery overlooking the Hudson River offers weekend tours of its fields, cellars, and small bottling plant, followed by samples of the wines produced there, including Amberleaf's noted chardonnay and cabernet.

For sumptuous dining in an elegant setting, try Hopewell Junction's **Le Chambord.** This restaurant's fine French nouvelle and classic menu changes three times a year, and is overseen by Henri Benveniste, a renowned French chef. Choices can include medallions of veal in a cherry and wine sauce, chateaubriand, grilled salmon bearnaise, and coquille St. Jacques. If you decide to extend your trip, lodging (in an 1863 Georgian Colonial mansion) is also available at Le Chambord.

DESTINATIONS

Dutchess County Tourism Promotion Agency, PO Box 2025, Rte 9, Hyde Park, NY 12538. 914/229-0033.

RESTAURANTS

Le Chambord (see Accommodations). 914/221-1941. Mon-Fri 11:30 am-2:30 pm, 6-10 pm; Sat 6-11 pm; Sun 11:30 am-2:30 pm, 5-9 pm.

ACCOMMODATIONS

Le Chambord, 2075 Rte 52, Hopewell Junction, NY 12533. 914/221-1941.

87 🍎 🍎

Sharing Of The Greene

East Durham, New York

Most Irish Americans will settle for a look at a St. Patrick's Day parade once every year or so. Not so the Irish of **East Durham, New York.** For them, Irishness is a business—a *serious* business. A majority of the community's 1,000 citizens are of Irish descent, and they may draw 10 times that many to their Catskills' hamlet during special Irish-themed events that they stage each year. Chief of these is the **Catskill Irish Festival,** always held over Memorial Day weekend, rain or shine. Bagpipes blare, step dancers step, and the pubs and dancehalls resound with the sound of music, all provided by people with such names as Frankie Curran, Dermot Henry, Tommy Mulvihill, and Martin Flynn. The Clancy Brothers and Paddy Noonan add a big-name touch to the Celtic sounds. Amateur songsters burst forth with lusty versions of "McNamara's Band," "Danny Boy," and "My Wild Irish Rose," while bartenders and waitresses hustle to keep up with the demand for Guinness Stout and Harp Lager. Little wonder that East Durham is often called the 33rd county of Ireland. (The other 32 are actually in Ireland.)

Music is the mainstay of the Memorial Day gathering, just as it is at other times of the year when the area celebrates its Irishness. On St. Patrick's Day, for example, you might find as many as 300 revelers crowded into a single pub, where the music is likely to be provided by a band with a name that's as Irish as a shamrock, such as Frankie Curran and the Evergreens. On the big day itself, it's over to nearby Greenville for the traditional parade sponsored by the Irish American Club and marched in by the Greene County chapter of the Ancient Order of Hibernians and the East Durham Kings of Columbus. Floats? How about a thatched roof Irish cottage float completely surrounded by children—all dressed in native costume?

In August the town puts on a typical Irish *feis* (pronounce it "fesh;" it means "festival"), with another relentless onslaught of Irish music, dancing, and carrying on.

Requirements for the wearing of the green (and applying that color to just about everything else) are relaxed somewhat at the **International Celtic Festival** on Hunter Mountain where, in addition to Irish music and events, you can also enjoy related cultural doings provided by people of Welsh, Scottish, and Breton ancestry. The Scots, of course, excel at Highland games, which involves various kinds of contests, most of which seem to consist of throwing things that weigh a lot and have strange names. Bretons are known for folk singing; the Welsh, for their lovely harp music.

One of the most impressive events of the festival occurs when all the bands gather high on the side of the mountain, then march down to the front of the Hunter Mountain ski lodge—all the while playing in unison. Food is never a problem here. Irish soda bread and corned beef is always available, along with other Celtic specialties such as Scottish shepherds pie. (Hunter is also the site of the biggest ski mountain south of New England—see trip #91.)

If you can't make it when one of the special events is on, don't worry. The Irish don't go away. They're just quieter at other times of the year. Many of them earn their livelihoods by running comfortable inns and resorts—Gavin's Golden Hill House, Keogh's, McGrath's Edgewood Falls, Mullan's Mount Spring Hotel, O'Dea's Riverside Inn, and Shamrock House. A popular restaurant is **Bernie O's Steak House,** which serves seafood as well as steaks. Other folks make ends meet by selling imported goods from Ireland. These establishments include Mullan's, the Shamrock and Heather Irish Import Gift Shop, and Guaranteed Irish. Items for sale include knits, tweeds, hand-engraved glass, Irish wild flowers, hand-blown glass, early Celtic sculpture in turf and clay, and china.

For some reason, this part of New York state loves ethnic festivals. If you don't fancy the Irish ones, you can take your pick of events with other ethnic themes. The organization that's responsible for most of them is called Exposition Planners (address below).

DESTINATIONS

East Durham Vacationland Association, Box 67, East Durham, NY 12423. 518/634-7100. **Greene County Promotion Department,** Box 467, Catskill, NY 12414. 518/943-3223. **Exposition Planners,** Bridge St, Hunter, NY 12442. 518/263-3800. **East Durham Irish Cultural & Sports Center,** PO Box 320, East Durham, NY 12423. 518/634-7209.

RESTAURANTS

Bernie O's Steak House, Rte 23, Cairo, NY 12413. 518/622-9998. Thu-Tue 11:30 am-9 pm.

ACCOMMODATIONS

Gavin's Golden Hill House, Box 6, East Durham, NY 12423. 518/634-2582.

88

The Sport Of Kings

Goshen, New York

Well-known among horse-racing aficionados is the

historic Saratoga Race Track in upstate New York, where thoroughbreds have been racing since 1863. But few realize that the Hudson Valley is home to a landmark of the sport of kings that stretches back even further and is a full quarter-century older than Saratoga. **Goshen Historic Track,** in **Goshen, New York,** has been playing host to trotters, pacers, and other standardbred horses and their trainers, riders, and fans since 1838, and still offers a slate of high-stakes racing each summer.

Standardbred racing in America dates back to the 1780s, when Messenger, a horse who came to be known as "the Father of Standardbred Racing" was shipped to the United States from England. His virility was legendary, indeed—it is estimated that his progeny included more than 600 foals in 20 years! Trotters (which move their legs in diagonal pairs—front right and rear left, then front left and rear right) and pacers (which move their legs by side—both right, then both left) developed from this line of breeding, and were raced at tracks in New York, New Jersey, and Pennsylvania. Only 50 years after Messenger's historic arrival, the Goshen Track opened. In 1967, it was designated a National Historic Landmark, the first sporting site of any kind in the U.S. to receive such an honor.

Today, the track offers a brief season of stakes racing, but attracts visitors year-around. The old place exudes a sort of country charm—a feeling of lazy days in the sunshine, sitting in the grass with a picnic lunch, as horses dash around the track or slowly tromp their way between the paddock and the racing oval. Most days of decent weather will find horses being worked out on the track, being shoed in the paddock, or being groomed in their stables. Visitors are welcome to wander the grounds of the track; children, especially, enjoy meeting, petting, and learning about the powerful, yet gentle horses.

Adjacent to the track is the **Hall of Fame of the Trotter,** the only trotting-horse museum in the world. Here you'll find displays tracing the history of the sport, a gallery of horse-race-oriented artwork (including an extensive collection of Currier and

Ives lithographs), and a Hall of Fame honoring the famous horses and men who have raced them in the two centuries that the sport has existed in America. A gift shop offers a variety of things equine.

In nearby Washingtonville is the **Brotherhood Winery,** claimed to be the oldest winery in the country. Opened the year after Goshen Track (1839), the winery has been producing fine New York wines ever since. It survived Prohibition, which ruined many historic wineries, by producing sacramental wines from 1920 to 1933. A guided tour takes you through Brotherhood's cave-like cellars, past huge wooden casks as old as the winery itself, and along the semi-modern production line where the bottles are filled and labelled. After the tour comes a chance to sample the varieties of chablis, burgundy, rose, and special seasonal wines that Brotherhood produces. All varieties are also available for purchase.

For lunch or dinner, journey to nearby Central Valley, New York, and **Gasho of Japan,** a hibachi-style steakhouse in a 400-year-old farmhouse imported from Japan. Appetizers of calamari, scallops, and eel, and entrees of steak, chicken, and shrimp are prepared tableside by your chef, with the familiar knife-flashing theatrical flourish of tepanyaki cooking. Round out your meal with a stroll through the restaurant's paper-lantern-lit Japanese garden.

DESTINATIONS

Goshen Historic Track, Box 192, Goshen, NY 10924. 914/294-5333. Racing May-Jul on selected weekends and weekdays. **Hall of Fame of the Trotter,** Goshen, NY 10924. 914/294-6330. Mon-Sat 10 am-5 pm, Sun 1:30-5 pm. **Brotherhood Winery,** 35 North St, Washingtonville, NY 10992. 914/496-9101. Daily Apr-Nov; weekends Dec, Feb, & Mar; as weather permits on Jan weekends; call for specific seasonal hours.

RESTAURANTS

Gasho of Japan, Rte 32, Central Valley, NY 10917. 914/928-2387. Mon-Fri noon-3 pm, 5:30-11 pm; Sat noon-3 pm, 5-11 pm; Sun noon-10 pm.

89

Hard-Working Waterway

Delaware and Hudson Canal Museum
High Falls, New York

Before the railroads criss-crossed America, much of
the commerce of the country was dependent on rivers and canals. If you wanted to go somewhere or
ship something, you often depended on some kind
of waterway to get the job done.

For a good part of the 19th century, one of the
busiest commercial waterways in the United States
was the Delaware and Hudson Canal. Coal from the
mines of Pennsylvania made its way along the canal
to the factories of New York. Cement went south-
ward, transhipped by Hudson barge to New York
City for use in creating bridges and skyscrapers.

The canal ran for 108 miles, moving heavily-laden
boats and barges quietly and efficiently—if somewhat slowly—to their destinations. Although the
locks, basins, and dams along the waterway were
marvels of 19th-century engineering, the trip from
one end of the canal to the other took six days.

It went on like this from 1820 to 1898. But years
before it finally shut down, the canal had outlived
its usefulness, made obsolete, just as the Mississippi
sternwheelers had been, by the faster and more flexible railroads.

Thanks to the **Delaware and Hudson Canal
Museum,** the era has not been lost. With the aid of
exhibits, artifacts, dioramas, and well preserved sections of the canal, you can get a very good idea of
the way it functioned and the important transportation role it played during the 70 years it was in operation. You can even get a good idea what the trip
was like for the men who worked on the boats and
lowered barges heaped with coal through the locks.

A self-guided tour along a system of hiking trails
takes you past a series of locks from lock No.16 to
lock No.20. Ask for a copy of the map and guide at
the museum. During the 45-minute walk you'll get

close-up views of such things as snubbing posts, weirs, loading slips, original stonework, and of the locks themselves.

Another good way to catch the flavor of the era and the area is to have lunch at the **DePuy Canal House.** The comfortable stone inn with its exposed-beam ceilings was built by Simeon DePuy in 1797, a generation before the canal itself got into full swing. Located only a few yards from the waterway, Canal House prospered during the years the canal was in operation, but when the canal fell on hard times, so did Canal House.

The present owner is John Novi, who bought and restored the place and then started operating it as a restaurant again in 1969. In the interim, it has become a favorite not only of casual visitors, but of the hard-bitten and hard-to-please fraternity of big city food critics. *The New York Times* bestowed a Four Star rating on it.

Canal House has five dining rooms, a bar, and numerous fireplaces. The menu changes frequently and includes such imaginatively prepared dishes as bluefish with oyster sauce, poached sole with salmon red pepper mousse, quail with sausage stuffing, Dijon rabbit, lobster bouillabaisse with saffron leek sauce, duck breast schnitzel with orange-tomato curry, and smoked salmon ricotta in pasta with basil cream.

DESTINATIONS

Delaware and Hudson Canal Museum, Mohonk Rd, High Falls, NY 12440. 914/687-9311. May-Oct Wed-Sun.

RESTAURANTS

DePuy Canal House, Rte 213, High Falls, NY 12440. 914/687-7700. Thu-Sat 5:30-9 pm; Sun 11:30 am-2 pm, 4-8:30 pm.

90

Wine Not?

Hudson River Wineries

In New York City, you can sit at a trendy midtown

wine bar, but less than a two-hour drive away, you can visit a clutch of wineries to learn how wines are made, to sample each vintner's output, and to buy rare and unusual wines from the source.

Route 9W, skirting the west bank of the Hudson, is the traditional wine road, but Hudson River wines are now understood to come from wineries a few miles inland as well. "Ulster," after the Catskills' southeasternmost county, has not yet taken on the same regional significance as "Burgundy" or "Bordeaux" in the wine world, but it's coming on strong.

A typical winery tour is free and includes an informative walk-through conducted by a knowledgeable guide who will show you where grapes are pressed, fermented, aged, bottled, and labeled. Your group will most likely consist of tyros taking their first winery tour and card-carrying oenophiles who make it a point to visit every vineyard on the map and cross-examine every wine maker about the intricacies of the art. At the tour's end, you'll be invited to sample the wines—and rare is the visitor who can resist the temptation to buy a few bottles of a favorite. A bottle directly from the winery makes a lovely gift at the next dinner party, or a splendid souvenir to serve with a special dinner of your own.

At many wineries, you may walk through the vineyards and feel that you are transported thousands of miles to the estates of Europe, or you may enjoy lunch at a picnic area with a view of the neat rows of vines. While Hudson River wines have become as American as the apple pie made from the bounty of thousands of acres of surrounding orchards, their roots go deeper. The wineries may be as old as four decades or as young as '80s children, but their practices and ambiance recall the finest traditions from various European wine countries.

The **Royal Kedem Winery** was founded in 1948 by Czech refugees who had been wine makers in pre-war Eastern Europe. It is now the largest of the score of Hudson River Wineries, producing kosher wines, including sophisticated, dry varieties. Royal Kedem wines have won gold medals in Vienna, Budapest, and Paris. The tour includes an entertaining and informative show in the winery's own theater, and children will get a tasty glass of Kedem grape juice while adults are sampling wines in the tasting room, a converted 120-year-old railroad station.

The **Benmarl Vineyards** were founded in 1957 using premium European wine grapes, but wine isn't the only attraction there. Stop at Benmarl's small gallery to see a unique collection of art, including original magazine illustrations from the '50s and '60s, and have a bite at the charming **Bistro,** the perfect spot for a French-accented light lunch. The Bistro will also make up a "Lovers' Picnic Basket" to enjoy on the vineyard's picnic ground.

When the **Brimstone Hill Vineyard** began in 1968, it was one of the first in the mid-Hudson area to plant French hybrid grapes. It specializes in wines that have what the wine maker calls a "French character," including those from Burgundy, the Alsace, and neighboring Switzerland. By contrast, the **El Paso Winery,** begun in 1977 by a Uruguayan vintner whose father ran a winery in South America, brings the Spanish tradition to the Hudson River area.

If you take a winery tour in summer or fall, you'll also reap the benefits of the bountiful harvest of berries, corn, melons, apples, pears, and other seasonal produce from the scores of farm stands which dot the roadsides of the area. Throughout the warm months, special events from strawberry festivals to barbecues are scheduled at most wineries, too.

DESTINATIONS

Hudson River Wineries information from the **Ulster County Public Information Office,** PO Box 1800, Kingston, NY 12301. 800/342-4826, 914/331-9300. **Royal Kedem Winery,** Milton, NY 12547. May 1-Dec 31 Sun-Fri, 10 am-5 pm, Sun only Jan 1-Apr 30; closed Sat and Jewish holidays. **Benmarl Vineyards and Winery,** Highland Ave, Marlboro, NY 12542. 914/236-4265. Daily 1-4 pm (except holidays). $5 per adult incl wine glass. **Brimstone Hill Vineyard,** RD 2, Box 142, Pine Bush, NY 12566. 914/744-2231. June-Aug Thu-Mon, 11 am-6 pm; Sep-May Sat, Sun, 11 am-6 pm. **El Paso Winery,** Rte 9W, Box 170, Ulster Park, NY 12487. 914/ 331-8642. Apr-Dec Mon-Fri, noon-6 pm, Sat, Sun, holidays, 10 am-6 pm (closed holidays).

RESTAURANTS

Bistro, Benmarl Vineyards (see Destination). Fri-Sun, 11 am-5 pm.

91

Hopping Around Hunter

Hunter Mountain, New York

Within easy weekend, even day-trip, distance of New York, you'll find the biggest ski mountain south of New England. It's a true New York ski area—a busy, bustling, crowded place that demands a lot and gives a lot. It demands the patience and challenge of mountain skiing (as opposed to sliding on a hill). You won't find it better, or closer.

Short on resort frills but long on the elements that constitute good skiing, **Hunter Mountain** is a huge, cone-shaped peak in the rugged northern Catskills. Onto its rocky front face and precipitous backside have been carved 46 trails served by 11 chairlifts and six surface lifts with a total uphill capacity of 18,000; the Starlite Express is the only high-speed quad chairlift in New York State.

The 1,600-foot vertical dwarfs all others in the Middle Atlantic States, and the icing on the cake at the self-proclaimed "snowmaking capital of the world" is a system that is a contender for the honors of the biggest around. This first-rate snowmaking gives Hunter a season that lasts from mid-November through early May, second in the East after Killington and one of the longest in the country.

At Hunter, there's not just skiing, there's tough skiing—lots of it. The fall-away precipice known as K27 is one of the steepest runs in the East, and the super-steep Hunter West trails challenge experts run after run. If you are a really good skier, you'll love swinging to Hunter's big beat. If you're a new skier, Hunter is for you, too. The tabletop smooth precincts of Hunter One, out of the way of skier traffic from above, is as tame and sheltered a novice area as you could want. Karl Plattner's 150-instructor army is ready to teach you the rudiments of skiing.

But most of Hunter is for most skiers—ranging from mildly challenging terrain for intermediates to moderately difficult runs for advanced, but not quite expert, skiers. Harking to its Big Apple roots, you'll find many runs sport familiar names. Boston Road, Madison Square, Fordham Road, and Grand Concourse are a few of the tame beginner paths at Hunter One. Park Avenue, Lower Broadway, and Fifth Avenue on the lower part of the main mountain are as heavily trafficked as their New York namesakes, as are Broadway, Seventh Avenue, and 42nd Street, which serve as the main routes up high. And Belt Parkway, fittingly, is the name for the easy two-mile boulevard along the rim of the peak, enabling even novices to ski from the top.

For three decades, Hunter has refined the art of handling hordes of skiers. Its constantly expanding base lodge now has a walk-through ticketing and rental area at ground level, so that you can buy your lift ticket, book your ski lesson, and get information in a straight shot between the parking lot and the lifts. After all, New Yorkers are an impatient lot, and when they want to ski, they want to ski.

Also at the lodge is a 300-seat full-service restaurant called, simply, **The Restaurant.** Hunter can feed the masses in a vast two-level cafeteria and has such specialty eateries as a pizzeria, deli, soup kitchen, and sushi bar.

In addition to recreational skiing for the multitudes, there always seems to be a special racing event going on. Nastar and Silver Series races, which anyone can enter, are scheduled throughout the season. Meets for serious amateur competitors and professional ski racers have long been a staple at Hunter, but there are lighthearted events, too: races for chefs in their *toques*, firefighters in their coats and helmets, police officers, nurses, and such.

Hunter attracts all ages, from families with preschoolers to members of the 70-Plus Ski Club, which started at Hunter and now has garnered free skiing privileges for septuagenarians and their elders at mountains all over the country. But most in evidence are the young adults from New York—gregarious socializers—for whom Hunter's great skiing is just part of the appeal. The ski area isn't just the "snowmaking capital of the world" and skiing capital of the Catskills—it's one of the apres-ski capitals of the East, too. The action starts fast and furious at the base-lodge bar (also a behemoth, of course), and when things wind down at the mountain, they move into the town of Hunter and on to Tannersville and Haines Falls.

To enjoy the mountain with fewer crowds and less furious nightlife, sneak up during non-holiday midweeks, when Hunter, like all Eastern mountains, is virtually empty. One-day bus trips by Scandinavian Ski Shop leave midtown Manhattan for day escapes. They are popular with doctors, lawyers, and hooky-playing executives. Try stretching a normal weekend into a three day version, or better yet, see if you can finagle a two or three day midweek getaway.

Another trick for relaxing in spite of Hunter's hopping scene is to ski on weekends but to live and dine well, mellowing out what can otherwise be a frantic ski experience. Most Hunter weekenders wedge into shared houses, a winter version of summering in the Hamptons, or stay in one of the many barebones lodges or motels in the area. However, you can overnight in great comfort and enjoy some commendable cuisine in the region, which for apres-ski and dining purposes extends toward Windham, another fine ski area 10 miles to the northwest.

Condo development has been slow coming to Hunter, but there are now townhouses comprising **Hunter Mountain Village,** and some are available for short-term rental. You might prefer **Scribner Hollow,** a luxurious hotel with great views, a good restaurant, and the Grotto, one of the most sybaritic hot tub/waterfall/soaking pool installations in ski country. Especially if you are skiing with youngsters in tow, you will like the casual **Villagio Resort,** an upgraded complex which now includes spacious rooms and suites, an indoor pool and game room, and a restaurant which serves mammoth portions of rich Italian food. Bring the family—and bring your appetites.

Because of Hunter's proximity to New York, a surprising number of restaurateurs and top chefs have second homes there, and the trend has spawned a surprising number of exceptional restaurants in a rustic and rural area. One of the first, and still one of the best, is **Auberge des 4 Saisons,** known for exceptional French cuisine and sparkling atmosphere. **Brandywine,** which features northern Italian food, has a country ambiance. **Chateau Belleview** prepares imaginative continental specialties and boasts an excellent wine list. **The Redcoat's Return,** an atmospheric British-style restaurant, is an absolute charmer.

Hunter Mountain's high season is winter, but summer activities abound as well. The Starlite Express operates the **Hunter Skyride,** providing a scenic chairlift ride to the mountain's 3,200-foot summit. The calendar is filled with specialty festivals—German, Irish, Polish, folk, and the like.

DESTINATIONS

Hunter Mountain, Hunter, NY 12442. 518/263-4223 general information; 800/FOR-SNOW ski conditions; 518/263-4723 central reservations. Lift tickets: adult full-day $32, half-day $23; junior (ages 7-12), full-day $24, half-day $18; child (to age 6), $7; Hunter One (beginner lifts), $18 (credit card prices; all tickets $1 less with cash). Consecutive multi-day tickets and coupon books also available.

RESTAURANTS

Auberge des 4 Saisons, Rte 42, Shandaken, NY 12480. 914/688-2223. Fri-Sun 6-10 pm (nightly Dec 24-Jan 2). **Brandywine,** Rte 23, Windham, NY 12496. 518/734-3838. Sun, Tue-Thu noon-10 pm; Fri & Sat noon-midnight. **Chateau Belleview,** Rte 23A, Hunter, NY 12442. 518/589-5525. **The Redcoat's Return,** Dale Lane, Elka Park, NY 12427. 518/589-6379. Fri-Wed 6-10 pm.

ACCOMMODATIONS

Hunter Mountain Village, Hunter, NY 12442. 518/263-4606. **Scribner Hollow,** Rte 23A, Hunter, NY 12442. 518/263-4211. **Villagio Resort,** Rte 23A, Haines Falls, NY 12436. 518/589-5000.

92

FDR's Not-So-Rustic Retreat

Hyde Park, New York

During the more than 12 years that Franklin Roosevelt served as president he operated his summer White House out of the mansion in Hyde Park where he grew up. Now it's called the **Franklin D. Roosevelt National Historic Site.**

Hyde Park was, and still is, a town. It was named for Edward Hyde, Lord Cornbury, the eccentric provincial governor of New York. Hyde gave a parcel of land along the Hudson to his secretary. Hyde's name was then given to an estate on the property, and later to the town, which was established in 1821. For years it remained a rather sleepy little trading center serving farmers and the wealthy eastern establishment families who built lavish estates overlooking the Hudson. Its role changed radically, of course, when Roosevelt was first elected president in 1932.

Roosevelt loved coming here: Not long before he was nominated by his party for the fourth time he wrote to the Democratic national chairman that he would serve if needed. But he added, ''All that is within me cries out to return to my home on the Hudson River.'' Roosevelt was born here, grew up here, and is buried here. He brought his wife Eleanor here in 1905 as a bride, struggled against polio here in 1921, and entertained Winston Churchill and other distinguished world leaders here during his presidency.

The house was built around 1826. Roosevelt's father bought it in 1867 and enlarged and remodeled it extensively in 1916. Inside the columned building you can see the room where Roosevelt worked. On a desk are the items that the world knew him by: the beloved fedora with the crease down the middle, the wire-rimmed glasses, and the cigarette holder that was often tilted at a jaunty upward angle. In this room in November, 1944, Roosevelt broadcast the last campaign speech he ever made. Roosevelt was born in the Blue Room. In his bedroom at the end of the hallway you can see the leash and blanket that once belonged to his famous dog Fala. Books and magazines are scattered about the room just as they were at the time of his last visit in March of 1945.

The adjacent museum contains extensive displays of FDR's life and career, including photos, personal objects, gifts, speeches, state documents, and official correspondence. Here you'll also see his famous blue Ford convertible with its hand controls.

For a meal fit for a head of state, make an executive decision and call in the CIA. Hyde Park's famed **Culinary Institute of America,** which trains chefs and restaurateurs in the fine arts of cooking and restaurant management, has several restaurants to choose from, including two in the gourmet category, the American Bounty and The Escoffier Room. The Bounty serves Hudson Valley veal cutlets, plus sausage and seafood specialties and fresh bread and pastries baked right on the premises. The Escoffier Room specializes in French and continental cuisines. Try the *canard la perouse.*

Two miles east is **Val-Kill,** the stone cottage that was built for Eleanor Roosevelt. The cottage contains many mementoes of Eleanor's own public career, especially those connected with her well-known humanitarian efforts and service as ambassador to the United Nations. A shuttle bus operates on a regular schedule between the FDR National Historic Site and Val-Kill.

A few miles up-river from the Roosevelt complex is the **Vanderbilt Mansion,** a Beaux-Arts limestone palace that was built around the turn of the century by Frederick W. Vanderbilt, the grandson of "Commodore" Cornelius Vanderbilt. Frederick filled the place with art treasures from around the world and furnished it with Aubusson tapestries, Venetian chairs, and oriental rugs. Mrs. Vanderbilt's bedroom is a replica of a French queen's bedchamber. The ornate rug, made especially for this room, weighs 2,300 pounds. Until the 1930s the family hosted lavish parties and balls for the wealthiest families of America and the nobility of Europe. The mansion is now a National Historic Site, and the barns have been taken over by the Hyde Park Festival Theatre.

The Roosevelt sites and the Vanderbilt estate are part of a 40-mile, self-guided driving tour that has been laid out by the Dutchess County Tourism Promotion Agency.

DESTINATIONS

Dutchess County Tourism Promotion Agency, 46 Albany Post Rd, PO Box 2025, Hyde Park, NY 12538. 914/229-0033. **Roosevelt-Vanderbilt National Historic Sites,** Rte 9, Hyde Park, NY 12538. 914/229-9115. **Eleanor Roosevelt National Historic Site,** Hyde Park, NY 12538. 914/229-9115. Access by shuttle bus only from FDR complex, daily Apr-Oct, weekends only, Nov & Mar. Closed Dec-Feb.

RESTAURANTS

Culinary Institute of America, Rte 9, Hyde Park, NY 12538. 914/471-6608. American Bounty & Escoffier: Tue-Sat noon & 12:30 pm seatings, 6:30-8 pm.

ACCOMMODATIONS

Montgomery Inn Guest House, 67 Montgomery St, Rhinebeck, NY 12572. 914/876-3311.

93

Music Maestro, Please

Caramoor Center for Music and the Arts
Katonah, New York

Approaching a footbridge that crosses a creek and leads to a leafy glen, you startle a deer. With a flash of white tail, it scampers into the woods. This is **Caramoor,** an expansive estate nestled in the rolling hills of Westchester County, its grounds accented by serene woodlands, colorful formal gardens, and an apple orchard perfect for picnics. Caramoor also is an Italianate mansion built in the 1930s and filled with priceless artwork that spans 2,000 years, one of America's premier private collections of European and Chinese art. And it is the site of a world-renowned music festival.

Every year from late-June through late-August the **Caramoor Music Festival** offers a series of concerts as well as special programs for children. You'll find chamber music and piano concerts and the likes of the Count Basie Orchestra, The Canadian Brass, The New York Trumpet Ensemble, and the Tokyo String Quartet. There's a little jazz and ragtime, and programs that range from "All J. S. Bach" and "All Mozart" to "Mostly Gershwin." A half-dozen or so children's events explore such art forms as American clogging, Irish step dancing, English hornpipes, African boot dancing, French Canadian broom dancing, and Georgia Sea Island hand clapping—with children and parents joining the troupe for a round of dancing.

Festival performances are held at two locations. Chamber music and small, intimate concerts are performed in the Spanish Courtyard. Flanked by the red-tiled roofs of the mansion, the courtyard has a fountain, orderly plantings of red, pink, and mauve impatiens, and statues of lions cast in Sienna, Italy from a 15th-century mold. Larger concerts are held at the Venetian Theatre, where all seats are covered. (In inclement weather, performances scheduled for the Spanish Courtyard are moved to the theater.) Entrance to the theater is through magnificent Swiss 18th-century iron-and-gilt gates with imposing gateposts surmounted with sculptured Pegasus heads.

Other events include a fall concert series held in the Music Room of the mansion and lectures on art, photography, and other subjects. Popular events in early December are a concert featuring holiday music and an open house, Holidays at Caramoor, offering a twilight tour of the house which is decorated for the holidays, strolling Renaissance musicians, refreshments, and seasonal items in the gift shop.

Inside this "Great House," entire rooms from

European villas and palaces are carefully preserved. Paintings, sculpture, textiles, jades, ceramics, stained glass, and furniture date from the Middle Ages. The library, circa 1678, is from a chateau in Burgundy and features a carved and gilded vaulted ceiling decorated with biblical scenes and contains a 15th-century folding chair from the household of Ferdinand and Isabella of Spain. The Great Music Room is stunning and baronial with a coffered ceiling, a huge 17th-century Ushak carpet, tapestries from the 15th and 16th centuries, and furniture upholstered in needlework from the 17th and 18th centuries.

Art treasures on display include Grecian urns from 500 B.C., a 16th-century Spanish brocade bedspread, Chinese objects in ceramic, ivory, enamel, jade, and hand-painted silk, and an extensive collection of 18th-century Italian and English lacquer furniture, 16th-century Italian Renaissance furniture, and tapestries and embroideries of the Middle Ages and the Renaissance. Doors have dual personalities—inside they match the decor of various rooms, outside they are designed to resemble the doors of a 16th-century Spanish monastery.

Picnicking is welcomed in the apple orchard *before* concerts. Pack your own goodies or have a picnic catered by **Leslie's Kitchen** (call two days in advance for delivery to Caramoor). Nearby dining suggestions include **Covington** and **Crabtree's Kittle House** (see trip #94).

DESTINATIONS

Caramoor Center for Music and the Arts. Girdle Ridge Rd, Katonah, NY 10536. 914/232-5035. May-Nov Thu & Sat 11 am-4 pm, Sun 1-4 pm, Wed & Fri by aptmt; Nov-May Mon-Fri by aptmt.

RESTAURANTS

Leslie's Kitchen, 25 Depot Plaza, Bedford Hills, NY 10507. 914/666-8222.

94

Home Sweet Homestead

John Jay Homestead
Katonah, New York

Above the pianoforte in the parlor of this handsome farmhouse is a portrait of John Jay in the robes he wore as the first Chief Justice of the United States Supreme Court, an appointee of President George Washington. Of all of the founding fathers, no other filled so many high offices, and a visit to the **John Jay Homestead State Historic Site** and a tour of the house, conducted by a knowledgeable guide in period dress and shawl, provides a good sense of the man and his times.

Born in 1745 to a family of self-exiled French Huguenots, John Jay went on to serve the nation as President of the Continental Congress, Minister to Spain, and Secretary of Foreign Affairs, and as author and key negotiator, with Benjamin Franklin and John Adams, of the Treaty of Paris which ended the Revolution. He also served two terms as New York governor, retiring in 1801 to the farmhouse on land purchased from Indians by his maternal grandfather, Jacobus Van Cortlandt. He lived there as a country farmer until his death in 1829. The house was occupied by five generations of the Jay family and today is largely furnished with original items used by them.

Furnishings include a handsome dry sink in the parlor as well as a sofa and chairs with original 18th-century French tapestry and, in the dining room, a reproduction of the original wallpaper and Delft tiles around the fireplace, each detailing a biblical scene. An 1801 kitchen is equipped with spider pots (mounted on legs to allow hot cooking cinders to be shoveled beneath them), a reflector oven, and a beehive baking oven. In the rear parlor is a windup pipe organ with music rolls and a whale-oil lamp that produced as much light as 20 candles.

Be sure to check the homestead calendar for unusual and fun events such as 18th-century country dances, and in June, the popular annual dog competition and Farm Day at the Homestead. The latter offers demonstrations of sheepshearing, carding, and spinning of wool and contests of strength between teams of oxen. The holiday season features evening candlelight tours of the Homestead and its decorations, concerts (including one by English handbell ringers), and workshops on such crafts as making marzipan treats, cooking for the holiday table (using recipes from Jay's family and period cookbooks), and creating such Christmas decorations as mantle greens, fruit topiary, and kissing balls.

On Main Street in nearby Armonk the **Covington** offers American and continental cuisine and piano music in the bar on Friday and Saturday evenings. Signature dishes include rack of lamb and veal chateaubriand with Bearnaise sauce. Other entries include grilled Cajun chicken, blackened shrimp, and angel-hair pasta with shrimp, tomatoes, and garlic. In Chappaqua, **Crabtree's Kittle House** offers the ambiance of a country inn and such entrees as roast duckling, poached Norwegian salmon, sautéed medallions of veal, and rack of American lamb. Starters include asparagus puffs, gravlax with dill sauce, and seafood ravioli with lobster sauce. Save room for dessert, baked daily on the premises and including country apple cake and white-chocolate mousse.

Another stellar attraction, literally a few minutes' drive of the homestead, is Caramoor. Its popular music festival and magnificent collections of fine and decorative arts are well worth a separate visit (see trip #93).

DESTINATIONS

John Jay Homestead State Historic Site, Rte 22, Box AH, Katonah, NY 10536. 914/232-5651. Apr-Dec Wed-Sat 10 am-5 pm, Sun 1-5 pm.

RESTAURANTS

Covington, 465 Main St, Armonk, NY 10504. 914/273-5700. Sun-

Thu 11:30 am-3 pm 6-10 pm, Fri-Sat 11:30 am-3 pm, 6-11 pm. **Crab-tree's Kittle House,** 11 Kittle Rd, Rte 117, Chappaqua, NY 10514. 914/666-8044. Mon-Thu noon-2:30 pm 5:30-9:30 pm, Fri noon-2:30 pm 5:30-10:30 pm, Sat 5:30-10:30 pm, Sun noon-2:30 pm 3-9 pm.

95

Capital Hudson Town

Kingston, New York

Thick black smokes curls from the stacks of the paddlewheeler, and three piercing blasts sound from her steam whistle. Steamships such as the *Homer Ramsdell*, along with a flotilla of ferry boats, tugs, barges, and scows create constant traffic at the busy harbor. This was the scene at **Kingston, New York,** during the 19th century when the Hudson River provided a major route between Albany and New York City. There were boat yards and rigging lofts, trolley lines, wharfside hotels and restaurants, and huge loads of coal shuttled by canal from the mines of Pennsylvania.

These were busy times in Kingston, but the town's heyday as a major Hudson port was but one phase in its long and checkered history. Today, Kingston relies for its prosperity on a thriving electronics industry—and upon tourism, as visitors find that Kingston is one of those special places where history seems to reach out to touch them.

Kingston was settled by the Dutch in 1652 when Peter Stuyvesant was provincial governor of New York. The town became the state capital 125 years later in 1777 when Gen. George Clinton was sworn in as the first state governor. The ceremony took place on the steps of the Kingston Courthouse, one of an incredible array of historic buildings that have been beautifully preserved here for more than two centuries.

The courthouse, as with many of the other historic structures in Kingston, is part of the **Stockade**

District. The stockade was built in 1658 on orders from Stuyvesant as a result of skirmishes with local Indians. The Dutch and other early settlers from Europe were required to build their houses within it, and they built them exceedingly well, using large blocks of local limestone. Although the stockade itself was gone by the early 18th century, many of the structures have survived. Some of the oldest of the original buildings date to the years between 1670 and 1750.

Although the British burned Kingston during the Revolutionary War, the stone houses of the Stockade District survived well enough to be reconstructed and repaired. Subsequent refurbishing and restoration work has helped to make this historic district and the adjacent neighborhood not only the focal point of Kingston, but the locus of one of the finest self-guided walking tours in the country. Its streets, brightened with tubs of flowers, contain a wealth of Dutch stone houses from the 17th and 18th centuries and pretty pastel-shaded buildings with overhanging balconies that provide covered walkways.

A map and guide, available from the Visitor Center, describes and locates 39 structures within and just outside the Stockade District. One of the most important is the **Senate House,** built in 1676. The New York State Senate met here for the first time on April 20, 1777, the same day that Governor Clinton was sworn in. Guides at Senate House provide a tour and explain the crucial role played by Kingston during the Revolutionary War. (The town was a hotbed of revolutionary activity and the area around it was known as the "Breadbasket of the Revolution," owing to the large quantities of food it supplied to the Continental Army.)

In the Senate House Museum you can admire paintings by John Vanderlyn (1775-1852), a Kingston native who is recognized as one of the first native American landscape artists, as well as a portrait painter of some distinction. The **Old Dutch Church,** built in 1852 from a Renaissance Revival design by the noted architect Minard Lafever, has a vaulted ceiling, a main altar window by Tiffany, and a framed letter from George Washington. The leafy churchyard, which includes the tombstones of early settlers and the grave of Governor Clinton, is a pleasant place for strolling and resting and listening to the musical pealing of the church bells. In spring, the churchyard is painted with the colorful blooms of thousands of tulips.

The corner of Crown and John streets owns a distinction that no other intersection in the country can claim. It's the only one with an 18th-century house on each corner. A house that once belonged to Dr. Luke Kiersted has the distinction of being the only pre-1800 dwelling with clapboard siding. The Judge Lucas Elmendorf House, built about 1790, is the best remaining example of a late 18th-century stone mansion. And Van Steenburgh House, on Wall Street, five blocks south of the Stockade District, is the only pre-Revolutionary stone house that the British spared when they burned Kingston in 1777. According to local legend, the British officer in charge was a friend of the owner's daughter.

Around the midpoint of your tour of the Stockade District, you'll come to **Hoffman House,** which was built prior to 1679 and is a National Historic Landmark. It was severely damaged when the British burned Kingston, and still has the char marks to prove it. In addition to qualifying as a bona fide historical attraction, Hoffman House now doubles as a restaurant, specializing in hot and cold luncheon plates, hot luncheon sandwiches, and various "melts," including one with pastrami.

With a family-owned butcher shop next door, you've got to know that the sausages at **Schneller's** are good, as are other entrees on the predominantly German menu. There's variety, too, with these wonderful wurst—weisswurst, fresh and smoked bratwurst, and knackwurst are among the popular German varieties, plus fresh Spanish choriza, spicy Italian sausage, and Polish kielbasa. At this comfortable eatery, you'll also find schnitzels, sauerbraten, goulash, pâtés, lebercase (head cheese), homemade breads, and a wide selection of beers. For dessert try blueberry pancakes, strudel, cheesecake, or torte.

The upstairs Victorian dining room is light and airy with tall, arched windows offering a nice view of an historic section of town. Downstairs is a recently-installed bar, a market with a tempting selection of meats and cheese, and a gift shop with German imports.

Beyond the Stockade District head for Rondout Landing and be sure to visit the living museum at the **Hudson River Maritime Center.** Here you can see boats being built and rigged, as well as various maritime exhibits, including the *William O. Benton*, a retired tugboat beached just back from the river. One of the best Hudson River cruises also leaves from here. It's aboard the *Marion T. Budd.* Scenery includes the wooded banks of the river, the distant Catskills, the Kingston-Rhinecliff Bridge, and the Esopus Light lighthouse. For a fascinating look at another mode of transportation, visit the **Trolley Museum** at the waterfront. It displays several vintage trolleys and, in season, provides rides along the waterfront. For unusual lodgings, stay at **Rondout II Lighthouse,** an actual working lighthouse that also functions as a B&B.

DESTINATIONS

Friends of Historic Kingston, PO Box 3763, Kingston, NY 12401. 914/338-5100. **Hudson River Maritime Center,** 39 Broadway, Kingston, NY 12401. 914/338-0071. May-Oct Wed-Sun noon-5pm. **Trolley Museum,** 89 E Strand, Kingston NY 12401. 914/331-3399. Mem Day-Oct.

RESTAURANTS

Hoffman House and Tavern, 94 North Front St, Kingston NY 12401. 914/338-2626. **Oehmceler's,** 61 John St, Kingston, NY 12401. 914/331-9800. Mon-Tue 11:30 am-3:30 pm; Wed-Sat 11:30 am-3:30 pm, 5-10 pm; Sun 5-10 pm.

ACCOMMODATIONS

Rondout II Lighthouse B&B, 25 E O'Reilly St, Kingston, NY 12401. 914/331-0682. **Holiday Inn,** 503 Washington Ave, Kingston, NY 12401.

96

Antiquing With Peter Piper

Millbrook, New York

Pity poor James Kirke Paulding, native of **Millbrook, New York.** This early-19th-century Renaissance man wrote well-regarded novels and plays and served as Secretary of the Navy under President Martin Van Buren. So why "pity?" Because, with all his achievements (including his staunch advocacy of the use of American locales and themes for native literary works) and creations, the one best known to the American public is a "tongue-twister" that he devised for a collection of light poetry. Paulding's name may not be familiar, but you know his words: "Peter Piper picked a peck of pickled peppers..."

His hometown has no such problem—Millbrook is best-known for its best feature: a profusion of fine antique shops, many of which are clustered on (or just off) Franklin Avenue. Together, these shops contain just about anything you'd ever want to collect—furniture, porcelain, paintings, tools, snuff boxes, lamps, candelabra, china, cookware, books, musical instruments, bottles, crocks, brass beds, oriental rugs, Art Deco pieces, and much more.

A particularly good shop is **Joyce Harris Stanton Antiques and Interiors.** The strong suit here is 18th- and 19th-century English and American furniture, in a variety of styles ranging from country to formal. You can also find oriental rugs, paintings, and brass items.

Other dealers in town include the following: **Wicker's Antiques,** specializing in Early American pattern glass; **Days of Yore Antiques,** offering estate jewelry, country and formal furniture, and silver and bronze pieces and accessories; **Bottle Shop Antiques,** featuring kitchenware, tools, crocks, and a large selection of various types of bottles; **The Village Antique Center,** which offers quilts, lamps, linens, pottery, porcelain, and other accessory items; and **Calico Quail,** specializing in furniture.

Millbrook also features a number of "Antique Malls," larger stores or exhibition areas that offer specialized material from a number of different independent dealers. Chief among these are **The Millbrook Antique Center,** with more than 45 dealers in one place, making it the largest operation of its kind in New York State, and the **Millbrook Antiques Mall,** representing nearly 40 dealers.

Millbrook is in Dutchess County (see trip #86), which is chock full of other small towns with large numbers of antique shops. If you're serious about collecting, you could schedule a visit to coincide with one of the large auctions. There are several places that hold them regularly, including **Rinaldi Auctions,** the **Eastern Dutchess Auction Gallery,** the **Pleasant Valley Auction Hall,** and **Country Fare Antiques, Arts Center, and Auction Barn.**

A lovely and convenient place for a refreshing pause is the **Silver Fox Inn** just outside Millbrook. This restaurant serves continental, nouvelle, and new American dishes in a charming country atmosphere. Try the duck with cherry sauce, the medallions of veal in a white sauce, or the variety of grilled fresh seafood entrees.

DESTINATIONS

Dutchess County Tourism Promotion Agency, 46 Albany Post Road, PO Box 2025, Hyde Park, NY 12538. 914/229-0033.

RESTAURANTS

Silver Fox Inn, Rte 44, Millbrook, NY 12545. 914/677-3919. Daily 7 am-midnight.

97

Magnificent Mohonk

Mohonk Mountain House
New Paltz, New York

Perched high atop the Shawangunk Mountains, looking for all the world like a sprawling European castle, lies an imposing romantic hotel, striking a fortress-like silhouette in the vast blue sky. The **Mohonk Mountain House,** near New Paltz, New York, has, in the more than 120 years since it was erected, established itself as one of the most picturesque and gracious hotels on the East Coast.

The hotel stands basically as its founder, Alfred Smiley, envisioned it in 1869. Smiley convinced his twin brother, Albert, to build a peaceful retreat on the site, so they scraped up the money to buy 300 acres and a run-down 10-room tavern, which they converted to a hotel. The following year they expanded to 40 rooms, and the Mountain House was on its way. Over the years, this resort has played host to an impressive list of famous visitors, including four U.S. presidents—Rutherford B. Hayes, Chester A. Arthur, Theodore Roosevelt, and William Howard Taft.

Today, the Mountain House is a magnificent 300-room hotel, designated a National Historic Landmark, stretching a quarter of a mile along the Shawangunk Mountains (pronounced locally, "Shawngump"). The Smileys were Quakers, and the hotel retains a somewhat strait-laced atmosphere, but is still a fun and relaxing spot for a getaway and is particularly known for its innovative theme weekends, often hosted by celebrity authors, cooks, and noted experts in other various fields. Although there is no bar, wine is allowed at dinner. Neat attire is requested during the day and jackets and ties are requested at dinner. The hotel offers classical concerts, prayer services, and afternoon tea. Smoking is not permitted in the dining room, parlor, or library, but is allowed in guest rooms.

The hotel's common rooms are appointed in antique furnishings; the guest rooms can be average to small, but command views of either Lake Mohonk or the surrounding mountains. The Mountain House has three dining rooms, 150 working fireplaces, 200 balconies, six parlors, and three verandas lined with rockers. The grounds feature gardens and greenhouses, picnic areas, a museum, stables, sports facilities, and an observation point known as Skytop

Tower. Two-night minimums are required on weekends, and three-night minimums are required for holiday periods including Memorial Day, Independence Day, Columbus Day, and President's Day. Special packages are offered, such as a "Midweek Sports Package," "Recreation Midweek Package," and "Golf Midweek Package."

Very popular at the hotel are special theme weekends. One that commands a lot of attention and excitement is the "Mystery Weekend," which the Mohonk was the first in the country to offer, back in 1977. On these weekends, "murders" are committed, and guests must use their wits to figure out whodunit. On hand for the event are impressive guests, usually best-selling authors, such as Stephen King, Elmore Leonard, or Mary Higgins Clark. The weekend is great fun.

Other theme weekends include: "The Wonderful World of Words," "Choral Singers Weekend," "Cooking Weekend" (hosted by national food writer, Adrianne Marcus), "Tower of Babble" (an immersion course in languages), and "Science Fiction" (which has had well-known writer Isaac Asimov as host). There are also programs on nature, pioneer crafts, hiking, tennis, holistic health, and stargazing. It's advisable to make your reservations very early.

But even if you don't participate in themed goings-on in the hotel, there's plenty to do. The hotel offers aerobics, fishing, golf, ice skating, square dances, yoga, tennis, croquet, carriage rides, children's programs, concerts, dances, movies, nature walks, swimming, jogging, and lectures.

The Mohonk Mountain House is snuggled into 22,000 acres of preserved land. On the sheer faces of the Trapps cliffs, rock-climbers from all over the world practice their skills. Perhaps less daunting than rock climbing is "rock scrambling" through terrain strewn with boulders. Even less demanding are scheduled walks led by naturalists.

More than 20 years ago, the Smiley family was instrumental in setting up the Mohonk Trust, an organization committed to protecting natural lands in the Shawangunks and to advance world peace through an understanding of the relationship between human beings and their environment. The trust evolved into the **Mohonk Preserve**, separate now from the Mountain House jurisdiction. Within the preserve's domain are miles of trails and carriage roads where visitors can hike, ride horseback, or cross-country ski.

The Shawangunks have three recreational lakes: Mohonk, Awosting, and Minnewaska. Mohonk is stocked with trout every year. Besides fishing, there are 135 miles of trails that double for hiking and prime cross-country skiing. Alfred Smiley built a resort at Lake Minnewaska, which is now separate from the Mountain House's holdings, and has been developed into **Lake Minnewaska State Park.** A waterfall, pine trees, and distant mountains provide spectacular scenery for skiers and hikers who visit its 10,000 acres, located about six miles from the Mountain House.

The Mountain House also offers special programs for children ages two to 13, based on the philosophy of "let kids be kids." Games and other activities are organized five days a week from mid-June through Labor Day, and on weekends and holidays the rest of the year.

Non-staying guests may hike on the grounds, but must pay a parking fee for the day. Meals are also available to visitors; reservations should be made in advance. The fare in the dining room features what the Mohonk calls "Hearty American cooking," which includes pork chops, baked ham, roast turkey, spring chicken, and, for dessert, a favorite pecan pie.

Nearby is the town of New Paltz, New York, famous for its beautiful 17th-century stone houses on what is called "the oldest street in America" (see trip #98).

DESTINATIONS

Mohonk Mountain House, Lake Mohonk, New Paltz, NY 12561. 914/255-1000 or 212/233-2244. **Mohonk Preserve,** Mountain Rest Rd (between Lake Mohonk and New Paltz), New Paltz, NY 12561. 914/255-0919. **Lake Minnewaska State Park,** Lake Minnewaska, NY 12561. 914/255-0752.

RESTAURANTS

Mohonk Mountain House (see Destination). Daily 8-9:30 am, 12:30-2 pm, 6:30-8 pm.

ACCOMMODATIONS

Mohonk Mountain House (see Destination).

98

America's Oldest Neighborhood

New Paltz, New York

No matter whether they are bathed in the bright sunshine of early summer or blanketed with a covering of fresh snow, the beautiful stone houses on the oldest street in America have an ephemeral, almost magical charm. **Huguenot Street,** just beyond the college town of **New Paltz, New York,** is a picturesque oasis of history with original buildings that date back to the 1690s.

Huguenot Street was founded by exiled members of the French Protestant restoration sect that King Louis XIV was persecuting for its religious and political beliefs. Fleeing their homes in Lille and Calais, the Huguenots first moved to Speyer and Manheim in Germany, in the province of *Die Pfalz*. Finally, they came across the sea and landed in the Dutch villages of Kingston and Hurley in the Hudson Valley. In 1677, 12 families pooled their resources and purchased nearly 40,000 acres of land from the Esopus Indians. Four months later, the English governor issued a patent for the land, and the settlers set up a unique form of government, called the *Duzine*, or rule of the elders. One representative from each family was elected to the *Duzine*. The family leaders were called "patentees," a word you'll see a lot around Huguenot Street. They called their home New Paltz, after their old home in Germany.

The first homes the settlers built consisted of one simple room with a cellar, but these soon were expanded. Many of the houses on the street were passed down through the families of the original owners, and still contain much of their original furnishings. For a good orientation of the history of the street, start your tour at **Deyo Hall.** Exhibits give information about the settlers; the hall also offers a museum and a gift shop.

On the guided tours, unique architectural features of the homes are noted, such as the ingeniously constructed, jambless fireplaces in the **Jean Hasbrouck House.** The variety of furnishings show the continuity of the settlement: pieces brought from France, items bought upon settling here, and pieces added by descendants.

Also noteworthy are the two churches on the street. The **Reformed Church** is the last in a series of churches built on its site, all torn down as the congregation grew. It is in the typical Georgian colonial style common to the Hudson Valley. If you look closely at the stone portion of the church, you'll find stones with names, dates, and initials, all from earlier churches.

Also on Huguenot Street, don't miss the church and little cemetery closest to Main Street. The first log cabin church was built in 1683. The church currently on the site is rebuilt from the French Church originally built in 1717. All the patentees and their families, save for two, are buried in this cemetery. The earliest tombstone is that of Andries LeFevre, a patentee, who died in 1714. Most of the patentees' tombstones are gone, but the Huguenot Society has placed markers commemorating them.

For lunch or dinner in an historic house, try the **Locust Tree Inn.** Located in a 1759 stone house, this restaurant has fireplaces in every dining room, and specializes in continental chicken, duck, and fresh fish entrees.

For other diversions, the area boasts a concentration of antique stores. Each August, the Ulster County Fair is held at the New Paltz Fairgrounds.

New Paltz is also home to the **Mohonk Mountain House,** a castle-like resort in the Shawangunk Mountains (see trip #97).

DESTINATIONS

Huguenot Street, c/o The Huguenot Historical Society, 6 Brodhead Ave, New Paltz, NY 12561, 914/255-1660 or -1889. Huguenot Street houses open Mem Day-Sep Wed-Sun 9:30 am-4 pm. Call for off-season availability. Guided tours available; prices vary. **Hudson River Valley Association,** 76 Main St, Cold Spring, NY 10516. 914/265-3066. **Ulster County Fair,** Ulster County Public Information Office, PO Box 1800, Kingston, NY 12401. 914/331-9300.

RESTAURANTS

Locust Tree Inn, 215 Huguenot St, New Paltz, NY 12561. 914/255-7888. Tue-Fri 11:30 am-2:30 pm, 5:30-10 pm; Sat 5:30-10 pm; Sun 11 am-8 pm.

99

Tasting The Little Orange

Orange County, New York

When most people think of a getaway to **Orange County,** they envision trips to the ones in California or Florida, world-famous as the homes of Disneyland and Walt Disney World, respectively. But New York has its own Orange County, and while you may not find any pumpkin coaches there, it is a Cinderella destination with a diverting assortment of attractions and activities. A little more than an hour's drive north of New York City, it is a perfect spot for a weekend getaway.

The county stretches west from the Hudson River to New York's borders with New Jersey and Pennsylvania, and has varied topography, ranging from mountainous woodlands in the north and west to the plunging valley along the river. Orange County is home to the stirring sights and storied traditions of the U.S. Military Academy at **West Point** (see trip #106), the **Historic Track** and **Hall of Fame of the Trotter** at Goshen (see trip #88), and a large portion of the Palisades Parks at **Bear Mountain** and **Harriman** (see trip #100).

The county's largest city is **Newburgh,** whose claim to everlasting historical fame may be that it was where George Washington strongly rejected a plan (fashioned by some of the men in his command) designed to make him the first American king at the end of the Revolutionary War. It happened in 1782, after the victory at Yorktown, but before the official declaration of peace, while the majority of the Continental Army was camped at the **New Windsor Cantonment** just outside of town. Washington was occupying Newburgh's Hasbrouck House, known since then as **Washington's Headquarters.** This 1750 stone house has been restored to the condition it was in when George and his wife Martha spent 16 months there in 1782-83. The Cantonment was the last encampment of the Continental Army, and has been recreated as a living history site. Costumed interpreters demonstrate aspects of 18th-century military life, including musket and cannon drills.

Southwest of Newburgh, in the town of Central Valley, is **Woodbury Common,** a shopping center of factory outlet stores. Although Woodbury is a recent addition to the county, its design of colonial-village-style storefronts and cobblestone sidewalks gives it a feeling of history. There, shoppers can find brand name items—from such designers and manufacturers as Anne Klein, Nike, Carter's Childrenswear, Corning, and American Tourister—at savings of 25 to 75 percent.

A 10-minute drive from Woodbury is a another unique area of shops—**Sugar Loaf Craft Village.** This hamlet of artists and craftspeople consists of restored 18th- and 19th-century houses (along with a handful of newer structures) along a half-mile stretch of Kings Highway. Stroll from shop to shop, and you'll find toymakers, leatherworkers, painters, jewelers, dollmakers, sculptors, and other talented and friendly artisans. Visit Sugar Loaf on Columbus Day weekend for the town's Fall Festival, offering music, food, art contests, and plenty of fine crafts, all framed by the colorful beauty of an Orange County autumn.

For dining in Newburgh, try the mainly Italian fare of **Chianti.** Specialties include homemade pasta dishes, veal Marsala, fresh seafood entrees, and aged steaks. In Central Valley, the choice is **Gasho of Japan,** which offers the flavorful food and tableside theatrics of tepanyaki-style cooking in a 400-year-old farmhouse imported from Japan (see trip #88).

DESTINATIONS

Eastern Orange County Chamber of Commerce, 47 Grand St, Newburgh, NY 12550. 914/562-5100. **Washington's Headquarters State Historic Site,** 84 Liberty St, Newburgh, NY 12550. 914/562-1195. Jan-Mar Sat 10 am-5 pm, Sun 1-5 pm; Apr-Dec Wed-Sat 10 am-5 pm, Sun 1-5 pm. **New Windsor Cantonment,** Box 207, Vails Gate, NY 12584. 914/561-1765. Apr-Oct Wed-Sat 10 am-5 pm, Sun 1-5 pm. **Woodbury Common,** Rte 32, Central Valley, NY 10917. 914/928-7467. Hours vary by season. **Sugar Loaf Craft Village,** Sugar Loaf, NY 10981. 914/469-4963.

RESTAURANTS

Chianti, 362 Broadway, Newburgh, NY 12550. 914/561-3103. Mon-Thu 11:30 am-2:30 pm, 4:30-9:30 pm; Fri 11:30 am-2:30 pm, 4:30-10 pm; Sat 4:30-10 pm. **Gasho of Japan,** Rte 32, Central Valley, NY 10917. 914/928-2387. Mon-Fri noon-3 pm, 5:30-11 pm; Sat noon-3 pm, 5-11 pm; Sun noon-10 pm.

100

Ah, Wilderness!

The Palisades Parks
Hudson Valley area, New York

When life starts getting too close, the noise too loud, and your nerves too jangled, it is good to remember the **Palisades Parks.**

In only an hour from Manhattan, you can be in the midst of sweet serenity, hiking down a path, maybe coming face-to-face with a white-tailed deer. On summer's hottest days you can splash in a cool lake, and there's a mountaintop to climb to survey the colors of fall or winter-white hills. **Bear Moun-**

tain and **Harriman** State Parks offer a peaceful and revitalizing retreat from reality in any season.

The 51,000 acres of these two parks are the bulk of the 81,000-acre **Palisades Interstate Park System,** which also includes parks along the Palisades cliffs of the Hudson River from Fort Lee north, and other sites at Lake Minnewaska, Goosepond Mountain, Highland Lakes, and more.

Bear Mountain was the site of Fort Montgomery and Fort Clinton during the Revolutionary War. Today, visitors can catch a glimpse of this period of history at **Knox's Headquarters,** a 1754 stone house from which Maj. Gen. Henry Knox commanded the patriot's artillery; today, exhibits recall the military skirmishes and campaigns that occurred in the area.

The more populated and developed of these two parks is Bear Mountain, which offers fishing, boating, hiking, and, every winter, a very popular ski-jump competition. Bear Mountain also plays host to a number of interesting festivals. The arrival of spring is heralded with "Festa Italiana," offering food, music, and games of old Italy; summer's "Country Music Festival" attracts top-name performers; and "Oktoberfest" brings beer, knockwurst, and lederhosen to the park each autumn. The most popular annual event is the "Christmas Festival," held throughout the month of December. The highlights of this yuletide celebration include a lavishly decorated 40-foot tree; a detailed Santa's Workshop for the kids to visit—complete with jolly old St. Nick himself; and the presentation of a living Nativity scene.

Harriman was originally intended to be the site of a state prison, but that idea was eventually quashed by influential people in the area. Today, Harriman is the quieter of the two parks, and boasts wilder country. There, you're likely to find a quiet spot even on the busiest of summer weekends, particularly somewhere along the glorious Seven Lakes Road, buttressed by mirror-still lakes on either side. Most popular are Sebago Beach and Lake Welch. Rustic cabins are available for rent at Sebago Beach, for a reasonable fee.

Also part of the park system is a stretch of land following the towering Palisades, north of the George Washington Bridge. The two main trails are the Long Path, which runs along the top of the cliffs, and the Palisades Shore Trail, which follows the Hudson River. Along the hundreds of miles of trails you may see deer, raccoons, woodchucks, and squirrels, and perhaps some of the preserve's rarer species, such as otters, minks, beavers, and bobcats. Overhead, you'll see some of the more than 240 species of birds that inhabit the area, including red-tailed hawks, great horned and screech owls, and scarlet tanagers.

A perfect way to top off a fine day is with dinner at the picturesque **Bear Mountain Inn,** dating from 1922. The big stone-and-timber lodge offers a beautiful panorama of pines and deciduous hardwoods surrounding Hessian Lake. The dining room offers generous helpings of basic American fare, such as fried chicken, baked ham, hearty soups, and homemade desserts. Especially popular is the Saturday night smorgasbord. On the grounds are places to hike, jog, picnic, swim, ice skate, and cross-country ski. Crafts fairs and a variety of other events are held throughout the year at the inn. If you choose to extend your trip to this area, overnight accommodations are also available at Bear Mountain. A dining alternative to the inn is the **Reef and Beef,** just across the Bear Mountain Bridge. Reef and Beef is a big, yet cozy and very friendly place with a great salad bar and a variety of fish and beef dishes.

DESTINATIONS

Bear Mountain and **Harriman State Parks,** c/o Palisades Interstate Park Commission, Bear Mountain, NY 10911, 914/786-2701.

RESTAURANTS

Bear Mountain Inn, Bear Mountain, NY 10911. 914/786-2731. Sun-Thu 8-11 am, noon-3 pm, 5-8 pm; Fri-Sat 8-11 am, noon-3 pm, 5-10 pm. **Reef and Beef,** Roa-Hook Rd, Peekskill, NY 10566. 914/737-8880. Sun-Thu 11:30 am-10 pm, Fri-Sat 11:30 am-11 pm.

101

Finders, "Kippers"

Poughkeepsie, New York

Twelve years after it declared its independence, the United States of America had become most notable for its disunity. The nation had devolved into 13 little nations, bickering over everything from land grabbing to voting rights to competing currencies. It was in **Poughkeepsie**, New York, that it all stopped. The courthouse where it occurred no longer stands, but its successor, opened in 1903, now occupies the site where New York delegates, in a tight vote, decided to ratify the U.S. Constitution, and provided the winning margin for its adoption.

Not many people outside of the State of New York give the city its correct pronunciation (po-KIP-see). That's because there's nothing logical about the way the Dutch tried to pronounce a Wampinger Indian phrase meaning "the reed-covered lodge by the little water place." The little water place, a spring, still exists, two miles south of Poughkeepsie city hall.

It was the Duke of York, the future James II, who sent Colonial Governor Thomas Dongan in 1683 to establish Dutchess County 60 miles north of the bustling port of New York City, and about the same distance south of the region the Dutch called Renssalaerwyck, surrounding Albany.

It wasn't the Dutch, however, who concerned the Stuart monarchs, but New Englanders to the east. They threatened to push the Connecticut colony line to the banks of the Hudson. Dutchess County and Poughkeepsie made sure the river remained in royalist hands after the restoration of the crown that followed Oliver Cromwell's reign in Mother England, 23 years before. The dutchess (old spelling) for whom the county was named was Maria Beatrice D'Este, wife of the future king.

Even though it found itself to be a crossroads, most of the county continued to exist as wooded hills invaded by nothing more threatening than the

occasional deer, pheasant, wild turkey, or grouse—
species that still make their homes here. It was virtually untouched by the American Revolution.

It wasn't until the 19th century that Poughkeepsie
and the Dutchess County became known for what it
is now known: Dutch vernacular, Federal, Classical
Revival, and Victorian mansions that recall names
such as Vanderbilt, Livingston, Astor, Schuyler and
Roosevelt; riverboats along the Hudson, covered
bridges across sleepy streams, and one of the most
famous of the "Seven Sisters," Vassar College. As
you might expect, the county is riddled with antique stores.

Besides Vassar, Poughkeepsie boasts the oldest
continuously published newspaper in New York
State (the *Poughkeepsie Journal,* founded in 1785),
the Union Street Historic District, the 1869 Barda-
von Opera House, stately houses along Lower Mansion Street and, just south of town, Locust Grove,
home of **Samuel F.B. Morse.** And riverboats, operated by **Riverboat Tours,** take seasonal sightseers
north as far as the foothills of the Catskills and
south to West Point.

For family style dining before setting off, try the
Palace Diner/Restaurant for continental fare or the
Village Diner for home-style cooking. Much of the
charm and tradition of Dutchess County is accessible by car. One two-hour loop drive takes you north
of Poughkeepsie to Hyde Park and Springwood,
Franklin D. Roosevelt's home, library, and museum.
Here too is the estate of Frederick Vanderbilt. The
first stop in Hyde Park, however, is the Culinary Institute of America which features four restaurants,
all of them staffed by faculty and students in their
final semester of training. Each restaurant features a
different cuisine: American bounty (American regional), Caterina de Medici (Italian), Escoffier
(French), and St. Andrew's Cafe (health related). Reservations are necessary.

Walk through the grounds of this former Jesuit
seminary and enjoy the Hudson view. Also visit the
bookstore which has an impressive collection of
cookbooks and cooking equipment (see trip #92).

From there, visit Norrie State Park and Yacht Basin in **Staatsburg,** and the Mills Mansion, built for Ogden and Ruth Livingston Mills in the styles of Louis XIV, Louis XV and Louis XVI of royal France.

Fifteen miles of winding, scenic roadway brings you to **Clinton Corners,** home of the Clinton Vineyards, and a four-mile stretch of the **Taconic Parkway,** truly one of the most beautiful in the country. The parkway was inspired by the European idea of making the most of the aesthetics on either side.

The loop takes you back to Hyde Park and Val-Kill, Eleanor Roosevelt's retreat a shuttle away from Franklin's home. Frederick's, also known as the Val-Kill Tea Room, contains a weaving shop and showroom, featuring examples of finely crafted furniture, pewter and handwoven items.

North of Staatsburg on Route 9, **Rhinebeck Village** begins a second two-hour drive. It takes you to Mill Road and the 16-Mile District, filled with outstanding examples of 18th and 19th Century natural and cultural landscapes, including the American Romantic Style distinct to the Hudson Valley. Along the way, you come to historic Annandale. Visit Montgomery Place, built for the widow of Gen. Richard Montgomery, a hero of the American Revolution. The home, situated on 400 acres, features a blend of the Federal and Classical Revival styles. It's located on River Road, and the Hudson can be viewed from the grounds.

Less than a mile to the north is **Red Hook,** named by Henry Hudson. Red Hook is home to Bard College, a gorgeous riverside campus founded in 1860. **Tivoli,** a mile further north, offers one of Dutchess County's most spectacular views of the Catskills. The drive takes you east and south back to Rhinebeck Village. A side trip along Stone Church Road brings you the **Old Rhinebeck Aerodrome** (see trip #102), where aircraft from World War I and the Lindbergh era are on display and in action, featuring open-cockpit rides and barnstorming.

DESTINATIONS
Dutchess County Tourism Promotion Agency, Rte 9, Box

NEW YORK – UPSTATE

2025, Hyde Park NY 12538. 914/229-0033. **Riverboat Tours,** 310 Mill St, Poughkeepsie, NY 12601. 914/473-5211. Early May to mid-Oct. Fares range from $9 for sightseeing to $25 for music, dancing, & dinner. **Old Rhinebeck Aerodrome,** 42 Stone Church Rd, Rhinebeck, NY 12572. 914/758-8610. Mid-May to late Oct: Daily 10 am-5 pm. Adults $3, children $1; weekends adults $7, children $3.

RESTAURANTS

Culinary Institute of America, Rte 9, Hyde Park, NY 12538. 914/471-6608. Reservations required. Escoffier & American Bounty: Tue-Sat 12 & 12:30 pm seatings, 6:30-8 pm; Caterina de Medici: Mon-Fri 6 pm seating; St. Andrew Cafe: Mon-Fri: 11:30-12:30 pm, 6-7:30 pm. **Palace Diner/Restaurant,** 194 Washington St, Poughkeepsie, NY 12601. 914/473-1576. Daily 24 hrs. **Village Diner,** 39 W Broadway, Red Hook, NY 12571. 914/758-6232. Sun-Thu 6 am-8 pm, Fri & Sat 6 am-9 pm.

ACCOMMODATIONS

Dutch Patroon, Rte 9, Hyde Park, NY 12538. 914/229-7141. **Inn at the Falls,** 50 Red Oaks Mill Rd, Poughkeepsie, NY 12601. 914/462-5770. **Scenery Hill Bed & Breakfast,** North Cross Rd, Staatsburg, NY 12580. 914/889-4812 or 4301.

102

Magnificent Flying Machines

Rhinebeck, New York

Driven back by whirring propellers, the wind whips at the open cockpit. Far below you, the shiny blue ribbon of a river snakes through patches of brown and green farmland dotted with specks of farmhouses. With a powerful roar, you dip closer to the ground, barely skimming the tops of trees and buildings. Such were the thrills of early aeronautics—the age of the plucky barnstormers. If the only flying you've experienced lately has been inside a sterile jumbo jet, make your way to **Rhinebeck, New York,** and the **Old Rhinebeck Aerodrome,** and relive the pioneering days of flight by soaring above the Hudson River Valley in an open-cockpit biplane.

While the planes of the first few decades of this century have long since been surpassed in terms of technology and speed, they remain outstanding examples of the spirit that characterized the early days of flight. And Cole Palen is a man who definitely felt that spirit; he created the aerodrome as a unique tribute to those magnificent flying machines. Palen had always loved airplanes, and, after World War II, he decided to become an airplane mechanic. While training as a mechanic at Roosevelt Field on Long Island, he noticed a hangar full of old planes and immediately fell in love with them. He snooped around them, and even sat in them during his lunch hour. And when the field was being turned into a shopping mall, he bid on some of the planes. He got six, including the Fokker D-VII he absolutely adored; the Smithsonian only got three. That was in the mid-1950s. Over the years, Cole's personal collection of airplanes has grown to about 50 and they are all on display at the aerodrome. The collection includes pioneer airplanes, World War I, and Lindbergh-era planes, covering the period from roughly 1900 to 1937. Also on display are old airplane engines (whenever Palen buys a plane, he tries to buy an extra engine, since spare parts are scarce), and classic motor vehicles, such as a venerable "Caddy" with tailfins and a collection of dusty motorcycles.

Most of the planes are functional, and from June to mid-October dogfights and airshows are staged. You can even take a ride in an open-cockpit 1929 New Standard D-25.

The Rhinebeck Aerodrome is just one attraction in this pretty, upscale section of the Hudson Valley. Between visiting mansions and antique-hunting, you may wish to devote an entire weekend sampling the offerings of this history-rich area. Stay at the **Beekman Arms,** established in 1700 and claiming itself America's oldest hotel in continuous operation.

The Beekman started out in the manner of many

historic inns—as a tavern. It is built with stone walls two-to-three feet thick, huge oak beams, and large floor planks. Its builders said it was as strong as a fortress and, during the ensuing years, it sometimes was used as one. During the Revolution, the infantry, led by Col. Henry Beekman Livingston, drilled on the Beekman Arms' front lawn. In those days, Gen. George Washington paced and conferred on those heavy floorplanks. Lafayette, Burr, Schuyler, Arnold, and Hamilton all planned and ate and slept at the Beekman. The inn also served once as a refuge for all the townspeople, who huddled in the basement anticipating an attack from the British—which never materialized.

After the war, the Beekman Arms was still the site of much high thinking. Among its guests were Horace Greeley, William Jennings Bryan, and Franklin D. Roosevelt, who lived in nearby Hyde Park.

Today the inn retains its original architecture and charm. The rooms are furnished in antiques, and many have fireplaces. The large gathering rooms feel rich yet cozy, and the furniture is beautiful. A dining room offers American cuisine, especially prime rib, duck, and chicken dishes. The Beekman also offers a very popular Sunday brunch; reservations are advised. You should also reserve well in advance for a room at this popular inn.

For a nearby adventure in fine dining, visit the Culinary Institute of America in Hyde Park (see trip #92). There you can sample exquisite cuisine prepared by chefs in training. The CIA offers four restaurants, each featuring different fare: American Bounty (American food), Escoffier (French), Caterina de Medici (Italian) and St. Andrew's Cafe (healthy, calorie- and cholesterol-conscious). Plan well ahead—they are sometimes booked months in advance for weekend meals.

The Beekman Arms is at the very center of the 16-mile stretch of the Hudson River that has been designated a National Historic Site. There are dozens of magnificent mansions, many built by members of the distinguished Livingston family, with some still occupied by Livingston descendants.

Visit **Clermont State Historic Park,** on County Route 6 just west of Route 9G. Clermont is the stately Hudson River mansion that was home to seven generations of Livingstons, beginning with Robert Livingston. A Scottish immigrant, he made his fortune in shipping and fur trading, and assumed influential positions in public life. In 1686 he was given a patent establishing the Manor of Livingston, a grant of 160,000 acres. Great buildings were built, landscaping was done, and important deals were made on this turf. Today, visitors can stroll the grounds, explore the mansion, and imagine the way people lived back then. There are trails for horseback riding and cross-country skiing.

To the north is another beautiful old mansion, recently refurbished. **Montgomery Place** in Annandale-on-Hudson was built by Janet Livingston Montgomery in 1805, after the death of her husband, Revolutionary War Gen. Richard Montgomery. The main house overlooking the Hudson was twice remodeled by the famous architect Alexander Jackson Davis and is a fine example of Federal architecture. Tours are provided by knowledgeable docents.

South of Rhinebeck are two more historic homes: the **Mills Mansion** in Staatsburg and the **Franklin D. Roosevelt National Historic Site** in Hyde Park (see trip #92). The former is an opulent Neoclassical style mansion designed by Stanford White for Ogden and Ruth Livingston Mills. It is filled with frilly furniture and decorated in a style of dandified finery. The latter is the birthplace of the former President. Roosevelt and his wife Eleanor spent a lot of time here, and it is permeated with small details of their historic lives. Just down the road from Roosevelt's home, and included in the admission fee, is the mansion built by Franklin's grandson, Frederick. It is a Beaux Arts structure of grand proportions, capable of entertaining hundreds, and boasting beautifully kept grounds. Just south, along the Hudson, are the diversions and attractions of Poughkeepsie (see trip #101).

DESTINATIONS

Old Rhinebeck Aerodrome, 42 Stone Church Rd, Rhinebeck, NY 12572. 914/758-8610. May 15-Oct 31. Air shows June 15-Oct 15. Daily 10 am-5 pm; air shows Sat & Sun only 2:30-4 pm. Weekends adults $7, children 6-10 $3. Weekdays and when there are no shows adults $3, children $1. Airplane rides, four-person minimum, $20 per 15-minute ride. **Montgomery Place,** River Rd, Rte 103, PO Box 32, Annandale-On-Hudson, NY 12504. 914/631-8200. Apr-Oct Wed-Mon 10 am-5 pm (10 am-sunset on summer weekends). Nov, Dec, & Mar weekends only. Closed Jan and Feb. Adults $5, seniors $4.50, children 6-17 $3. **Mills Mansion State Historic Site,** off Rte 9, Staatsburg, NY 12580. 914/889-4100. May-Oct Wed-Sun 9 am-5 pm. **Franklin D. Roosevelt National Historic Site,** Rte 9, Hyde Park, NY 12538. 914/229-9115. Apr-Oct daily 9 am-5 pm, Nov-Mar Thu-Mon 9 am-5pm. Adults $3.50; 12 and under, or 62 and over free. **Clermont State Historic Site,** RR 1, Box 215, Germantown, NY 12526. 518/537-4240. Mansion open Mem Day-last Sun in Oct, Wed-Sun, hours vary. Grounds open all year 9 am-sunset.

RESTAURANTS

Beekman Arms (see Accommodations). 914/876-7077. Mon-Sat 8-10 am, 11:30 am-3 pm, 5-10 pm; Sun brunch 10 am-2 pm, dinner 3:30-8 pm. **Culinary Institute of America,** Route 9, Hyde Park, NY 12538. 914/471-6608. Reservations required. Escoffier & American Bounty: Tue-Sat 12 & 12:30 pm seatings, 6:30-8 pm. Caterina de Medici: Mon-Fri 6 pm seating. St. Andrew's Cafe: Mon-Fri 11:30 am-12:30 pm, 6-7:30 pm.

ACCOMMODATIONS

Beekman Arms, Route 9, Rhinebeck, NY 12572. 914/876-7077.

103

Resort For All Seasons

Arrowwood Resort
Rye Brook, New York

Even if it were not so convenient, this luxury resort in the wooded countryside of southeastern

Westchester County would be an ideal getaway destination. But consider that **Arrowwood** is located just 23 miles from the hustle and bustle of midtown Manhattan, only 45 minutes away by car or train, and you have a resort that is close enough to provide a country weekend retreat without the hassle of extended travel.

Folded into 114 acres of rolling woodland and open meadows, Arrowwood is constructed of warm-colored wood and stone, with a handsome cedar-shake facade. It is set at five different levels into the sloping hills, so it may come as a surprise to find that your fifth-floor room is on the same level as the ground-floor lobby—and then find yourself looking down on a pretty wooded view from a three-story-high window! Atriums and skylights blend the rich interior with the natural outdoors.

During the week (and increasingly on weekends), Arrowwood functions as a conference center, providing state-of-the-art audiovisual services and meeting facilities for business and corporate groups. As a carryover from this conference-center orientation, each guest room is equipped with a large work table, a special, wall-mounted corkboard with a built-in writing surface, large, comfortable "18-hour" chairs specially designed for long conference sessions, and a dictionary and thesaurus.

On weekends, guests are more inclined to be visiting with pure leisure in mind. Amenities include: a par-35, nine-hole golf course (with adjacent practice range); Olympic-size indoor/outdoor pool with a swim-through heat lock; racquet sports, including four lighted tennis courts, two racquetball courts, a squash court, and two platform tennis courts; a well-equipped weight room; saunas, steam, and massage rooms; and miles of wooded trails for walking, jogging, and bicycling. Bicycles are available for loan, as well as cross-country skis, toboggans, and sleds. Those in search of less-energetic pursuits will find pool tables and game tables in the game room of **The Pub,** which also offers burgers, sandwiches, and giant-screen television.

Dining at Arrowwood is a story in and of itself

and includes a highly-rated destination restaurant, **Mallards.** It's a spot for elegant dining, with club-like appointments such as roomy seating, classical game prints, and a hunter-green decor with handsome mirrors etched with cattails. Mallards is formal, yet comfortable enough to entice guests to linger over a long meal—beginning with a selection of warm breads served with a trio of sweet and herbed butters and ending with a hard-to-resist selection of desserts, including tarte tatin, chocolate praline torte with pistachio sauce, and a nicely rendered profiterole. Starters include escargot wrapped in chicken breasts served on angel-hair pasta with a creamy sauce of shiitake mushrooms, tomatoes, and spring onions, and a rich lobster bisque flavored with tarragon and brandy. Creative salads include chilled medallions of lobster and melon presented on a bed of endive with a citrus mayonnaise. In keeping with its name, Mallards offers two duck specialties—roast Long Island duckling, halved and boned and extremely tender, and flavorful grilled sliced breast of Muscovy duck. A selection of unusual sauces includes green peppercorn brandy, raspberry and fresh currant, honey almond with amaretto, and bourbon maple with chestnut. Your server will gladly provide samples of several or all and, while this may sound more appropriate to a pancake house, it is an intriguing idea. Other options include beef selections, blackened scallops, filet of salmon with a watercress cream, and roast rack of lamb with a rosemary glacé.

In contrast, **The Atrium,** as its name suggests, is an open, multi-tiered restaurant with a window that climbs three stories and looks out onto a pretty, three-acre pond. With lush ferns, planters full of colorful blooms, and large ficus trees, which, after dark, sparkle with miniature lights, the restaurant is visually appealing with huge circular lighting and sweeping, curved decks. It features a breakfast buffet, including eggs cooked to order and a lavish Sunday brunch with live jazz. Standard items on the regular menu include rich clam chowder full of chunky vegetables, a good selection of fish, and prime rib with horseradish sauce. Popular touches include a between-courses sorbet served in a miniature cone, and a belt-busting, all-you-can-eat dessert bar with a selection of pies, tarts, cakes, and build-'em-yourself sundaes.

A visit to the dessert bar could make you a prime candidate for exploring the system of trails that winds through forest and fairways. Borrow a bicycle—or stroll over to nearby PepsiCo, Inc. Although a corporate headquarters may seem an unlikely destination, consider that **The Donald M. Kendall Sculpture Gardens at PepisCo** provides a tranquil setting for a world-renowned collection of sculpture.

Started in 1965, the collection includes 40 pieces by 20th century artists set in approximately 112 landscaped acres. Included are works by Alexander Calder, Henry Moore, Henri Laurens, Auguste Rodin, Alberto Giacometti, Isamu Noguchi, and Joan Miro. The gardens, designed by Russell Page, an internationally famous garden designer, are an art form in their own right. Included are: A garden planted with sweet-scented azaleas that bloom in shades of white, cream, yellow, and orange; an Ornamental Grass Garden with grasses and sedges in a range of colors, shapes, and textures; a collection of spring-flowering crabapples, cherries, and magnolias; and waterlily pools. There is the Gold Garden with golden conifers that glow brightly in the sun; a collection of many species of oak, edged in summer by white and blue hydrangeas; another collection of 13 species of birch trees, originating from different parts of the world; and the Fall Garden, a collection of plants notable for their autumn foliage and colorful fruits.

Of special botanical interest are specimens of Franklin trees, which in late summer bear white, camellia-like flowers. This is one of the world's rarest trees, discovered around 1756 in Georgia, but now thought to be extinct in the wild.

Arrowwood also is ideally located for short auto trips to many nearby attractions. These include the Caramoor House Museum and Music Festival, the

mansions of Sleepy Hollow, and Lyndhurst, the famous gothic mansion on the banks of the Hudson
(see separate descriptions).

Weekend packages are offered at Arrowwood, beginning at about $80 per person per night. A unique
concept, the Luxury Weekend Club, is a 12-month
package priced from $2,300 per couple and good for
any 10 weekends.

DESTINATIONS

Arrowwood, Anderson Hill Rd, Rye Brook, NY 10573. 914/939-
5500, NY 800/633-6569. **The Donald M. Kendall Sculpture
Gardens at PepsiCo,** Purchase, NY 10577. Daily dawn to dusk;
free.

RESTAURANTS

Arrowwod (see Destination). **The Pub,** 914/939-5500. Mon-Sat
11:30-2 am, Sun noon-2am. **Mallards,** 914/939-5500. Tue-Thu
11:30 am-2pm, 5:30-9:30 pm; Fri 11:30 am-2 pm, 5:30-10:30 pm.
Sat 5:30-10:30 pm. **Atrium,** 914/939-5500. Daily 6:45 am-2:30
pm, 5:30-10:30 pm.

104

Rip Van Winkle Slept Here

Historic Hudson Homes
Tarrytown, New York

For a haunting Halloween treat head for the **Sleepy
Hollow Restorations** near **Tarrytown, New York**
(preferably with youngsters in tow). The "Legend of
Sleepy Hollow Weekend" presents classic film versions of Washington Irving's spooky tale at both
Philipsburg Manor and **Sunnyside.** Included are
storytellers, puppet shows, and tours of the Old
Dutch Church and the graveyard Irving used as the
setting for his macabre story (and where the author
is buried).

In Washington Irving's famous tales, the Headless
Horseman chased Ichabod Crane along the scenic

hills of the Hudson, and Rip Van Winkle admired
the river before falling asleep in the Catskill Mountains. Irving often remarked that in all of his European travels he had seen nothing to compare with
the view of the Hudson from the porch at Sunnyside.

The author created his home on the banks of the
Hudson in 1835, transforming a small Dutch farm
cottage into a picturesque country home he called
his "snuggery." With red gabled roof, weather
vanes, turrets, chimneys, and gnarled wisteria vine
draping the front door, the charming stone mansion
is, in Irving's words, "as full of angles and corners
as an old cocked hat." The house is full of the author's belongings—his writing desk and favorite
chair, pipes and flute, walking stick and cloak.
Linger for views of the river, and picnic beside a
pretty pond with swans.

Philipsburg Manor sits on a 50,000-acre estate
built by an enterprising Dutch immigrant carpenter.
In its heyday flour and other goods were shipped
from its wharf to ports across the world. Today,
young visitors enjoy watching both the antics of
spring lambs on the farm, and early American technology at work in the water-powered grist mill.
Tours of the mill include a description of the miller's trade and a chance to purchase freshly-ground
flour and loaves of whole-wheat bread. Tours of the
18th-century fieldstone manor are conducted by
costumed guides.

Third of the sites that comprise the "restorations"
(a discounted ticket provides multiple admission to
all three) is the vast **Van Cortlandt Manor.** Built
close to 300 years ago and owned by one of the most
influential families in the emerging nation, the
house is known for its elegant period furnishings
and extensive, restored 18th-century gardens. Furnishings in this baronial mansion include Chippendale, Queen Anne, and Federal pieces.

In total contrast is **Lyndhurst,** a Gothic castle with
sweeping views of the Hudson. Built in 1838, the
mansion (managed by the National Trust) has handsome landscaped lawns and a comprehensive col-

lection of Victorian decorative arts. Designed for former New York City mayor William Paulding, it is considered one of America's finest examples of Gothic Revival architecture.

These Hudson mansions provide a bounty of special events. Lyndhurst's full calendar includes shows respectively featuring antiques, dogs, and crafts, Rose Day, and celebrations for Christmas and Halloween. The Pinkster Festival (May) at Philipsburg Manor recalls the early Dutch celebration of spring with music, dancing, storytelling, and food and drink. On October weekends Van Cortlandt Manor recreates an 18th-century open-air market with apples, pears, cider, pumpkins, baked goods, and crafts. Candlelight tours at Sunnyside celebrate Christmas with caroling by a bonfire, hot cider and cookies, and a tour of the house decorated for the holidays.

In downtown Tarrytown, **Lago di Como** is a handsome northern Italian restaurant with forest-green wall coverings accented by colorful abstract watercolors and *Vogue* posters. Try the pasta-and-bean soup, select from seven different kinds of *risotti*, the famous Northern Italian rice dish, or perhaps choose a pasta sauced with four Italian cheeses.

DESTINATIONS

Sleepy Hollow Restorations, c/o Historic Hudson Valley, 150 White Plains Rd, Tarrytown, NY 10591. 914/631-8200. Hours (all three) Apr-Nov daily 10 am-5 pm, Dec-Mar Wed-Sun 10 am-5 pm. Adults $5, seniors $4.50, students $3 (20% discount on multiple admissions). **Lyndhurst,** 635 S Broadway, Tarrytown, NY 10591. 914/631-0040. May-Oct & Dec Tue-Sun 10 am-5 pm, Jan-Apr & Nov Sat-Sun 10 am-5 pm. Adults $4, seniors $3, children $2.

RESTAURANTS

Lago di Como, 27 Main St, Tarrytown, NY 10591. 914/631-7227. Tue-Sat noon-3 pm 5-10 pm, Sun noon-1:30 pm 5-10 pm.

105

Knight And Day

The New York Renaissance Festival
Tuxedo, New York

All eyes are on the queen for some sort of signal. Then quietly and without warning, she gives a small nod. Soon knights in armor are thundering toward one another on snorting steeds. Lances splinter and crack on shields as the knights fight to maintain their mounts. One of them cries out, then falls heavily to the ground. Shortly he struggles to his feet and calls for his sword—just about the time you thought he was done for.

Of course, there won't be any blood shed by these knights. This "duel-to-the-death" is one of many medieval entertainments performed at the **New York Renaissance Festival** in Tuxedo, New York. Sprawling across 65 acres of festival grounds, the event is a spirited recreation of a 16th-century English country fair.

Over the past two decades, dozens of Renaissance festivals and fairs have sprung up across the country, many presenting good value and quality entertainment, others a mere collection of pseudo-Olde English souvenir stands with "entertainment" by amateur mimes and jugglers of limited ability. The New York Renaissance Festival puts the emphasis on theatrical presentation—albeit theater that runs seven hours at a time and is only loosely scripted. It boasts 200 craftspeople and more than 250 professional performers who dance, sing, joust, perform magic, and generally interact with the festival's visitors. From the moment you pass through the festival's gates and cross the bridge to the main grounds, their mission is to transport you to a kingdom that recreates all the splendor and pageantry, the color and cacophony of life during the Renaissance: banners flutter from flagpoles and turrets, bagpipes blare, minstrels sing, and gaily costumed gypsies beckon you to dance.

Theatrical entertainment includes Shakespearean plays (as well as performances of individual scenes and sonnets from the works of the Bard), *Tales of the Decameron*, a *Punch and Judy* show, *Scenes From the Queen's Court*, and other diversions. With five outdoor stages, there's almost always something happening.

Music includes madrigals, bagpipes, Irish harps, dulcimers, lutes, flutes, bells, drums, recorders, and herald trumpets—not to mention liturgical numbers and several faintly bawdy airs. And just when you're least expecting them, a band of strolling troubadours may burst upon you in full voice.

If you like dancing, take your pick of maypole, English country, court, galliards, gypsy, Morris, Celtic, or a lively jig; watch the performers, or try your hand (or foot, actually) at one of these traditional dances. For visitors with a bent for games, the festival offers everything from archery and axe throwing to Dunk the Fool.

As you stroll the tree-shaded grounds, you'll be tempted by stands and stalls offering almost every conceivable comestible known to Renaissance man. How about a Cornish meat pastie? Or some Scotch eggs, crab cakes, fish 'n' chips, or bangers and wursts? If these won't do, you could consider "dragon ribs" (meaty pork ribs), "steak on a stake," or maybe just a simple French crepe. Wash it all down with iced tea, lemonade, or a cooler—or, if you've a taste for something stronger, a glass of ale or mead.

If you've come to buy—or even just to look—you'll likely be entertained by and perhaps tempted to buy from the 150 artisans who sell and demonstrate their art here. The items run from apple-head dolls and blown glass to unicorn sculpture and zodiac amulets. You'll also find flutes, lace, jewelry, pottery, scrimshaw, tapestries, weaving, batik, brooms, brass, calligraphy, coats of arms, pewter, puppets, macrame, and miniatures.

This is a popular family outing. Kids are fascinated by this lively (if somewhat freewheeling) interpretation of life in Tudor Times—life without designer jeans, cassette tape players, or television. Not only will they have a great time, but, who knows, they may even glean a historical fact or two at this entertaining event.

DESTINATIONS

New York Renaissance Festival, PO Box 844, Tuxedo, NY 10987. Information from **Creative Fairs, Ltd,** 134 5th Ave, New York, NY 10011. 212/645-1630. Late Jul-mid-Sep Sat & Sun 11 am-6 pm. Adults $12, seniors $10, children 6-12 $5.

RESTAURANTS

New York Renaissance Festival (see Destinations).

106

Officers And Gentlemen

U.S. Military Academy
West Point, New York

Except for Niagara Falls and New York City, the **U.S. Military Academy** at West Point receives more visitors per year than any other destination in the state of New York. You may find your level of patriotism increasing as you explore the academy, for West Point is one of the great traditions in U.S. history.

The drive to West Point follows the scenic cliffs of the Hudson River on Route 9, then crosses Bear Mountain Bridge. The area around the academy has been of military importance since the days of the American Revolution. George Washington's last encampment was near West Point, and in 1778, a great iron chain was strung across the Hudson at the bend in the river below the present site of the academy to stop British ships. The following year, the revolutionaries built Fort Putnam, which has been fully restored and can be visited just outside the academy gates. This modest fortification houses a display on the life and duties of Revolutionary War-era soldiers. After the war, the academy was founded by an act of Congress. In 1802, the academy's first year, its entire student population was 10 cadets; today, more than 4,500 young men and women train and learn there.

The federal government has acquired the adjacent campus of closed Ladycliff College, and moved the **West Point Visitor Center** and the academy's extensive **Military Museum** onto the property. The Museum houses the largest collection of military artifacts in the Western Hemisphere, including uniforms (those worn by generals Grant, Patton, and Eisenhower are on display), firearms and swords, flags and banners, and some of the giant iron links that once formed the chain that blockaded the river. Also at the museum are scale replicas of military fortifications, including a frontier fort and a World War I trench.

Visitors are also welcome to attend most services at West Point military chapels. There are four chapels, in all, but be sure not to miss the **Cadet Chapel.** Perched on a hill overlooking the campus, this church is a fine example of an architectural style that has been dubbed "Military Gothic." Stone arches soar toward the ceiling, historic American Army flags hang from the walls, and stained glass windows depict notable warriors of the Bible. The chapel has the largest pipe organ in the world, containing 18,000 pipes. If the Cadet Chapel Choir is performing when you visit, stop to listen—you are guaranteed a patriotic lump in your throat.

Most of the academy's monuments to our country's great military men can be found at **Trophy Point,** a scenic spot high above the Hudson near the center of the campus. The largest of these monuments is dedicated to officers and soldiers killed in the Civil War. More recent memorials commemorate Eisenhower, MacArthur, and Patton.

Seasonal activities at West Point include fall football games at Michie (pronounced "MY koo") Stadium, and cadet parades in spring, late summer, or fall. The parades are especially notable—the sight of these crisply uniformed cadets marching in unison is something to remember, and the great open-air chorus of trumpets and drums is a sound to stir the soul.

The academy includes the venerable **Hotel Thayer,** where the American hostages stayed after they were released from Iran. The hotel's dining room offers a variety of chicken, beef, and seafood dishes for lunch and dinner, as well as a popular champagne brunch on Sundays.

DESTINATIONS

U.S. Military Academy, West Point, NY 10996. 914/938-2638. Visitor Center open daily 8:30 am-4:15 pm.

RESTAURANTS

Hotel Thayer (see Accommodations). 914/446-4731. Daily 7-10 am, 11:30 am-4 pm, 5:30-9 pm.

ACCOMMODATIONS

Hotel Thayer, West Point, NY 10996. 914/446-4731.

107 🍎
Scenic Soaring

Wurtsboro Airport
Wurtsboro, New York

It is an eerie feeling—flying silently, effortlessly, like a lazily circling hawk soaring high above the mountains. There are lots of ways to experience the beauty and majesty of the Catskills, but none quite compares to gliding over them in a sailplane. **Wurtsboro Airport,** in Wurtsboro, New York, claims to be the oldest soaring site in the United States, a declaration that's hard to challenge when you consider that planes without engines have been floating over the landscape here since 1927, the same year Charles Lindbergh made his dramatic solo flight across the Atlantic.

To experience the joy and freedom of a sailplane flight, sign up for a demonstration ride (for as little as $25) originating at the Wurtsboro Airport. The only engine noise you'll hear is at the beginning of your ride as you're towed (in a world-famous Schweizer sailplane) to soaring altitude by a high-performance single-engine Cessna. Once you're released, the only sound you'll hear is a slight whistling of the wind. For company you have only your sailplane pilot (who will have an FAA commercial rating) and a few curious birds.

Introductory lessons are also available. You'll learn the fundamentals of soaring and go through the basic flight controls. In addition to programs for beginning students, there are private and commercial programs, power-pilot transition courses, and programs for advanced commercial and instructors ratings. Airport spokeswoman Pat Claussen said that it takes the average sailplane student 30 flights before he or she is ready to solo. Of the people who begin soaring lessons at Wurtsboro (as opposed to those who simply take the demonstration ride), Claussen estimates that more than 80 percent actively continue in the sport. Rates are the same for demonstrations and lessons: a $20 per hour charge for use of the plane and a $15 per hour charge for a pilot or instructor (both these amounts are pro rated; you are only charged for actual time spent in the air), plus a flat $14 charge per each tow. Depending on the weather and wind conditions, each flight can last from 15 minutes to the full hour (or beyond, if so desired).

A good way to celebrate your first flight is with lunch or dinner at **The Repast.** The restaurant specializes in country gourmet cooking in a Victorian atmosphere, with such specialties as veal Marsala, baked French onion soup, stuffed breast of chicken, and homemade pies and pastries for dessert. Adjoining the restaurant is **Canal Towne Emporium,** originally built as a dry-goods store in 1845. The structure has been restored to its appearance circa 1880, and on the shelves you'll find not only jams, jellies, and cheeses, but items made of pewter and tin, plus shoes, fabrics, toys, stationery, and candles.

DESTINATIONS

Wurtsboro Airport, Route 209, Wurtsboro, NY 12790. 914/888-2791. Flights daily (weather permitting). **Canal Towne Emporium,** Sullivan and Hudson Sts, Wurtsboro, NY 12790. 914/888-2100. Daily 10 am-5 pm.

RESTAURANTS

The Repast, Sullivan and Hudson Streets, Wurtsboro, NY 12790. 914/888-2100. Mon-Wed 11 am-2:30 pm; Thu-Sun 11 am-2:30 pm, 5-9:30 pm.

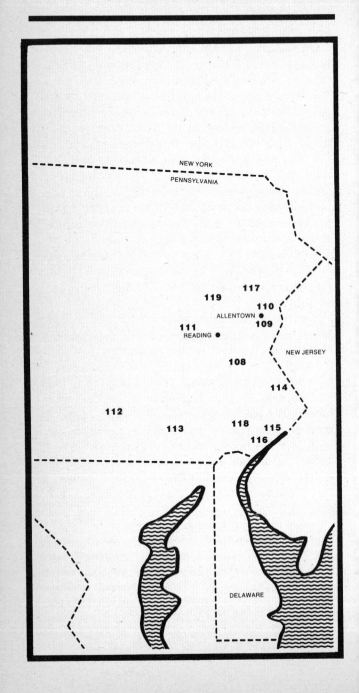

PENNSYLVANIA

108

A Mixed Bag Of Treats

Allentown, Pennsylvania

It began as North Hamptontown, although everyone called it "Allen's town," after founder William Allen. But it was the arrival of immigrants from southern Germany, misnamed the "Pennsylvania Dutch" (a corruption of "Deutsch"), whose industrious and sometimes unusual customs gave a lasting quality to the city and especially the surrounding area of rolling farmlands in the Lehigh Valley. Their tidy farms, often with hex signs painted on barns, still dot the countryside. A visit to **Allentown, Pennsylvania,** as well as short car trips to some of the neighboring points of interest, brings the full bounty of Pennsylvania Dutch country into view.

A number of German immigrants had already arrived in the Lehigh Valley, when, in the fall of 1777, American patriots smuggled the Liberty Bell from Philadelphia to "Allen's town," barely ahead of the British army. Together with the bells from Philadelphia's Christ Church, the Liberty Bell was hidden under the floor of the second Zion Church in the heart of town until the summer of the following year. That church is gone now, replaced by the somber stone structure of **Zion's Reformed United Church of Christ,** built in 1905 at 6th and Church Streets. In the 1950s, local historians created a shrine in the basement of that building to indicate where the enduring symbol of freedom was kept. The exhibit includes a full-size replica of the bell and an account of its journey.

The **Old Court House County Museum,** at 5th and Hamilton streets, is just a few blocks from the Reformed Church. Home of the Lehigh County Historical Society, the first floor houses exhibits explaining the history of Lehigh County from prehistoric days to the present. The Trexler Library on the second floor contains a large collection of documents about local history and genealogy. A geology garden in the rear explains the mineral history of the Lehigh Valley. A few blocks south and east is **Trout Hall,** also maintained by the county historical society. The two-and-a-half-story stone house was built in the early 1770s by James Allen, son of the city's founder, and is the oldest home still standing in Allentown. Free tours are given by the society on Tuesdays through Sundays April through December.

A few other downtown attractions are worth seeing if time permits. The **Allentown Art Museum** at 5th and Linden streets includes a library room from a Frank Lloyd Wright house and art from the Renaissance to the 20th century. The Albertus Meyers Bridge at 8th and Union streets was, at the time of its construction by a trolleycar firm in 1913, the largest concrete bridge in the world. Headquarters of the Lehigh Portland Cement Company, which provided the cement for the bridge, are at the corner of Hamilton and 7th streets. The **Old Allentown Historic District,** extending northward from 8th and Linden, contains some fine old Victorian row houses and other structures, some of which have been converted to restaurants and shops.

A most intriguing destination about 15 miles east of Allentown is the **Canal Museum** and **Hugh Moore Park,** in the city of Easton. This wooded riverland combines scenic interest and history, with a nod at America's nearly forgotten canal-building era of the late 1700s and early 1800s, when some 1,200 miles of canals were built in Pennsylvania alone. The Canal Museum, located at the confluence of the Lehigh and Delaware rivers, contains artifacts, exhibits, and audiovisual displays about canal life. From the grounds, it is possible to see both rivers as well as three different canals: the Lehigh Canal (which parallels an often unnavigable part of the river), the Delaware Canal, and the entrance to New Jersey's Morris Canal.

About four miles east of the museum, following the Lehigh River and Canal, is the Locktender's House in Moore Park. The first floor of this restored house is a museum depicting the lifestyle of a locktender and his family during the 1890s. On the grounds is some of the primitive machinery used to maintain the system. A canal boat dock and boat rental area is located along the canal about a 10-minute walk east of the Locktender's House. There, up to 88 people can ride on the *Josiah White*, a mule-drawn canal boat. Pedalboats, canoes, and bicycles can also be rented.

About 35 miles west of Allentown (the drive, along Interstate 78 or even more scenic back roads, takes visitors through the heart of Pennsylvania Dutch country) is the town of Shartlesville, home of the largest known indoor miniature village in the world. **Roadside America,** as it is called, is the product of 60 years of work by one man, Laurence Gieringer. In exquisite detail, he has recreated not one but actually a series of whole towns, industries, and transportation networks as they appeared at various times over a period of two centuries. There is continual movement throughout the enormous display, with operating trains, trolleys, airplanes, fountains, mines, and mills, among other things. It's a particular treat for children.

Several seasonal festivals are worth attending in the Allentown area. In late June or early July is the **Kutztown Folk Festival,** a celebration of Pennsylvania Dutch culture, crafts, cooking, music, and dance. Little Kutztown is about 18 miles southwest of Allentown on Route 222. Later in July is the Allentown **Balloon Festival,** featuring sky-diving demonstrations and balloon flights at the Queen City Airport. The city's big **Das Awkscht Fest** is held in early August as literally thousands of antique cars compete for attention with more traditional arts and crafts. Neighboring Bethlehem has a number of Christmas exhibits which should not be missed (see trip #109).

Regardless of the time you visit, be sure to enjoy a meal at one of the area's exquisite inns. On the less expensive side, the **King George Inn** features American and European cuisine. The **Ballietsville Inn,** in neighboring Ballietsville, is highly regarded for its French and Swiss cooking. Dover sole and roast rack of lamb are two noteworthy offerings. You might also try sampling some inexpensive traditional Pennsylvania Dutch dishes at any of the four **Dempsey's Restaurants,** located in Allentown, Bethlehem, Easton, and Whitehall.

Eight miles northwest is the 1500-hundred-acre **Trexler-Lehigh County Game Preserve,** bequeathed to the county in 1909 by Allentown businessman and farmer Harry C. Trexler. Visitors to the preserve drive past herds of bison and palomino horses, ford (quite safely) Indian Creek near a covered bridge, and then drive up to a hilltop for a glorious view of the Lehigh Valley. In both open and closed settings, the preserve is home white-tailed deer, zebras, gnus, antelope, camels, llamas, monkeys, and a variety of birds, including geese, ducks, and swans. Children can pet animals on a model farm, and the entire family can watch nature films in the preserve's theater.

DESTINATIONS

Lehigh Valley Convention & Visitors Bureau, Inc., PO Box 2605, Lehigh Valley, PA 18101. 215/266-0560. **Zion's Reformed United Church of Christ,** Hamilton and Church Sts, Allentown, PA 18101. Daily mid-Apr to mid-Oct Mon-Sat. **Trexler-Lehigh County Game Preserve,** Schnecksville, PA 18078. 215/799-4171. Daily 10 am- 5 pm Mem Day-Lab Day. Sundays only during May and Lab Day-Nov. Nominal admission fee. **Canal Museum,** and **Hugh Moore Park,** 200 S Delaware Dr, PO Box 877, Easton, PA 18044. 215/250-6700. Museum: Mon-Sat 10 am-4 pm, Sun 1-5 pm. Adults $1, children 50 cents. Locktender's House: Mem Day-Lab Day Wed-Sun 12-4:30 pm; weekends only in Sept. Canal Boat Rides: Mem Day-Lab Day Wed-Sat 11 am, 1, 2:30, & 4 pm; Sun 1, 2:30, & 4 pm; Sept, Sat-Sun only 1, 2:30, & 4 pm. Admission (includes Locktender's House) $4 adults, $2 children 5-12. **Roadside American** Rte 22 at I-78, Shartlesville, PA 19554. 215/488-6241. Jul-Lab Day Mon-Fri 9 am-6:30 pm, Sat-Sun 9 am-7 pm; Sep-Jun Mon-Fri 10 am-5 pm, Sat-Sun 10 am-6 pm. Adults $3.25, children 6-11 $1, under 5 free.

RESTAURANTS

King George Inn, 3141 Hamilton Blvd, Allentown, PA 18103. 215/435-1723. Mon-Thur 11:30 am-10 pm, Fri & Sat to 12 pm, Sun 4-9 pm. **Ballietsville Inn,** Ballietsville, PA 180327. 215/799-2435. Mon-Sat 5:30-10 pm. **Dempsey's Restaurant,** 2027 Hamilton St, Allentown, PA 18104. 215/432-3713. Daily 24 hrs.

ACCOMMODATIONS

Allentown Hilton, 904 Hamilton Mall, Allentown, PA 18101. 215/433-2221. **George Washington Lodge,** 1350 MacArthur Rd, Allentown, PA 18052. 215/433-0131.

109 🍎 🍎

Christmastime Town

Bethlehem, Pennsylvania

Long before a giant industry made the name

Bethlehem nearly synonymous with steel, this developing city was a haven for the devout followers of an eastern European Protestant sect. The churches, homes, and other buildings these early residents constructed, many dating back to the 1700s, still stand and are interesting at any time of year. But it is during the Christmas season that Bethlehem attracts the greatest number of visitors. For more than 50 years, civic leaders, businesses, churches, and residents have cooperated to create a month-long celebration that is traditional, glittering, yet decidedly non-commercial.

As the name suggests, **Bethlehem, Pennsylvania** was founded by Christians, in particular the Unity of Brethren, who because of their European roots later became known as the Moravian Church. On Christmas Eve, 1741, members of the Unity of Brethren met in the area's only building and sang a hymn celebrating Bethlehem, giving rise to the name of the town they were founding. The area remained exclusively Moravian for about a century, eventually opened up by other groups primarily because of the economic opportunities provided by Bethlehem Steel.

The **18th-Century Industrial Area,** just beyond the southern end of Old York Road in the heart of the city, is a 10-acre site with historic exhibits that testify to the industriousness of the early Moravian settlers. Included is a portion of a tannery built in 1761 and the reconstructed mechanisms of the 1762 waterworks, believed to be the first municipal water pumping system in the American colonies.

Directly north is the restored Luckenbach Mill, built in 1869 and now the headquarters of the **Bethlehem Visitors Center** and the Chamber of Commerce. In addition to providing maps and tour information, the center also operates as a museum. A short distance east is the **Moravian Museum** housed in the 1741 Germein Haus, the city's oldest building. It has an outstanding collection of early Moravian antiques, including furniture, musical instruments, clocks, silver, and religious articles. Other historic buildings downtown include the beautifully restored Goundie House, built in 1810 by a Moravian brewer, the Sun Inn, constructed in 1758, the Old Chapel (1751), the Central Church, built from 1803 to 1806, and a number of 18th-century homes. Group tours can be arranged through the Visitors Center. However, it is easy for individuals to follow the brown-and-white "Historic Bethlehem Walking Tour" signs which begin at the Visitors Center, where a brochure can be purchased for a nominal fee.

No visit to Bethlehem can be complete without having lunch or dinner at one of the most famous inns in America. Built in 1758 and lovingly maintained, the **Sun Inn** hosted members of the Continental Congress and was visited by every president from Washington to Lincoln. John Adams called it "the best inn I ever saw." It is typically Moravian, with its clean, simple style and muted tones, but the cuisine is quite the opposite, with unusual ingredients and complex sauces. Try the veal Normandy, cooked with apples and apple brandy in cream sauce, or the shrimp noir, the beef au poivre, or salmon amandine. The fixed price ($19.95) menu gives you a four-course meal beginning with soup served from a copper tureen. Don't miss the museum downstairs, with a restored kitchen, bedroom suite, and guest room.

The city of Bethlehem hosts a number of festivals in the spring and summer. The best known of these is the Bach Festival, held in mid-May at **Lehigh University's Packer Memorial Church.** Other May celebrations include the Sidewalk Art Show and the Shad Festival, and old-fashioned fishbake in the 18th-Century Industrial Area. The Moravian Antique Show is held in June. As interesting as these and a few others may be, by far the most famous of Bethlehem's festivals is the one that attests to the city's self-proclaimed titles of "Christmas City, U.S.A."

Each December, city officials expect about 700 tour buses, and untold thousands of independent visitors, to arrive in Bethlehem to see America's most elaborate city-wide Christmas festival. During the holiday season, a special **Christmas Tour and Information Center** is open to provide information and maps to visitors. On the first Sunday of Advent, 60,000 lights on more than 500 trees are lit in the downtown and outlying areas, white lights on the north side, colored on the south. Many homes and businesses begin observing the Old Moravian custom of placing a single candle (now mostly electric) in windows. A huge Star of Bethlehem, with rays up to 81 feet long, is displayed on South Mountain overlooking the city.

Another Moravian custom preserved today in three city churches and the Moravian Museum, all open to the public, is the building of a Christmas Putz, a miniature nativity scene often made from hand-carved figures. Of more recent origin is the live Christmas Pageant, complete with costumed characters, animals, narration, and music, usually performed on both days of a mid-December weekend at the Community Pavilion on Lehigh Street. There are also a number of seasonal concerts, including one by the Bach Choir at the First Presbyterian Church and a performance of "The Messiah" at Packer Memorial Church on the Lehigh University campus.

Reservations for two different Christmas tours can be made through the Visitors Center. **Night Light Bus Tours,** led by guides in Moravian costumes, provide a one-hour journey through three centuries of architectural history and pass by many of the city's most colorful Christmas displays. Conducted through December except on Christmas Eve and Christmas, the tour attracts tens of thousands of people annually. On selected December evenings, **Lantern Walking Tours** of Church Street are conducted by the Moravian Museum and the Kemerer Museum.

DESTINATIONS

Bethlehem Visitors Center, 459 Old York Rd, Bethlehem, PA 18018. 215/868-1513. Mon-Fri 9 am-5 pm year-around, also, Sat 10 am-4 pm Apr-Dec only. **Christmas Tour Information Center** (in the lower level of Lehigh Valley Bank, Broad & Guetter Sts. during Dec only). 215/694-0737. **Moravian Museum,** 66 W Church, Bethlehem, PA 18018. Tue-Sat 1-4 pm; closed Jan. Adults $1, students 50 cents.

RESTAURANTS

Sun Inn, 564 Main St, Bethlehem, PA 18018. 215/867-1761. Tue-Sat 5-10 pm, Dec 11:30 am-2 pm also. Building tours: Tue-Fri 12:30-4 pm, Sat 10 am-4 pm. Adults $2, students $1.50, children under 6 free.

ACCOMMODATIONS

Bethlehem Hotel, 437 Main St, Bethlehem, PA 18018. 215/867-3711. **Comfort Inn,** 3191 Highfield Dr, Bethlehem, PA 18017. 215/865-6300.

110   🍎 🍎

Agape At The Gap

Delaware Water Gap National Recreational Area
Near Stroudsburg, Pennsylvania

Even in the early 1800s, the more than one-mile notch in the Kittatinny Mountain Range cut by the Delaware River was one of the best known natural landmarks in the United States. The meandering, S-shaped gap near the southeastern edge of the Poconos was so breathtakingly scenic that large resort hotels sprang up around it catering to vacationing 19th-century businessmen and their families. Most of the old resorts are gone now, a few converted to other uses. The entire area, encompassing land in both Pennsylvania and New Jersey along a 37-mile stretch of the Delaware River, was declared a protected national recreation area by Congress in 1965. The emphasis by National Park managers and rangers today is on preserving the unspoiled beauty of the area, a paradise for nature-loving sightseers, hikers, bicyclists, and boaters.

The fastest way for people driving from the vicinity of New York City to see the **Delaware Water Gap** is to drive right through it on Interstate 80, the most direct route from the east. The highway parallels the Delaware River for about five miles, following the S-curve through the gap before crossing the river and continuing westward. The view of the tree-covered valley is magnificent, especially during June, when the mountain laurel is in bloom, and again in the fall, when the entire area is ablaze with color. Along the highway before it crosses the river is the **Kittatinny Visitor Center,** a good place to plan a more detailed itinerary and to enjoy a leisurely view of the valley from the Kittatinny Overlook.

Although overnight camping is permitted in a few designated areas for boaters on the Delaware River and hikers on the nearby **Appalachian Trail,** the entire recreation area, including the gap itself at the southern end, is intended primarily for day use. There are 13 different hiking paths in the area, but the longest by far is a leg of the famed Appalachian Trail, which stretches more than 2,000 miles from Georgia to Maine. This segment follows the eastern boundary of the park for about 25 miles and stops at the parking area by the Kittatinny visitor center. Of the others, one of the more interesting is the Dunnfield Hollow Trail, actually an old logging road following Dunnfield Creek to its headwaters. It, too, is easily reached from the visitor center parking lot.

Popular with all who enjoy canoeing, tubing, and rafting, the relatively calm Delaware River provides paddlers with magnificent scenery, passing through canyons towering up to 700 feet above water level. Access points have been established at eight- or 10-mile intervals along the river throughout the recreation area, sometimes more frequently, making day trips simple to plan. Note, however, that safe drinking water is available only at the Milford Beach, Kittatinny, and Smithfield Beach access points. Nearly two dozen commercial liveries rent a variety of river-running equipment. At 10 am on most Saturdays, park rangers lead free-hour canoe trips on the Delaware River which stress safety skills and the natural and cultural history of the river. There is no charge, but visitors must supply their own canoes. Reservations are necessary and can be made by calling 717/828-7802.

Many miles of scenic roads, clearly marked on maps available from the visitor center, can be enjoyed not only from automobiles but on bicycles and, in some cases, on horseback as well. The very best views of the Water Gap are from three scenic overlooks along Route 611 just south of Interstate 80. Information on good places for picnicking, swimming, fishing, bicycling, hunting, rock climbing, snowmobiling, ice skating, ice fishing, cross-country skiing, and even, for the truly adventurous, hang gliding can be found at the Kittatinny visitor center.

A number of specific attractions within the recreation area are worth a special visit. **Dingman's Falls,** well north of the Water Gap, is a series of picturesque cascades cut by Delaware River tributaries through deeply forested land. A few miles south of the falls is the **Pocono Environmental Educational Center,** a converted resort now used by ecology students. Organized groups of adults and students can make arrangements to stay at the center for any length of time.

One of the most interesting destinations in the recreation area is **Millbrook,** a partially restored and partly recreated mill town from the late 1800s. The historic community includes a number of modest homes, a church, school, general store, shoe shop, and a weaving shop. Weekends are the time of greatest activity, when the village blacksmith and some of his neighbors can be seen practicing their crafts. "Millbrook Days," usually the first weekend in October, feature even more elaborate demonstrations of traditional American crafts.

More of the skills of yesteryear, with a number of modern twists, are practiced at **Peters Valley Craft Village,** where courses in wood, clay, metal, textile, and photographic handicrafts are taught by resident craftsmen. Appointments are needed to tour the working studios, but an information center and store are open to all visitors. A craft fair is held on the last weekend in July.

Since restaurants and accommodations are unavailable within the Delaware Gap Recreation Area, a good home base for a weekend stay is the nearby town of **Stroudsburg, Pennsylvania,** itself a fascinating place to visit for its history as well as its Pocono Mountains charm (see trip #117). The first log cabin in the area was built in 1730 at what is now the corner of Ninth and Main. Jacob Stroud acquired 5,000 acres of land here 31 years later and built a mansion by the site of the original cabin. In 1799 he announced that he was founding a town named, appropriately enough, Stroudsburg.

The downtown district, between Second and Tenth Streets just northwest of I-80 and McMichaels Creek, is filled with historic buildings, including the original **Jacob Stroud Mansion.** A detailed walking-tour guide of the district is available from the Pocono Mountains Chamber of Commerce. Good eateries in Stroudsburg include **Beaver House,** whose specialty is fresh Maine lobsters, and the **William Penn Restaurant,** in the Best Western Pocono Inn, which offers standard American fare, including chicken and beef specialties. There are a number of conventional accommodations in and around Stroudsburg, but one of the most picturesque and romantic, in an 1842 building nestled in a country setting of hills and fields, is **The Inn at Meadowbrook.** The **Manitou Mountain Resort,** another out-of-the-ordinary choice, is a collection of deluxe housekeeping cottages in the middle of a pine forest.

DESTINATIONS

Kittatinny Point Visitor Center (at I-80 and the Delaware Water Gap). 201/496-4458. Apr-Oct daily 9 am-5 pm; Nov-Mar weekends only 9 am-4:30 pm. (Direct written requests for info to: Supt, Bushkill, PA 18324). **Pocono Mountains Vacation Bureau,** 1004 Main St, Stroudsburg, PA 18360. 717/421-5791. **Pocono Environmental Education Center,** RD2, Box 1010 Dingman's Ferry, PA 18328. 717/828-2319.

RESTAURANTS

Beaver House, 1001 N. Ninth St, Stroudsburg, PA 18360. 717/424-1020. Mon-Sat 11:30 am-10:30 pm, Sun 1 pm-8 pm (9 pm in summer). **William Penn Restaurant** (Best Western Pocono Inn), 7th & Main Sts, Stroudsburg, PA 18360. 717/421-2200. Daily 11:30 am-9 pm.

ACCOMMODATIONS

The Inn at Meadowbrook, RD 7, Box 7651, East Stroudsburg, PA 18301. 717/629-0296. **Manitou Mountain Resort,** Stroudsburg, PA 18360. 717/421-4510.

111

Old King Coal

Hazelton and Jim Thorpe, Pennsylvania

Nestled among tree-covered rolling mountains just west of the Poconos, **Hazelton, Pennsylvania,** is steeped in the lore of King Coal. A few retired coal miners (and some of their widows and children) still live in the valley towns and mountain slopes around the area, living reminders of a gritty, giant industry that is mostly displaced now by oil wells, natural gas pumps, hydroelectric and nuclear power-plants, and surface coal mines located elsewhere. Today, most visitors come here to get away from the cities to the east, to try white-water rafting or horse-back riding in the summer, downhill skiing in the winter. The big-time mine operators, coal buyers, union organizers, and union busters are gone. But some people still take the time to explore a number of nearby museums recalling the lives and labors of Pennsylvania's hard-coal miners.

Less than 10 miles northeast of town is **Eckley Miners' Village,** a 100-acre living museum that is still home for a few dozen retired miners and their families. Established in 1854, Eckley was a company-owned town until 1971. Now an Historic District listed in the National Register, it is virtually surrounded by black-silt ponds and strip-mining pits and is administered by the Pennsylvania Historical and Museum Commission.

A few miles in the opposite direction from Hazelton is the **Anthracite Museum at Ashland,** administered by the same state commission. Tools, machinery, and historic photographs show in detail how anthracite (hard) coal was once mined in the area.

Nearby is an actual mine shaft that visitors can enter for a first-hand glimpse of the coal miner's grim working conditions; the Pioneer Tunnel Mine Tour and Lokie Ride is also operated by the museum.

Hazelton is a small city, with just over 27,000 people recorded in the 1980 census (down more than 3,000 from the 1970 census). Most of the area's tourist attractions, aside from the city's quiet historic charm and the **Greater Hazelton Historical Society Museum,** open on weekend afternoons only, are found in the surrounding areas. The Chamber of Commerce can provide information on nearby skiing, white-water rafting, and horseback riding.

As the crow flies, it's less than 15 miles from the center of Hazelton to the town of **Jim Thorpe, Pennsylvania.** But driving southeast along winding Route 93 across the Broad Mountains, the only direct route, makes the scenic journey seem longer. The effort is well worth it, however, because the town, consolidated from Mauch Chunk and East Mauch Chunk in 1954, is one of the most unusual mountain settlements in America. It's built in three distinct neighborhoods, each beginning at the Lehigh River and extending away into the surrounding hills. Toward the hills, the valleys become so narrow that houses and little shops are crowded along a single street, back yards rising quickly above the rooftops.

The town is named after the legendary Fox Indian athlete Jim Thorpe, an Olympic pentathlon and decathlon champion who became both a professional baseball player and one of the original iron men in pro football. His grave is along Route 903.

A glorious view of the town and a curving stretch of the Lehigh Valley can be seen from the top of Flagstaff Mountain about three miles to the north. On a clear day, you can see New Jersey. The **Flagstaff Mountain Park Resort,** a combination inn, restaurant, and dance pavilion, is perched on the hilltop. The sprawling establishment is now somewhat faded, but half a century ago thousands of people packed the house to listen and jitterbug to the bands of Jimmy and Tommy Dorsey, two local boys who found worldwide fame. Dances are still sponsored at the Flagstaff by local organizations.

The town may be named after Jim Thorpe, but it was wealthy Asa Packer, founder of the Lehigh Valley Railroad and Lehigh University, who left the most enduring mark on the area. His 20-room Italianate home, **Asa Packer Mansion,** was built in 1861 on a hill overlooking what is now called Lower Jim Thorpe, bequeathed to Mauch Chunk by his daughter, and dedicated as a National Landmark in 1986. A second mansion built for Asa's son, Harry Packer, is next door. A few blocks down the hill on Race Street is **Old Stone Row,** a series of 16 stone rowhouses Asa built for engineers and foremen of the Lehigh Valley Railroad. Some of the buildings, a number of which are now little shops, are open to the public. Just a block away along Broadway is an area known as **Millionaire's Row,** with townhouses built between 1860 and 1890. You can't view the interiors, but the richly ornamented exteriors of these bygone business leaders' homes are worth seeing.

Along the banks of the Lehigh River near Asa Packer Park is the **Jersey Central Railroad Passenger Station,** built in 1888 for the once-booming passenger trade. Today, things are a little slower. A steam-engine passenger train runs on weekends only from spring through fall, giving passengers a half-hour trip through the valley. The station also houses Jim Thorpe's **Visitor Welcoming Center.**

A typical dining spot in the area is the **Stage Coach Inn,** a no-nonsense meat-and-potatoes kind of place with a rustic, western-style atmosphere. Steaks, seafood, and huge burgers with "the works" are popular choices.

DESTINATIONS

Greater Hazelton Chamber of Commerce, Northeastern Bldg, Hazelton, PA 18201. 717/455-1508. **Jim Thorpe Area Chamber of Commerce,** PO Box 164, Jim Thorpe, PA 18229. 717/325-4563. **Eckley Miners' Village,** Rural Rte 2, Box 236, Weatherly, PA 18255. 717/636-2070. Mon-Sat 9 am-5 pm, Sun 12-5 pm. Adults $2, seniors $1.50, children 6-17 $1. **Anthracite Museum at Ashland,** 17th & Pine Sts, Ashland, PA 17921. 717/

875-4708. Daily 9 am-5 pm, Mem Day-Lab Day; rest of year Tue-Sat 9 am-5 pm, Sun 12-5 pm. Adults $2, seniors $1.50, children 6-17 $1. **Jim Thorpe Rail Tours,** Rail Tours, Inc, PO Box 285, Jim Thorpe, PA 18229. 717/325-3673. May 30-Sep 1: trains depart at 1, 2, 3, & 4 pm Sat, Sun & holidays. (Fall autumn leaf specials announced in season.) Dates may vary, so call ahead. Adults $3.50, children 6-11 $2.50, under 6 free.

RESTAURANTS

Stage Coach Inn, Rte 309, Hazelton, PA 18201. 717/788-9980. Mon & Tue 4-10 pm, Wed-Sun 11:30 am-10 pm.

ACCOMMODATIONS

Genetti-Best Western Motor Lodge, Rt 309, Hazelton, PA 18201. 717/454-2494. **Hotel Switzerland,** 5 Hazard Sq, Jim Thorpe, PA 18229. 717/325-4563.

112

Chocolate Town, U.S.A.

Hershey, Pennsylvania

To most Americans the name "Hershey's" is synonymous with candy bars and foil-wrapped chocolate "kisses." But there's more. There is the man, the town, and the many Hershey-named attractions in the town. At **Hershey, Pennsylvania,** the name also means entertainment.

The entire empire can be traced back to the sweet dreams of one man: Milton S. Hershey. Born in Dauphin County, Pennsylvania, in 1857, Hershey apprenticed as a confectioner in Lancaster. After failing to establish his own candy-making businesses in both Philadelphia and New York City, he returned to Lancaster and founded the Lancaster Caramel Company, which was a considerable success. In 1900, he sold the company to its chief competitor for $1 million, and decided to concentrate on developing and manufacturing the perfect chocolate bar.

In 1903, in the southeastern corner of the county

of his birth, Hershey's chocolate factory was built. Shortly thereafter, the town where he made his home, and to which he gave his name, began to grow around the factory. Today, the influence of Hershey's legacy on the town is widespread: there are streets named Chocolate and Cocoa, and the town's streetlights are in the familiar bell-like shape of Hershey's Kisses. But what has had the most impact on the town has been Milton Hershey's and the Hershey Foods Corporation's winning combination of community commitment and money.

Visitors can learn about the history of the Hershey Foods Corporation and the manufacture of chocolate at the Hershey's Chocolate World visitor center. Attractions here include a simulated multi-media chocolate-factory tour, the expanded Hershey Cafe and Chocolate Fantasies Dessert Bar (offering ice cream, brownies, breads, pastries and other sweet treats), and shops offering candy, clothing, and other Hershey-oriented keepsakes and gifts.

The genesis for Hershey's most popular attraction came in 1907, when Milton Hershey commissioned a large athletic field to be constructed behind the factory. On Memorial Day of that year, a crowd of employees and residents gathered to play and watch a baseball game. Thus was born **Hersheypark.** In the more than 80 years since that day, the park has grown and been refined from a casual picnic-and-recreation area into one of America's most popular theme parks. The park spreads over 87 acres, and includes seven themed areas, seven different shows, seven full restaurants, and over 50 snack locations. Notable theme areas and attractions are: the Frontier Chute-Out and Canyon River Rapids water rides of the Pioneer Frontier area; the Pennsylvania Dutch food, crafts, and entertainment of Der Deitschplatz; the turn-of-the-century carnival rides of Carrousel Circle; and the special playland for younger children of Kaptain Kid's Kove.

Adjacent to Hersheypark (and included in the park's admission fee) is **ZooAmerica North American Wildlife Park.** This 11-acre walk-through zoo displays native plants and animals in five climatic regions of America, representing prairie, woodland, northwoods, desert, and grass marsh ecosystems. In the area just north of the park and the zoo are the separate sporting and entertainment facilities of Hersheypark Stadium and Hersheypark Arena. These are used for sports, concerts, ice shows, and other special events.

Also near the park is the **Hershey Museum of American Life.** The museum's diverse exhibits focus mainly on the portrayal of American life and culture in the 18th and 19th centuries, especially the history of central Pennsylvania and its strong German influence. Begun as Milton Hershey's private collection of Indian and Eskimo artifacts, the museum now traces the life and career of its founder and primary benefactor in an extensive exhibit called "The Man Behind the Chocolate Bar."

Another attraction with a direct and personal connection to Milton Hershey is the **Hershey Gardens.** In 1937, he requested that "a nice garden of roses" be planted on the site. The original three-acre plot consisted of a gorgeous display of more than 7,000 roses. Today, the gardens have grown to 23 acres with geometrically arranged beds containing more than 120,000 flowers, shrubs, and plants. Separate internationally-themed environments contain English and Japanese gardens.

The two most exciting and popular times to experience the attractions of Hershey are during the Christmas season and February's Great American Chocolate Festival. The month-long Christmas celebration includes one of the state's largest and most impressive light displays, special holiday gift and craft shops, an animated elf show, and a 60-foot-tall Christmas tree. The centerpiece of the holiday extravaganza is Christmas Candylane at Hersheypark, with more than 100,000 lights illuminating a Tudor-style shopping village, strolling carolers, horse-drawn carriage rides, and Santa's village.

After the luster of the holidays has faded into the doldrums of February, return to Hershey for the sweet pick-me-up of the Great American Chocolate Festival. Exhibits, contests, tastings, and other activities focus on chocolate in its many delectable forms. Learn a new recipe, join the Certified Chocolate Lovers' Club, or just sample the varied goodies you'll encounter at nearly every turn.

Hershey offers world-class lodging and dining in the four-star-rated **Hotel Hershey** resort. Designed in an attractive Spanish motif at Milton Hershey's request, the resort features luxurious guestrooms, a championship nine-hole golf course, tennis courts, horseback riding, indoor and outdoor pools, and nightly entertainment. The resort's Circular Dining Room serves fine cuisine, with accents on veal and cornish hen, in an elegant Old-World-style dining room overlooking a picturesque formal garden. A good choice for family lodging is the **Hershey Lodge,** which offers affordable accommodations and extras including two pools, a playground, a movie theater, an exercise room, and available bicycle rentals.

Another fine choice is the **Union Canal House** in nearby Union Deposit. Housed in a 1782 roadhouse, its antique-decorated restaurant is popular for its Black Angus beef and fresh seafood. It also offers bed-and-breakfast lodging in nine guestrooms.

DESTINATIONS
Hershey Entertainment & Resort Company, 400 W Hersheypark Dr, Hershey, PA 17033. 800/HERSHEY.

RESTAURANTS
Circular Dining Room (see Accommodatins, Hotel Hershey). 7-10 am, noon-2pm, 6-9 pm. **Union Canal House** (see Accommodations). Mon-Thu 4-10 pm, Fri & Sat 4-11 pm.

ACCOMMODATIONS
Hotel Hershey, PO Box BB, Hershey, PA 17033. 717/533-2171 or 800/533-3131. **Hershey Lodge,** Chocolate Ave at University Dr, Hershey PA 17033. 717/533-3311 or 800/533-3131. **Union Canal House,** 107 S Hanover St, Union Deposit, Hershey, PA 17033. 717/566-0054.

113

Pennsylvania Dutch And Such

Lancaster, Pennsylvania

In places where the "Plain People" live, time seems to have stopped more than a century ago. In the towns and farmlands of Lancaster County, Amish families still travel to church in horse-drawn buggies, a bearded father holding the reins, attired in simple black clothing, the women in plain frocks held together with straight pins, hair tucked neatly into white prayer bonnets. In the local schools, one teacher is still responsible for eight grades, and parents clean and repair the building. A barn-raising is still a social event, and dinners feature such dishes as chicken corn soup, snitz-and-knepp (a kind of meat pie with ham and apples), shoofly pie, and funnel cakes.

The Amish, Mennonites, and Brethren are living their lives according to their literal interpretation of the Bible. But for tourists who just want to mingle with them for a while, there are ample opportunities to sample their lifestyle. In Lancaster and its environs, you can ride in an authentic Amish buggy, visit old-fashioned farms and homesteads, see museums devoted to Amish culture and history, and sample their plainly delicious food.

The city of **Lancaster, Pennsylvania,** is near the center of Lancaster County, the heart of Pennsylvania Dutch country. Start a weekend visit at the **Pennsylvania Dutch Convention and Visitors Bureau Information Center** in Lancaster, where staff members can help plan a personalized itinerary. In addition to supplying maps and lots of printed information. A 36-minute motion picture depicting the Pennsylvania Dutch lifestyle is shown on the hour to help enrich your visit.

Several living history museums depicting Amish life in great detail are located within minutes of downtown Lancaster, many of them just to the east. Less than two miles southeast of the information center is the **Amish Homestead,** a 71-acre dairy farm. Guided tours of the house and farm buildings emphasize the Amish way of life. **The Amish Farm & House,** a few miles farther east, is also an operating farm. Guided tours are conducted regularly through all 10 rooms of the 19th-century stone farmhouse. A few more miles to the east, in neighboring Strasburg, is **The Amish Village,** where visitors can see a microcosm of Amish life and enterprise. Included are guided tours of a house, one-room school, blacksmith shop, operating smokehouse and waterwheel, and more.

While in Strasburg, you might want to climb aboard the **Strasburg Rail Road,** billed as "America's oldest short-line." A steam locomotive pulls wooden coaches along a 4-1/2-mile journey. The **Railroad Museum of Pennsylvania,** where visitors can enter the cab of a steam locomotive, is opposite the station.

The city of Lancaster, founded in 1718, claims to be the oldest inland city in America. For a single day, as the Continental Congress met here while fleeing from advancing British troops, it was also the capital of the United States. The many places to see, as well as the unusual nature of so many of the attractions, makes a comprehensive visit difficult for people with limited time. For a quick view of area attractions, you might consider one of a number of guided tours through the area.

A self-guiding, 90-minute cassette tape leads drivers past some area highlights and can be purchased at a number of places along U.S. 30, including Holiday Inn East in Lancaster. Ninety-minute walking tours of the downtown historic area are conducted by costumed guides daily during warm months. Call 717/392-1776 for specific information. Conestoga Tours (717/299-6666) and Dutchland Tours (717/392-8622) offer bus excursions covering a larger area, most lasting from two to four hours. From June 1 through October 1, and occasionally at other times, you can even see the beautiful Amish countryside from the air. Call Glick Aviation (717/394-6476) for details.

If you would like to tour the farmlands near Strasburg as the Amish do, rides can be arranged through Abe's Buggy Rides (Route 340, one-half mile east of Route 896) or Ed's Buggy Rides (717/687-6600). Whether you travel with a guide or on your own, remember that many Amish people, and members of some other Pennsylvania Dutch religious sects, consider it a sin to have their photographs taken.

Free buggy rides across the longest covered bridge in Lancaster County are offered at **Mill Bridge Village,** but only after you have paid admission. This colonial-style attraction, one of the more popular in the area, includes an operating, restored mill built in 1738, a number of restaurants serving local specialties, and demonstrations of a variety of old-fashioned crafts. The historical spirit is somewhat eclectic, mixing such things as nickelodians from the 1890s into the fun.

You needn't spend a dime to see the regional 18th- and 19th-century furniture, rifles, quilts, fraktur (a form of decorative calligraphy), and other artifacts on display at the **Heritage Center of Lancaster County** downtown on Penn Square. While in the downtown historic district, be sure to take a look at the **Fulton Opera House,** built in 1852. Sarah Bernhardt and John and Ethel Barrymore are among the historic stars who shined on the old stage. Another nearby attraction with free admission is in the gift shop called **Dutch Indoor Village.** The shop displays a colorful and magnificently detailed pewter model of a village created by Michael Anthony Ricker. The 10-by-30-foot exhibit, presented by President Gerald Ford, weighs more than five tons and is valued at over $250,000. While in a presidential spirit, you might want to visit **Wheatland,** an 1828 structure that served as the home of James Buchanan from 1848 to 1868.

Lancaster and the surrounding county are noted for their shops, from large factory outlet malls to smaller bakeries, specialty stores, and craft shops, some specializing in traditional Pennsylvania Dutch treats. The entire area is well geared for the tourist trade; sometimes making choices of restaurants and accommodations difficult due to the sheer number of options, some truly interesting, others less than tasteful. In addition to hotels and motels at all price levels, there is a variety of old inns, bed and breakfast establishments, tourist houses, and farm homes, most with day and weekly rates. At places such as **Lime Valley Cottage** and **Rose & Crown B&B,** you can rent a period house in the middle of the Amish farmlands. The Lancaster Information Center can provide a long list of tourist and farm homes. For a closer view and better understanding of area people and customs, inquire at the Information Center to arrange a stay with a Mennonite family.

While food can be found to suit every imaginable palate, most visitors enjoy sampling some genuine Pennsylvania Dutch cooking. The bright red and white **Amish Barn Restaurant,** midway between the towns of Bird-in-Hand and Intercourse, offers a variety of old favorites. One of the specialties of the house, or barn, is apple dumpling dessert. Hearty, farm-style dishes are served at the **Willow Valley Family Restaurant,** part of the large Willow Valley Resort just south of town.

DESTINATIONS

Pennsylvania Dutch Convention and Visitors Bureau Information Center, 501 Greenfield Rd, Lancaster, PA 17601. 717/299-8901. "Lancaster Experience" film shown hourly 9 am-4 pm Apr-Nov; Sat only 10 am-3 pm in Dec; Feb-Mar Sat & Sun 10 am-3 pm; by appointment only Jan-Feb. Admission fee. **Amish Homestead,** Hwy E, Lancaster, PA 17602. 717/392-0832. Tours daily 9 am-4 pm. Adults $3.75, children 6-11 $1.75. **The Amish Farm & House,** 2395 Rte 30 E, Lancaster, PA 17602. 717/394-6185. Daily 8:30 am-4 pm. Adults $3.90, children 5-11 $2, under 5 free. **Mill Bridge Village** (on S Ronks Rd off Rte 30). 717/687-6521. Mon-Thu 9 am-5 pm, Fri-Sun 9:30 am-5 pm. Candlelight tour Fri & Sat 6-9 pm. **Heritage Center of Lancaster County,** Penn Square, Lancaster, PA 17603. 717/299-6440. May to mid-Nov Tue-Sat 10 am-4 pm. **Dutch Indoor Village,** 2191 Lincoln Hwy E, Lancaster, PA 17602. 717/299-2348. Mon-Sat 9:30 am-9 pm, Sun to 8 pm. **James Buchanan's Wheatland,** 1120 Marietta Ave, Lancaster, PA 17603. 717/392-8721. Daily Apr-Nov.

RESTAURANTS

Amish Barn Restaurant, Rte 340 between Bird-in-Hand and Intercourse. 717/768-8886. Mon-Thu 11 am-4 pm, Fri-Sun 8 am-7 pm. **Willow Valley Family Restaurant,** 2416 Willow Street Pike, Lancaster, PA 17602. 717/464-2711. Mon-Sat 6 am-11 pm.

ACCOMMODATIONS
Holiday Inn East, 521 Greenfield Rd, Lancaster, PA 17601. 717/299-2551. **Lime Valley Cottage,** 1107 Lime Valley Rd, Lancaster, PA 17602. 717/687-6118. **Rose & Crown B&B,** 44 Frogtown Rd, Paradise, PA 17562.

114

Fine Arts And Fine Wine

New Hope, Pennsylvania

If you would like to spend a day leisurely browsing through art galleries and unusual shops, sampling wine, even traveling on a mule-powered river barge or on a steam railway, but you don't quite know where to go, there is **New Hope** in Pennsylvania. Listed in the National Register of Historic Places, the little Delaware River town is just the spot to pack a number of unique experiences into a one-day excursion from New York.

Dozens of shops line the four main streets of downtown New Hope, all within easy strolling distance of each other. Even for a town catering to tourists, the scope of these little establishments is remarkable, offering goods ranging from jewelry to gingerbread, from handmade crafts and homemade candy to unique clocks and hand embroidered frocks. India, Ireland, Japan, and Scotland are even represented by their own import stores. Of the more than a dozen art galleries in New Hope, the best known is the **Golden Door Gallery.** This gallery is housed in a 200-year old building of brick floors and stone walls. Its collection highlights many of the fine artists who reside in and around New Hope.

Visitors to New Hope can take advantage of two almost forgotten modes of transportation that provide scenic as well as historically interesting rides. From April through October, mule teams pull barges up and down the old Delaware Canal, built in 1831 right through the middle of town. For a modest fee, you can climb aboard and travel in the fashion of one of the area's early farmers. Barge trips begin at the dock along the canal just north of the intersection of South Main Street (Route 32) and New Street. Scenic excursions to nearby Lahaska and back aboard an old-fashioned steam engine train take place on weekends only from May through November. The train station is located near the canal just north of Bridge Street (Route 179). If these excursions are a little too tame, check out an alternative offered by **Point Pleasant Canoes**—rafting or tubing along lively stretches of the Delaware River.

New Hope is home to one of America's oldest theaters, the **Bucks County Playhouse,** which stages musicals and plays from April through mid-December. The company is housed in a remodeled mill built in the 1700s along the Delaware River. A block or so west of the playhouse, across South Main Street, is **Parry Mansion,** built in 1784. The mansion is decorated with priceless antiques, which are displayed in period rooms ranging from the mid-1700s to the early 1900s. Tours are conducted May through early September on Friday, Saturday, and Sunday afternoons.

Wine lovers should be sure to visit the **Bucks County Vineyards and Winery,** just three miles southwest of town on Route 202. Well-informed tour guides lead their guests through the cold cellars, the bottling room and aging areas, a museum, and, of course, the wine and cheese tasting room. Bucks County wines are produced using Old World methods from French-American hybrid grapes, grown locally. The vineyard's specialty is a fruity Pennsylvania Dutch Apple Wine.

Even the most militant teetotalers may want to visit the winery just to see the newly opened **Broadway Costume Museum.** Arthur Gerold, founder of the winery, was also the owner of America's largest theatrical costume house. Costumes on display, most from his personal collection, were once worn in stage or motion picture productions by stars including Audrey Hepburn, Mary Martin, Lily Tomlin, Carol Channing, Richard Burton, Rock Hudson, Kate Smith, Ginger Rogers, and many others.

For a uniquely scenic dining experience, journey seven miles north of New Hope to the **Black Bass Hotel,** in Lumberville. The dining area of this 1740 structure is in a screened veranda offering panoramic vistas of the gently flowing Delaware Canal. Specialties include crabmeat in white wine sauce with a variety of cheeses and smoked breast of duck.

DESTINATIONS

New Hope Information Center, South Main and Mechanic Sts, New Hope, PA 18398. 215/862-5880. Open seven days a week. **Point Pleasant Canoes,** PO Box 6. Point Pleasant. PA 18950. 215/297-8181. **Bucks County Vineyards & Winery,** US Route 202, New Hope. PA 18938. 800/523-2510 (in PA: 215/794-7449). Mon-Fri 11 am-5 pm, Sat & holidays 10 am-6 pm, Sun noon-6. Adults $1 weekends & holidays only; children free.

RESTAURANTS

Black Bass Hotel, Rte 32, Lumberville, PA 18933. 215/297-5770. Mon-Sat noon-3 pm, 5:30-9 pm; Sun 11 am-3 pm, 4-8 pm.

115

The Philadelphia Story

Independence National Historical Park
Philadelphia, Pennsylvania

W. C. Fields once said that he wanted his epitaph to read, "On the whole, I'd rather be in **Philadelphia.**" Fields was making a joke about a city he found less than desirable, but perhaps the joke would be on him if he knew just how many people would "rather be in Philadelphia" today. And one of the major reasons they come to the city is to visit **Independence National Historical Park,** a collection of colonial buildings and sites in central Philadelphia that has been called "the most historic square mile in America."

Philadelphia was the capital of the United States until 1800. For a century it was the second-largest English-speaking city in the world (behind only London). The "City of Brotherly Love" is where the American Revolution was fermented and where the Declaration of Independence was penned. Consequently, the city is the locale of a large number of American "firsts." Philadelphia was the site of the first American magazine, Shakespearean performance, manufactured locomotive, botanical garden, paper mill, waterworks, and, this perhaps more lost to the mists of time than even the others, the first house-call by a doctor.

The main area of the "park" (which is only its official designation; it's more of a district or region within the city than a separate entity) extends from 2nd Street to 6th Street, between Market and Walnut streets. A visitor center is located at the corner of 3rd and Chestnut, and offers tour maps, brochures on the sites, and a 30-minute orientation film on the present-day park and the historic roles of the attractions included within. Also available are tape-recorded tours of the park, complete with pleasant harpsichord music, but even better are the free guided tours led by knowledgeable and enthusiastic park staffers. One guide will dress as a printer, authentic down to his ink-smeared apron, and demonstrate on old-fashioned presses how the word of rebellion (and, eventually, independence) was passed on to the colonies' population. Another guide, outfitted in a period dress, will tell visitors about why opinions about the Revolution differed sharply, and were hotly debated in the city. Almost as if they lived back then, the guides impart gossip about the loud arguments between clashing personalities and egos, as well as the serious funding problems the Founding Fathers faced. In the very rooms where history was made more than 200 years ago, the guides make you aware of the pros and cons of going to war, describe who sat where at the signing of the Declaration of Independence, and even tell you which taverns the men repaired to afterward.

The centerpiece of the park, both physically as well as spiritually, is **Independence Hall.** This graceful brick building is perhaps the most historically notable structure in the country. Here, in the hall's Assembly Room, the Declaration of Independence was signed, the Second Continental Congress met on and off for eight years, George Washington accepted command of the Continental Army, and the U.S. Constitution was written and formally adopted. Today, the Assembly Room has been restored to its 1775-to-1787 appearance, including the inkstand used while the Declaration was being signed and the chair Washington sat in while he presided as president of the Constitutional Convention in 1787. Across the street from the hall is the **Liberty Bell Pavilion,** where the historic bell was moved to on Jan. 1, 1976, after more than 210 years in Independence Hall.

Flanking Independence Hall on either side are **Congress Hall** and the **Old City Hall.** Congress Hall was the home of the Senate and House of Representatives from 1790 to 1800, and was also the site of the inaugurations of presidents George Washington (for his second term) and John Adams. The chambers are restored to their original appearance, and furnished with a mixture of original and other period pieces. The Old City Hall was both the center of Philadelphia's government and the first home of the U.S. Supreme Court. The building's exterior has been restored; inside is an exhibit on Philadelphia during its period as the national capital. Other buildings of note in the park include the **First Bank of the United States; Carpenter's Hall,** where the first Continental Congress met in late 1774, and **Franklin Court,** on the site of Benjamin Franklin's home, which includes a museum focusing on Franklin and restorations of his Market Street businesses.

The historic park is perfectly compact and, with its stately Colonial buildings, lovely gardens, and verdant lawns, is pleasant for strolling. Well-kept paths connect most of the buildings, maintaining an island of 18th-century history in the middle of modern-day Philadelphia. For lunch or dinner in the same mode, stop at **City Tavern,** at the corner of 2nd and Walnut, within the boundaries of the park. This is an accurate reconstruction of the saloon where the Founding Fathers gathered for food, drink, and spirited discussion. Then, John Adams called it "the most genteel tavern in America;" today it specializes in fish and fowl dishes that were typical of 18th-century America. Also on Walnut Street is one of the classic Philadelphia restaurants. **Old Original Bookbinders** (not to be confused with the new Bookbinders Seafood House) is a popular choice for locals and visitors alike. Both come for the hearty seafood, especially the jumbo Dungeness crabs and the fresh snapping turtle soup, which are Bookbinders' unquestioned specialties.

DESTINATIONS

Independence National Historical Park, 3rd & Chestnut Sts, Philadelphia, PA 19102. 215/597-8974. Daily 9 am-5 pm. Free.

RESTAURANTS

City Tavern, 2nd & Walnut Sts, Philadelphia, PA 19106. 215/923-6059. Sun-Thu 11:30 am-3:30 pm, 5-9 pm; Fri & Sat 11:30 am-3:30 pm, 5-10 pm. **Old Original Bookbinders,** 125 Walnut St, Philadelphia, PA 19106. 215/925-7027. Mon-Sat noon-10 pm, Sun 1-9 pm.

ACCOMMODATIONS

Bed & Breakfasts of Philadelphia, PO Box 680, Devon, PA 19333. 215/688-1633. **The Four Seasons Hotel,** 18th St & The Parkway, Philadelphia, PA 19103. 215/963-1500 or 800/828-1188. **Westin Bellevue Stratford,** Broad St at Walnut St, Philadelphia, PA 19102. 215/893-1776 or 800/228-3000.

116

Yo, That's Italian

South Philly and the Italian Market
Philadelphia, Pennsylvania

Back in 1638, the Swedish were the first to settle

Philadelphia. The Italians, mostly from Sicily, came later, but more than made up for lost time. Thanks to the *Rocky* movies, nearly everyone has heard of **Little Italy** in South Philly. This neighborhood, said to be "as noisy as Naples," is full of small rowhouses with marble steps, clustered around 9th Street, between Wharton and Christian streets. These houses may look plain on the outside, but inside are often such baroque touches as gilded mirrors, ornate cherubs, and Renaissance prints.

Of the 109 (at last official count) neighborhoods in Philadelphia, this ethnic enclave is probably the most popular with visitors. And although visitors come and go, the locals have very deep roots. It's not uncommon for three generations of one family to live within blocks of each other, if not in the same house. Older family members may not have visited the Center City (as Philadelphians call their downtown area) for years, even though it's only a few miles away.

Another reason the neighborhood is so well known is because of its local boys who made good. Check out neighborhood restaurants and bars, and you'll often see photos, gold records, and other memorabilia pertaining to performers such as Frankie Avalon, Jimmy Darren, Fabian, Eddie Fisher, Joey Bishop, and Bobby Rydell. And although you may find them kitschy, don't dare make a disparaging comment about the black velvet paintings of Frank Sinatra and Sylvester Stallone that many stores display in their windows.

A neighborhood park is dedicated to another famous local son, Mario Lanza, the tenor and actor best-known for his movie portrayal of Caruso. Legend has it that he was moving a piano into the Academy of Music when he was inspired to sing on stage, and was soon discovered. The park is also home to a museum that commemorates his accomplishments.

The heart of South Philly is the five-block open market, which makes up most of Little Italy. The **Italian Market** is a wonderful mosaic of sights, smells, and sounds—and *especially* sounds. The din of hawking, dickering, and general commerce is amplified by the tin awnings that cover many of the stalls of vegetable vendors, bakers, spice salesmen and pasta- and mozzarella-cheese-makers. A typical line: "You want cheese, honey? We got it all." Claudio, self-styled King of Cheese, may not have it all, but does offer a wide selection. Visit the "King" to nibble a taste or purchase a whole wax-covered wheel.

There are live crabs and caged chickens, and butchers who seem to offer every bit of their animals, from snouts to shanks. The area's newest immigrants—Asians—are among the vendors selling housewares, T-shirts, and handbags from rickety-looking card tables. Check out beautifully-wrought Vietnamese, Thai, and Cambodian folk art.

You'll want to keep moving—if for no other reason than to keep your food intake in bounds. Sampling is encouraged and, almost without realizing it, it's easy to munch your way through the market: on olives, pepperoni, cannoli, string cheese, fresh bread, and stromboli.

Once out of the market, be sure to stop by the Samuel S. Fleisher Art Memorial, an art school that offers free instruction. You may ask what a name like "Fleisher" is doing so prominently displayed in Little Italy, but you'll know once you enter the 19th-century Romanesque basilica next door to the memorial. Fleisher was a German Jew who bought the basilica to prevent it from being made into a warehouse. Then he commissioned altar scenes of the life of Moses, modeled after paintings displayed in basilicas in Italy. This beautiful treasure has been something of a well-kept secret that relatively few native Philadelphians have seen.

After all this exploring, you may discover that the snacks you munched on at the market were merely appetizers. In South Philly, gustatory matters are paid the utmost attention, and you can find a meal to suit whatever it is that you're craving (particularly if it's Italian).

For the ubiquitous Philly cheese-steak sandwich (thinly sliced fried beef, slathered with sticky melted cheese—usually of the Cheez Whiz variety—and layered with sauteed onions on an Italian roll), try **Pat's Steaks** on Passyunk Avenue. If it's a full Italian meal you want, head for **Dante's and Luigi's,** just north of the market, and run by the same family for more than 80 years. Try the ravioli or the spaghetti with gravy (Philly lingo for tomato sauce). **Ristorante La Grolla** is a good choice for homemade pastas, fish dishes, and venison (in season). **La Famiglia** is well regarded for its veal entrees and its extensive wine selection.

Philadelphia has many fine hotels. For a change of pace in city accommodations, stay at **The Earl Grey B&B,** located in an 1860s landmark structure. Named not for the historical figure or the tea, but rather the owners' cat, the Earl Grey features antique-filled rooms, a gourmet breakfast, and a friendly, homey atmosphere.

DESTINATIONS

Visitors Center of the Philadelphia Convention and Visitors Bureau, 1525 John F. Kennedy Blvd, Philadelphia, PA 19102. 215/636-1666. **Italian Market,** 9th & Christian Sts, Philadelphia, PA. Tue-Sun 7 am-4 pm. **Fleisher Art Memorial,** 709-721 Catherine St, Philadelphia, PA 19147. 215/922-3456. Mon-Thu 12-5 pm, 7-9:30 pm; Sat 1-3 pm.

RESTAURANTS

Pat's Steaks, 1237 E Passyunk Ave, Philadelphia, PA 19147. Daily 24 hours. **Dante's and Luigi's,** 762 S 10th, Philadelphia, PA 19147. 215/922-9501. Sun-Tue 11:30 am-8:15 pm, Wed-Sat 11:30 am-8:45 pm. **Ristorante La Grolla,** 782 S 2nd St, Philadelphia, PA 19147. 215/627,7701. Daily 5 pm-midnight. **La Famiglia,** 8 S Front St, Philadelphia, PA 19106. 215/922-2803. Tue-Fri 12-2 pm, 5:30-9:30 pm; Sat 5:30-9:30 pm; Sun 4:30-8:30 pm.

ACCOMMODATIONS

The Earl Grey B&B, 2121 Delancey Pl, Philadelphia, PA 19103. 215/732-8356.

117

Inn The Poconos

Pocono Mountains, Pennsylvania

Geographers report that this famous mountain chain actually extends from the Wyoming Valley area, west of the Susquehanna River, northward to New York's Catskill Mountains, but it is really just the heart of the Poconos, in northeastern Pennsylvania, that is one of the favorite weekend getaway spots and romantic rendezvous in the eastern United States. The wooded hills and valleys, in some places covered with blooming mountain laurel in the spring, are dotted with lakes, streams, small towns, and large and small resorts that cater to visitors during all four seasons.

Winter travelers bound for the Poconos on I-84 often can be spotted by the skis strapped to their cars, a sure sign that they are being lured to the frosty hills of one of more than a dozen major ski areas in northeastern Pennsylvania. Most of the ski resorts have both downhill and cross-country trails, modern snow-making machines, and a variety of lifts, as well as full accommodations, restaurants, and night club- and discotheque-style apres-ski entertainment. The largest and best known of all is the **Camelback Ski Area,** a part of Big Pocono State Park near Tannersville, with a network of 25 trails (completely covered by a massive snowmaking system) down an 800-foot vertical drop, 11 different lifts, extensive instruction courses for beginners or experts, and even a free child-care center.

Some skiers prefer to purchase complete packages, including all room, board, and trail fees, offered at most of the major ski areas (mid-week rates are generally less expensive). Others enjoy a more serendipitous approach, skiing their favorite hills in the day and visiting neighboring restaurants in the evening, or, perhaps, lodging in any of the numerous inns sprinkled throughout the area. Information on specific country inns, bed and breakfast establishments, and just about anything else in the Poconos can be obtained from the Pocono Mountains Vacation Bureau. In addition to ski areas, there are indoor ice skating rinks (one is open year-around at Penn Hills Resort in Analomink), lakes for ice fishing and ice sailing, snowmobile trails, toboggan slopes, and indoor tennis facilities.

If you come to the Poconos in the warmer months, you'll find even more activities to choose from. Many people visit during the warm season simply to relax and enjoy the scenery, perhaps with a hike along a quiet country trail. Many of the major winter ski areas, including Camelback, welcome guests in the summer, although hours may be limited to weekends during some off-season months. Ride the lifts to the top of a mountain for a spectacular summertime view.

There are a total of seven Pennsylvania State parks in the Poconos, a number of which are particularly popular with summer campers, hikers, and visitors interested in water sports. Two of them are north of Mount Pocono: **Tobyhanna State Park and Gouldsboro State Park** (both 717/894-8336). These two parks contain lakes and provide camping sites. The largest by far of the state-owned facilities is the 15,500-acre **Hickory Run State park** (717/443-9991) near White Haven. The park provides land and water to pursue just about every summer and winter sport except downhill skiing. Other state parks are located near Hawley and in Dingman's Ferry.

A number of outfitters offer whitewater rafting tours on the Lehigh River and quieter trips on the Delaware. Some will rent canoes and rafts to those who choose to go out on their own.

Golfers can choose from more than 100 courses scattered throughout the Poconos, most open from early spring to late fall. One of the most highly regarded is at the **Hershey Pocono Resort.** Horseback riding stables are located in or near the towns of Mt. Pocono, White Haven, and Shawnee. More exotic animals can be seen, and sometimes touched, at **Claws 'n' Paws Wild Animal Park** and at **Pocono Snake and Animal Farm.**

The single most famous scenic attraction in the Poconos is the **Delaware Water Gap** at the Delaware River near I-80 and Sroudsburg (see trip #110). The unusually wide valley may have been created by huge quantities of rock and debris pushed through the Kittatinny Mountains by melting glaciers and runoff water. Much of the area is maintained by the National Park Service, and numerous scenic lookout points are positioned along Rt. 611. Also of great scenic interest is **Bushkill Falls,** about eight miles south of Milford on Rt. 209. The two main falls, Dingman's and Silver Thread, are the highest in the Poconos. A path through rustic bridges crossing mountain streams leads visitors to a half dozen more waterfalls.

There are a number of exhibits in the Poconos that should appeal to history buffs. **Memorytown, U.S.A** (Mt. Pocono, PA 18344; 717/839-7176) is a commercialized vintage Pennsylvania Dutch village with typical businesses of a bygone era and some unrelated, but often entertaining, activities as well. Visitors can tour a restored 19th-century gristmill at **Milford Upper Mill.** The working waterwheel is 24 feet in diameter and the entire structure is on the National Historic Register. Replicas of trolley cars that once were in service near the Delaware River Gap-Shawnee area take riders on a scenic tour that includes information on Indians and early white settlements.

The nine-day **Pocono Winter Carnival,** an area-wide festival including downhill and cross-country ski events, torchlight parades, fireworks, snowmobile rallies, ice fishing and snow sculpturing contests usually begins on the last weekend in February. Restaurants in the Poconos can be found in the big resorts and the little towns. Among numerous charming inns are the **Cliff Park Inn** in Milford and the Overlook Inn in Canadensis. Jackets and ties are required in the restaurants of each of these establishments, both originally 19th-century farmhouses. The Cliff Park Inn's continental menu includes stuffed quail and coquille St. Jacques. Filet mignon and rack of lamb are among the Overlook Inn's specialties.

DESTINATIONS

Camelback Ski Area, Box 168, Tannersville, PA 18372. 717/629-1661. Open daily Dec-Mar, Jul-Aug; weekends only other times. **Pocono Mountains Vacation Bureau,** 1004 Main Street, Stroudsburg, PA 18360. 717/421-5791. 24-hour Ski Hotline (in season): 717/421-5565. **Adventure Tours Canoe Trips,** Box 175, Rte 209, Marshalls Creek, PA 18335. 717/223-0505. **Whitewater Challengers,** Box 8, White Haven, PA 18661. 717/443-9532. **Milford Upper Mill,** Water & Mill Sts, Milford, PA 18337. 717/296-6313. **Water Gap Trolley,** Box 159, Delaware Water Gap, PA 18327. 717/476-0010.

RESTAURANTS

Cliff Park Inn, Mill Road, Milford, PA 18337. 717/296-6491. Serving breakfast 8-10 am, lunch noon-3 pm, dinner 6-9 pm. **Overlook Inn,** Dutch Hill Rd, Canadensis, PA. 717/559-7519. Mon-Sat 6-9:30 pm. Sun 5-8:30 pm. **Hershey Pocono Resort,** Box 126, White Haven, PA 18661. 717/443-8411.

ACCOMMODATIONS

Crescent Lodge (junction 191 & 940), Paradise Valley, Cresco 4, PA 18326. 717/595-7486, 800/392-9400). **Pinecrest Lake Resort,** Box 220, Old Rte 940, Pocono Pines, PA 18350. 717/646-1200.

118

Washington Schlepped Here

Valley Forge National Historical Park
Valley Forge, Pennsylvania

No place is more associated with the American Revolution than **Valley Forge, Pennsylvania.** Even though no battles took place in the huge, makeshift winter camp, about 2,000 soldiers of the Continental Army died from typhus, pneumonia, and other diseases during the winter of 1777-1778, the darkest days of the American Revolution.

The famous name for the historic site comes from an iron forge built in the 1740s along Valley Creek, a tributary of the Schuykill River. The park straddles both sides of Schuykill for several miles just west of the town of King of Prussia, but most of the public land, and all of the important historic sites and interpretive centers, are located south of the river. Park officials encourage guests to begin at the **Visitor Center,** located at the eastern edge of the grounds. Staff members are always on hand to help plan a visit, and there are a number of exhibits, including Washington's sleeping tent, as well as a 15-minute introductory film. Information on other nearby points of interest is also available.

Although America's first soldiers were in little position to appreciate it, the rolling, wooded land of Valley Forge is lovely, making hiking a pleasure. But since walking to and around all of the important places requires a hike of 10 miles or more, most visitors opt for the self-guided automobile tour in which one-way roads connect to most of the important sites and historical structures. From late spring to early fall, recorded cassette tapes and tape players can be rented at the visitor center for self-guiding tours. Bus trips with recorded narratives are also available during the same seasons. Most of the notable exhibits around Valley Forge are staffed by interpreters who will explain the historical importance of each site and answer questions. (Of course, if you try to bring home a Revolutionary War souvenir, they will turn on you faster than on a British Redcoat at a New England town meeting.)

For a change of pace in good weather, try bicycling along specially designated trails that usually parallel the car routes. Bikes can be rented daily at the visitor center during June, July, and August, and on weekends in May, September, and October. Cyclists will have to walk to follow the foot trail and one-way road along Valley Creek, but virtually all of the other sites of interest to the general public are accessible by bicycle. The park also contains about 10 miles of bridle paths.

After passing the reconstructed soldiers' huts on the site where Gen. Peter Muhlenberg's brigade guarded the perimeter of the camp, the tour trail leads to the massive **National Memorial Arch.** Dedicated in 1917, the arch overlooks the point on

Gulph Road where the Continental Army first marched into the encampment. One side of the graceful structure bears an inscription of General Washington's statement made February 16, 1778: "Naked and starving as they are, we cannot enough admire the incomparable patience and fidelity of the soldiery."

A few miles farther along the route, near the northeast corner of the grounds, is the beautifully maintained home of Isaac Potts, which served as **Washington's Headquarters** during the encampment. The picturesque stone building is virtually unchanged since its construction, circa 1770. Still farther along is **Artillery Park,** where most of the cannons available to the Continental Army were massed under the command of Brig. Gen. Henry Knox. A number of the old weapons are still there. Near a statue of General Steuben is the refurbished farmhouse used as Gen. James Varnum's headquarters. Located on private property within the park grounds near the end of the tour are the **Washington Memorial Chapel** and the **Museum of the Valley Forge Historical Society,** the latter housing many war-related artifacts.

Four times each year, park workers prepare special reenactments commemorating events during the six-month encampment: December 19, when the Continental Army first marched into Valley Forge; May 6, French Alliance day; June 19, when the army left camp (exactly six months after it arrived); and Washington's Birthday. A number of interpretive programs are scheduled during the summer months, when the three picnic areas are also popular. No open fires are permitted, but Betzwood picnic area has barbecue grills available on a first-come, first served basis.

There are no restaurants or overnight accommodations within the park. Best bets for both are in nearby King of Prussia. Restaurants serving standard dishes can be found in the Hilton, Sheraton, Stouffer's, and Holiday Inn hotels there. Also near the park are several sites of historic interest. **Mill Grove,** just three miles northwest of Valley Forge, is a 160-

acre wildlife refuge built around the first home of James Audubon. **Harriton House,** about six miles southeast of King of Prussia, was once the home of Charles Thomson, who served as Secretary of the Continental Congress. If you wish to make a short drive to Reading, you can see the **Daniel Boone Homestead.** Specific information on these and other area points of interest can be found at the park visitor center.

DESTINATIONS

Valley Forge National Historical Park, PO Box 953, Valley Forge, PA 19481. 215/783-7700. To arrange for audio tape or bicycle rentals or bus tours, call the Visitor Center at 215/783-5788. Park buildings open daily except Christmas 8:30 am-6 pm. Visitor Center and Washington's Headquarters open to 6 pm Memorial Day-Labor Day. Self-guided auto tour open daily 6 am-10 pm. Admission $1 for adults 17-61, but limited to a maximum of $3 per car.

RESTAURANTS

Stouffer's Valley Forge, 480 N Gulph Rd, King of Prussia, PA 19406. 215/337-1800. Daily 24 hrs.

ACCOMMODATIONS

Sheraton-Valley Forge, North Gulph Rd at First Ave, King of Prussia, PA 19406. 215/337-2000. **Hilton Valley Forge,** 251 W Dekalb Pike, King of Prussia, PA 19406. 215/337-1200.

119 🍎 🍎

The Little City That Could

Wilkes-Barre, Pennsylvania

Few cities in America have had as troubled a past as **Wilkes-Barre, Pennsylvania.** Burned by British and Indian forces during the American Revolution and burned again a few years later by Connecticut settlers protesting Pennsylvania's claim to it, the settlement was revived by the area's anthracite coal industry. But the once booming coal town suffered serious decline during the early 20th century as Pennsylvania anthracite mining operations dramatically declined. But even all these setbacks pale in comparison to the devastation the city suffered in 1972. It may be an unusual destination for a weekend getaway, but even a brief sketch of its recent troubles and the economic turnaround that followed will show why Wilkes-Barre is fascinating enough to attract visitors willing to explore a contemporary urban success story.

In the late 1950s and 1960s, city planners were desperately searching for new businesses to replace the vanishing coal industry. These efforts yielded few lasting results, and the city's prospects were soon to worsen. In June, 1972, torrential rains created by Hurricane Agnes flooded the Susquehanna River. At Wilkes-Barre, the river rose 14 feet above flood level, devastating nearly half the city and causing property damage of more than half a billion dollars. The flood demolished the downtown business district. On Public Square, out of 57 properties that were there the day of the flood, only three survived into the 1980s.

Remarkably, the flood turned out to be a blessing in disguise. Federal and state governments supplied $190 million dollars in relief and the Small Business Administration offered practically interest-free loans with the first $5,000 written off. Streets, sidewalks, and utility lines were repaired, and much of the once-aging downtown district was rebuilt. A comprehensive development plan attracted major new businesses and government offices.

Any visit to this phoenix-like metropolis almost has to begin with a walk through the central district, including at least passing glances at the historic buildings that survived the flood and a look at the four-block area of downtown restaurants and shops covered by lighted glass canopies. At the center of town, dividing South Main from North Main, is Wilkes-Barre's **Public Square,** with its fountain, amphitheater, and monument to the city's namesakes: John Wilkes and Colonel Isaac Barre, two Members of Parliament who supported the American colonies' struggle for independence. In May, the

Square is the site for the Fine Arts Fiesta, the oldest art fair in the state. A farmers market is conducted at the square on Thursdays during the summer.

The area between Public Square and the Susquehanna River, two blocks northwest, has been designated the **River Street Historic District** and in 1985 was placed on the National Register of Historic Places. Extending for four or five blocks along the river, the district includes a number of notable 19th and early 20th century buildings that survived the 1972 flood. While in the district, allow an hour or so to visit the **Wyoming Historical and Geological Society Museum.** The 1893 building houses permanent and changing exhibits depicting the natural and cultural history of the area.

When you leave the museum, walk a block north on Franklin Street to see the exotic **Irem Temple Mosque,** built in 1907 along the lines of the Middle East's Mosque of Omar. A detailed brochure describing a self-guiding walking tour of the downtown area can be acquired from the Chamber of Commerce in the building at 69 Public Square. In late April and early May, a Cherry Blossom Festival is held to celebrate the flowering of more than 100 Japanese cherry trees in River Common Park.

A good home base for touring the city and surrounding attractions is **The Woodlands Inn & Resort,** near the banks of bubbling Laurel Run Creek. The resort's **Left Bank Restaurant** offers continental cuisine and a fine view of the creek and surrounding woodlands. Specialties include rack of lamb, veal citron (sautéed veal medallions with mushrooms in a lemon butter sauce), and seafood melange (lobster, shrimp, scallops, mussels, clams and salmon poached in seasoned butter). Guests can enjoy indoor and outdoor swimming pools, a well-equipped exercise complex including one of the world's largest Jacuzzi tubs, jogging trails, tennis courts, and a flashy discotheque. If you would prefer to stay right in the heart of the reborn city, the **Sheraton-Crossgate** hotel is an example of one of the many fine buildings that have been constructed around the once-devastated Public Square. Another restaurant choice is the fresh pasta and Italian seafood dishes of **Aldino's Manor.**

Among the fascinating places to visit within an hour's drive of Wilkes-Barre is the historic and tourist-oriented village now called **Jim Thorpe,** about 30 miles south via Rte 9 (see trip #111). Directly to the northeast is Scranton and environs where a number of museums depicting Pennsylvania's coal mining past are located. Among them are the **Anthracite Museum of Scranton** and the **Scranton Iron Furnaces.** Some of the largest and best mountain resorts of the Poconos are also just minutes away (see trip #117).

Midway between Scranton and Wilkes-Barre is **Montage Mountain,** a major ski resort with 18 trails and five lifts. "Long Haul," a triple chair lift serving two steep trails, is nearly a mile long. The area near the summit affords a panoramic view of both Wilkes-Barre and Scranton and can be reached via the lifts even during the summer.

DESTINATIONS

Chamber of Commerce of Greater Wilkes-Barre, 69 Public Square, Wilkes-Barre, PA 18701. 717/823-2101. **Wyoming Historical and Geological Society Museum,** 69 S Franklin St, Wilkes-Barre, PA 18701. 717/823-6244. Closed Sun, Mon & holidays; free admission. **Anthracite Museum of Scranton,** RD 1, Bald Mountain Rd, Scranton, PA 18504. 717/961-4804. Tue-Sat 9 am-5 pm, Sun noon-5 pm; closed Mon and holidays. **Scranton Iron Furnaces,** Cedar Ave, Scranton, PA 18504. 717/961-4804. Tue-Sat 9 am-5 pm, Sun noon-5 pm; closed Mon and holidays. **Ski Montage,** Montage Mountain Rd, P.O. Box 3539, Scranton, PA 18505. 717/969-7669. (Ski conditions: PA: 800/468-7669; 800/847-7669.)

RESTAURANTS

Left Bank Restaurant (in the Woodlands Inn & Resort—see Accommodations). 717/824-0931. 7 am-11 pm daily. **Aldino's Manor,** 601 Kidder St, Wilkes-Barre, PA 18702. 717/825-8581. Mon-Fri 11 am-midnight, Sat 11 am-1 am, Sun 8 am-10 pm.

ACCOMMODATIONS

Woodlands Inn & Resort, 1073 Hwy 315, Wilkes-Barre, PA 18702. Toll-Free reservations: 800/556-2222; PA: 800/762-2222. **Sheraton-Crossgate Hotel,** 20 Public Square, Wilkes-Barre, PA 18701. 717/824-7100.

RHODE ISLAND

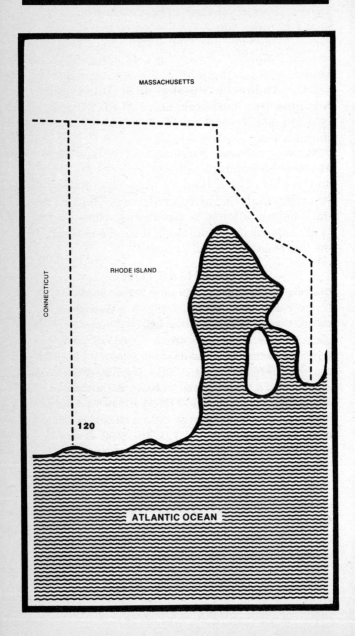

120. Westerly—Various Attractions

120

Prevailing Westerly

Westerly, Rhode Island

If the next time you play Trivial Pursuit, you encounter the question, "Which state has the longest name?" hesitate before you guess Mississippi or Massachusetts. Give thought to the *smallest* state in the union—Rhode Island. Or, more accurately, "The State of Rhode Island and Providence Plantations," the state's full name (leftover from its days as a colonized territory). Although the Ocean State contains little more than 1,000 square miles, it does boast more than 400 miles of coastline—and nowhere are the beaches lovelier and the scenery more appealing than in and around the village of **Westerly,** less than a mile east of the Connecticut-Rhode Island border.

According to legend, two lovers, John and Mary Babcock, were the village's first settlers, Westerly being the site of their elopement in 1648. But this romantic antecedent and the town's tranquil surroundings—it is, today, a delightfully romantic getaway destination—belie the tumult of its past. Connecticut and Rhode Island fought boundary wars against each other, on and off, for more than half a century, with Westerly often being caught in the middle. British privateers raided and rampaged throughout the area during the American Revolution. **Watch Hill,** a hamlet five miles south of Westerly, in fact, got its name as a lookout point against British pirates, whose booty was often lost in the treacherous seas around **Block Island,** nine miles south of the mainland. Today, Block Island is a popular resort area, and is connected by ferry to the Rhode Island mainland, New York, and Connecticut. Activities on this laid-back island (well worth an overnight side trip, or at least a day excursion) are mostly ocean-themed, including surf-fishing, boating, and swimming. The view from the island's Mohegan Bluffs, which soar 200 feet above the sea, is breathtaking. The colorful history of the island, from pirates and smugglers to society dandies, is displayed by the **Block Island Historical Society,** at Old Town Road and Ocean Avenue.

The town of Watch Hill, designated a Historic Landmark Community, has been a popular retreat since the 1860s, and one of the original grand hotels, the wooden Ocean House, still remains (if in a bit of a run-down condition). Several sites in Watch Hill document the area's 340-plus years of history. For example, the ruins of a colonial fort on Napatree Point are not far from Watch Hill's operating lighthouse, a granite tower built on land purchased by the government in 1807. The harborside statue of Ninigret, Chief of the Narragansett Indians, has been the "Guardian of Watch Hill" since it was erected in 1914. Also in Watch Hill, at the beach, is the nation's oldest merry-go-round, the Flying Horse Carousel, dating back to 1850; visitors can still ride the original carved wooden horses.

The waters of Long Island Sound, worthy of world-class boating, are Westerly's chief attractions today—along with gorgeous white-sand beaches that are perfect for an afternoon's lounging and tanning and for fishermen who cast into the surf for scrappy bluefish. Numerous deep-sea fishing boats are available for individual or group charter, most notably for excursions to battle marlin and bluefin tuna. Ponds, rivers, and streams are stocked with brook and rainbow trout, northern pike, and largemouth bass. The Rhode Island Tuna Tournament is a major event held each Labor Day weekend, which attracts anglers from throughout New England and the East Coast. One of the region's most enjoyable summer events is Stonington, Connecticut's "Blessing of the Fleet," held the first weekend in July. Festivities in this town only three miles southwest of Westerly include a block dance and shore dinners, as well as street and boat parades.

A drive along US 1 from Westerly to Pawtucket, on a portion of scenic highway designated as the New England Heritage Trail, will take you by or near numerous historic sites and scenic vistas. A stately collection of restored colonial homes and sprawling Victorian seaside "cottages" dot the roadside, as do shops filled with antiques, collectibles, and crafts. A major historic home in Westerly is the **Babcock-Smith House,** which was built in 1732, and was frequently visited by Benjamin Franklin, who was friends with Joseph Babcock, the home's original owner. Westerly also makes a convenient headquarters to use while seeing other sites in southwestern Rhode Island or southeastern Connecticut. In nearby Mystic, you can tour the Mystic Seaport, an authentic New England whaling village (see trip #5). Charlestown, adjacent to Westerly, also is home to the Audubon Society's **Kimball Wildlife Refuge,** a sanctuary for birds and endangered wildlife species. This 30-acre site offers hiking trails and various nature and interpretive programs throughout the year. Charlestown is also the tribal headquarters of the Narragansett Indians, many of whom continue their traditional crafts and celebrations, including an annual pow-wow, at the **Long House.**

Dining choices in Westerly range from casual waterfront cafes to more elegant, formal dining. But one constant is the availability and variety of fresh seafood. Drop in at the casual **Olympia Tea Room** in Watch Hill for a rundown of all the local gossip and some tasty seafood—perhaps the special shrimp salad served with homemade bread. **Villa Trombino** is a fine Italian restaurant, offering homemade pasta and a variety of veal and seafood dishes; the linguine with fresh clams (in season) is locally popular. For a particular treat, try the homemade pizza at **The Deck Bar & Grill** at the **Watch Hill Inn.** For more traditional fare, sample the Deck's award-winning New England clam chowder.

The picturesque Watch Hill Inn, which sits high on a hill overlooking Little Narragansett Bay, has long been one of the focal points of Watch Hill resort life. The inn's original structure was built around 1890, and has been recently remodeled; it is noted as an ideal spot for a romantic getaway, particularly in autumn, as the foliage bursts into vibrant colors.

DESTINATIONS
Westerly Area Chamber of Commerce, 159 Main St, Westerly, RI 02891. 401/596-7761. **Block Island,** Block Island Historical Society. Old Town Rd & Ocean Ave, Block Island, RI 02807. 401/466-2481. **Babcock-Smith House,** 124 Granite St, Westerly, RI 02891. 401/596-5704. **Kimball Wildlife Refuge,** Watchaug Pond, PO Box 908, Charlestown, RI 02812. 401/364-6151.

RESTAURANTS
Olympia Tea Room, Bay St, Watch Hill, RI 02891. 401/348-8211. Daily 8 am-10 pm. **Villa Trombino,** 106 Ashaway Rd, Westerly, RI 02891. 401/596-3444. Tue-Sun 4-10 pm. **The Deck Bar & Grill,** Watch Hill Inn (see Accommodations). 401/348-8912. Daily 5-10 pm.

ACCOMMODATIONS
Watch Hill Inn, 50 Bay St, Watch Hill, RI 02891. 401/348-8912. **Pine Lodge,** Rte 1, Westerly, RI 02891. 401/322-0333. **Ocean House,** Watch Hill, RI 02891. 401/348-8161.

INDEX